British Sign Language

Language, Education and Society

General Editor
Michael Stubbs
Department of Linguistics
University of Nottingham

British Sign Language

Margaret Deuchar

Lecturer in Linguistics
University of Sussex

Routledge
Taylor & Francis Group

NEW YORK AND LONDON

First published in 1984
by Routledge & Kegan Paul plc

Simultaneously published in the USA and Canada
by Routledge

711 Third Avenue, New York, NY 10017

Reprinted 1996, 2000 by Routledge
2 Park Square, Milton Park, Abingdon, Oxon, OX14 4RN

Transferred to Digital Printing 2005

First issued in paperback 2013

Set in Times, 10 on 12pt, by
Input Typesetting Ltd, London

Routledge is an imprint of the Taylor & Francis Group, an informa business

British Library Cataloguing in Publication Data
A catalogue record for this book is available from the British Library

Library of Congress Cataloguing in Publication Data
Deuchar, M. (Margaret)
British sign language.
(Language, education, and society)
Bibliography: p.
Includes index.
1. Deaf—Education—Great Britain—English language.
2. Sign language. I. Title. II. Series.
HV2469.E5D48   1984   419´.0941   83-9538

ISBN 978-0-415-15127-6 (hbk)
ISBN 978-0-415-86794-8 (pbk)

Contents

General Editor's preface

Simply a list of some of the questions implied by the phrase *Language, Education and Society* gives an immediate idea of the complexity, and also the fascination, of the area.

How is language related to learning? Or to intelligence? How should a teacher react to non-standard dialect in the classroom? Do regional and social accents and dialects matter? What is meant by standard English? Does it make sense to talk of 'declining standards' in language or in education? Or to talk of some children's language as 'restricted'? Do immigrant children require special language provision? How can their native languages be used as a valuable resource in schools? Can 'literacy' be equated with 'education'? Why are there so many adult illiterates in Britain and the USA? What effect has growing up with no easy access to language: for example, because a child is profoundly deaf? Why is there so much prejudice against people whose language background is odd in some way: because they are handicapped, or speak a non-standard dialect or foreign language? Why do linguistic differences lead to political violence, in Belgium, India, Wales and other parts of the world?

These are all real questions, of the kind which worry parents, teachers and policy-makers, and the answer to them is complex and not at all obvious. It is such questions that authors in this series will discuss.

Language plays a central part in education. This is probably generally agreed, but there is considerable debate and confusion about the exact relationship between language and learning. Even though the importance of language is generally recognized, we still have a lot to learn about how language is related either to educational success or to intelligence and thinking. Language is also a central fact in everyone's social life. People's attitudes and

most deeply held beliefs are at stake, for it is through language
that personal identities are maintained and recognized. People are
judged, whether justly or not, by the language they speak.

Language, Education and Society is therefore an area where
scholars have a responsibility to write clearly and persuasively, in
order to communicate the best in recent research to as wide an
audience as possible. This means not only other researchers, but
also all those who are involved in educational, social and political
policy-making, from individual teachers to government. It is an
area where value judgments cannot be avoided. Any action that
we take – or, of course, avoidance of action – has moral, social
and political consequences. It is vital, therefore, that practice is
informed by the best knowledge available, and that decisions
affecting the futures of individual children or whole social groups
are not taken merely on the basis of the all too widespread folk
myths about language in society.

Linguistics, psychology and sociology are often rejected by non-
specialists as jargon-ridden; or regarded as fascinating, but of no
relevance to educational or social practice. But this is superficial
and short-sighted: we are dealing with complex issues, which
require an understanding of the general principles involved. It is
bad theory to make statements about language in use which cannot
be related to educational and social reality. But it is equally
unsound to base beliefs and action on anecdote, received myths
and unsystematic or idiosyncratic observations.

All knowledge is value-laden: it suggests action and changes
our beliefs. Change is difficult and slow, but possible nevertheless.
When language in education and society is seriously and systematically studied, it becomes clear how awesomely complex is the
linguistic and social knowledge of all children and adults. And
with such an understanding, it becomes impossible to maintain a
position of linguistic prejudice and intolerance. This may be the
most important implication of a serious study of language, in our
linguistically diverse modern world.

In this book on *British Sign Language*, Margaret Deuchar makes
two kinds of contribution which are central to the series. She
advances linguistic research by providing a clear and systematic
description of a language. And, by disseminating up-to-date information, she advances rational debate on a matter of social and
educational importance.

She provides an excellent account of the sign language used by
the deaf community in Britain: what BSL is, its varieties and uses,
how it is acquired by children, its differences from American Sign
Language, and the educational issues involved in its use. BSL
provides a striking example of a topic about which clear and
straightforward information is badly needed by educators and
policy-makers, since there is widespread ignorance and confusion
about what deaf signing is. It is often thought to be mere random
manual gestures, imitative and transparent in meaning, a crude
and primitive communication system, unlike 'real' language. Or
it may be confused with finger spelling, which is a derivative from
normal written English. Deuchar shows just how inadequate such
views are. It is unfortunate, but inevitable, that in the area of
language, education and society, much effort has to go into
combating deeply held, but confused, myths. The case of BSL
provides, in fact, one particular example of the incomprehension
and rejection which attend non-standard dialects and minority
languages of all kinds.

Deuchar's book will be of great interest to linguists. Much
linguistics is based on the study of a very narrow range of the
world's languages: in some respects, BSL *is* very different from
'normal' spoken languages, and its study increases our understanding of human linguistic competence. It will also be of interest to
social psychologists and all those interested in non-verbal communication. And, of course, it provides crucial information for
anyone working with the deaf community, or indeed members of
the deaf community itself.

Michael Stubbs
Nottingham

Preface

This book is intended as an introduction to British Sign Language (BSL) from a linguistic point of view. It is hoped that it will be of interest to students of linguistics, deaf and hearing sign language researchers, teachers and social workers to the deaf, as well as to the general reader. It will be helpful if readers have some knowledge either of sign language or of linguistics, but those who have a background in neither may find it worth their while to read selectively. Chapters 1, 2, 7 and 8 are particularly suitable for the general reader, while chapters 3, 4 and 5 are of a more technical nature. The final chapter (9) is particularly aimed at linguists who wish not merely to know something about the nature of a language in a visual mode, but also to discover the implications of sign language research for linguistic theory, which hitherto has been based largely on spoken languages.

The reader will notice that throughout the book there is considerable reference to American Sign Language (ASL), and that there is even a chapter (6) comparing ASL with BSL. The reason for this is that ASL has been more extensively researched by linguists than any other sign language, and therefore is useful for comparison.

Sign language is in fact a very new area of investigation for linguists, for even in the United States it only became established as such in the 1970s. In Britain virtually no work had been done on BSL by 1976–7, when I did my own doctoral research in a British deaf community (reported in Deuchar, 1978a). However, soon after that time two fully funded BSL research projects were set up in Bristol and Edinburgh, and a national workshop began to meet regularly. In 1980 the first national conference on sign language to be held in Britain took place in Lancaster, and was attended by over 100 people. (The proceedings are published in

Woll et al., 1981.)

Apart from the proceedings of the Lancaster conference, there has at the time of writing been no book published specifically on British Sign Language, and it is this gap which the present book is intended to fill. The fact that the book appears in a series on 'Language, Education and Society' is indicative of the social and educational context which a study of BSL cannot ignore, even if the main aim is a linguistic analysis. Chapters 2 and 6 pay particular attention to the context in which BSL developed and is used.

My own introduction to BSL was originally through a practical course in ASL while a graduate student of linguistics in the United States. This led me to wonder about the existence of a sign language in Britain, and eventually to choose this as my PhD research topic. I had had no contact with British deaf people before my research in a British deaf community, and it must be emphasized, for the purposes of evaluating this book, that I have learned BSL only as a second language. Both because research on BSL is still in its early stages, and because I am not a native signer, the findings presented here are still tentative, and open to revision and modification. It is hoped that they will nevertheless be a stimulus to further research and interest in this topic.

Thanks are due to many people for their help in completing this book. Drafts were read and commented on by Richard Coates, Margaret Davison, Susan Fischer, Pierre Gorman, Helen James, John Lyons, Davina Merricks, Trevor Pateman, Suzanne Romaine, and Michael Stubbs. Davina Merricks also acted as a most helpful native signer consultant. Sharon Gretton typed the entire book onto the Sussex University computer; Helen James prepared the bibliography and did much of the editing, as well as helping in many ways in the final stages of the book's preparation. Davina Merricks and Sergio Solera provided the roughs for the illustrations, and I am also grateful to Sergio Solera in his capacity as a highly supportive spouse.

I should also like to acknowledge with thanks the support of the British Academy: without the help they provided from their Small Grants Research Fund in the Humanities, the completion of this book would have been infinitely more difficult. The British Deaf Association and the Reading deaf community must be acknowledged for their part in my original research into BSL, some of which is reported here. The illustration of the manual

alphabet on p. 9 is reproduced by kind permission of the Royal
National Institute of the Deaf.

Margaret Deuchar
Brighton, December 1982

1
What is BSL?

This chapter is intended as an introduction to British Sign Language (BSL) for those who have little previous experience of it. I shall attempt to answer the general question posed by the title of this chapter by trying to answer a series of questions of the kind typically asked by hearing people coming across sign language for the first time.

Let us start, however, with a rough definition of the term 'BSL' as it is used in this book. 'BSL' refers to a visual-gestural language used by many deaf people in Britain as their native language. The term 'visual-gestural' refers to both the perception and production of BSL: it is produced in a medium perceived visually, using gestures of the hands and the rest of the body including the face. Although the term 'manual' is sometimes used to describe BSL, I have avoided it here because of the implication that only the hands are involved. As we shall see, it is true that most research has concentrated on what the hands do, but recently we have become more aware of the important role played by body stance, head movement and facial expression.

BSL is used by many deaf people: we do not know exactly how many, though an estimate of 40,000 has been made, based on a survey in the early 1970s, of the number of deaf people attending clubs or known to social workers (Sutcliffe, personal communication). These people are mostly born deaf, to either deaf or hearing parents (but also hearing people born to deaf parents), and learn BSL either from their parents (if deaf), deaf siblings, or deaf peers. I have described BSL as these people's 'native language' because it is the language they know best and are most comfortable with. It may not necessarily be the first language they are exposed to, however. The particular way in which BSL is acquired will be discussed in chapter 7.

I shall now try to give some more idea of what BSL is like by attempting to answer the following questions: (1) Is sign language universal? (2) Is BSL based on English? (3) Is BSL iconic (or pictorial)? (4) Is BSL a language?

Is sign language universal?

People who ask this question are generally interested in knowing whether sign language, as used by the deaf, is universal in the sense of being the same all over the world. When told that it is not they are usually surprised and say that it should be. The idea that sign language must be universal seems to be very widespread, so it is interesting to consider why this should be so. I would suggest that the idea is based on one or more of the following erroneous assumptions: (i) sign language developed in a way radically different from spoken language; (ii) sign language is natural, instinctive and pictorial, so need not be learned; (iii) because deaf people from different countries appear to be able to communicate with one another, then they must be using the same language. Let us consider these assumptions.

It is well known that despite similarities in grammar or vocabulary between certain spoken languages, there are a large number of spoken languages of different types. Estimates of the exact number vary, largely because of the difficulty of determining how dialects or varieties of language should be grouped together, but one estimate is 'more than three thousand' (see Fromkin and Rodman, 1978, p. 350). Many spoken languages are mutually unintelligible, which means that the speaker of one language will not be able to understand the speaker of another language when each is using his or her own language. Languages develop in communities, through contact between speakers, so communities that are geographically separated from one another are likely to have different languages. This will apply to sign languages as well as to spoken languages.

We have little information about the origin and history of sign languages, but they seem to have developed where there were communities of deaf people, usually linked to deaf schools or welfare institutions. Before such institutions were formed (in the eighteenth and nineteenth centuries in Britain: see next chapter), deaf people would have been rather isolated from one another, although it is very likely that some kind of signing would have been used in various families. As a deaf community became established in a country, through links between various institutions, we may assume that a national sign language gradually developed, although differences related to different schools, for example, would have survived (see chapter 6 on variation in BSL). Deaf people would have had very little contact with one another across national boundaries, however, so there would have been no reason for an 'international' sign language to develop.

It may be argued that there was nevertheless some contact between educators of the deaf in different countries, the best documented link being that between France and the USA in the early nineteenth century (see next chapter). It is thought that because French manual methods were introduced into the first American school for the deaf, that American Sign Language (ASL) is descended from French Sign Language (FSL). There are certainly similarities between the two sign languages, but it seems likely that some kind of American Sign Language was already in existence, and that it was influenced by, rather than descended from, French Sign Language (cf Woodward, 1978). The effect of contact between deaf communities, or lack of it, is illustrated by the fact that ASL appears to be more similar to FSL than to BSL.

Linguistic research on spoken language has focused on similarities as well as differences in languages, searching for what may be universal or common to all languages. It may be that sign languages will turn out to have certain features which they share with one another and with spoken languages, but further research is needed to establish this. For the moment we can note that sign languages appear to differ from country to country in a similar way to spoken languages, and to have grown up in separate communities.

The second assumption, that sign language is 'natural and instinctive' may come from hearing people's association of the term 'sign language' with 'body language' or non-verbal communication. Non-verbal communication is not usually recognized as part of spoken language, and yet at least part of it seems to be learned and culture-specific (cf Hinde (ed.), 1972, Morris et al., 1979). Japanese people beckon with the palm down rather than up, for example, so that the gesture looks a little similar to the Western person's farewell gesture. Another common interpretation of the term 'sign language' is as an ad hoc gesture system used to communicate with people whose language one does not speak. This kind of system is usually closely tied to the immediate context (e.g. relying heavily on pointing to concrete objects) and used for conveying only limited messages, and is invented when it is required. This is not true of deaf sign language, however, which is not limited to the immediate context and can be used to communicate about a wide variety of topics. Nevertheless, its visual medium may lead people to expect it to be iconic and pictorial, or 'natural' in the sense of there being a 'natural' relationship between signs and what they represent. Meanwhile, however, we may note that the difficulty often experienced by hearing people in learning sign language means that it cannot be entirely 'natural' and 'instinctive'.

The final assumption, that deaf people from different countries must be using the same language because they can communicate with one another, was empirically tested by Jordan and Battison (1976), using subjects attending a World Federation of the Deaf Congress in Washington, D.C. Signers from different countries were asked to watch video tapes in various sign languages (American, Danish, French, Hong Kong, Italian and Portuguese), describing one of an array of pictures in front of them. Their accuracy in selecting the correct picture was measured. The results showed that for each single picture that the subject had to pick out, the percentage of errors was higher when the description was in a sign language other than the subjects' own. The conclusion, that 'deaf signers can understand their own sign language better than they can understand sign languages foreign to them' (p. 78), seems simple and uncontroversial, but at least it is evidence against the myth that sign languages are the same everywhere.

So how is it that we can observe signers communicating across national boundaries? It seems likely that deaf people are using a kind of compromise sign system, assessing the differences between their own sign languages and modifying them accordingly, borrowing signs from one another's languages and using mime where necessary. Deaf people are in fact quite expert at using mime on an ad hoc basis, through continual experience of trying to communicate with hearing people. Also, because their native sign languages generally have lower social status and fewer prescriptive norms attached to them than many spoken languages, I would suggest that deaf signers might be less inhibited about modifying their sign languages for ease of communication than would, say, speakers of English or French.

So sign language is not universal, and we are gradually finding out more and more about the sign languages of different countries. ASL has been investigated in the most detail (see e.g. Siple (ed.), 1978, Klima and Bellugi, 1979, Wilbur, 1979), but other sign languages currently being investigated apart from BSL include Japanese Sign Language (see Tanokami et al., 1976), Chinese Sign Language (see Klima and Bellugi, 1979), Swedish Sign Language (SSL) and Danish Sign Language (see e.g. Ahlgren and Bergman (eds), 1980). There has also been some research done on sign languages in less developed countries where deaf people tend to be less institutionalized and more integrated with hearing people (see e.g. Washabaugh, 1980, 1981).

As a final illustration of the fact that sign languages differ, at least on the level of vocabulary, here are some examples of different signs used to translate the English words 'woman' and 'England':

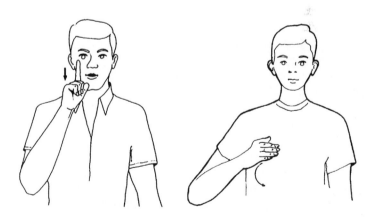

BSL WOMAN: index finger   *SSL WOMAN: cupped hand*
stroking right cheek   *outlining breast*

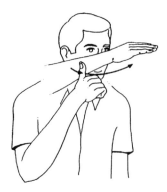

ASL WOMAN: thumb stroking cheek, then flat palm at eye level, neutral space

BSL ENGLAND: rubbing of fingerspelled 'e'

SSL ENGLAND: thumb and index finger clasping chin

ASL ENGLAND: hands clasped, palms down, moving back and forth

These examples illustrate the same English word being translated into different forms in different sign languages. In addition, the same form may have different meanings in different languages. For example, the sign meaning 'true' in BSL means 'stop' in ASL and 'right' or 'correct' in SSL. Also, the signs for 'good' and 'bad' in BSL mean 'male' and 'female' respectively in Japanese sign language.

Is BSL based on English?

People who do not expect sign language to be universal often seem to expect BSL to be based on English. They may assume, like some of those who think sign language is universal, that sign languages do not develop spontaneously like speech, but in addition, they tend to assume that BSL must have been invented by hearing people to help deaf people communicate or learn English. BSL should not be confused with the Paget Gorman Sign System (PGSS) which was indeed invented as a contrived system to help deaf people learn English. PGSS is a manual representation of English designed to be used simultaneously with speech, and is used in a few British schools for the deaf. There is also some discussion currently about the possible role of BSL in schools for the deaf, but BSL is not widely accepted in the classroom (see chapters 2 and 7). In some schools signs from BSL are used simultaneously with spoken English, but in this case the syntax of the signs is modified to fit the structure of English (as in 'Signed English': see chapter 2, p. 37).

However, BSL as used natively by deaf people is quite different from English. Individual signs in BSL are roughly equivalent to words in English and are translatable as such, but they do not directly represent either the sounds or meanings of English words. The only part of BSL which directly represents English words is the fingerspelling system, or manual alphabet. This alphabet is two-handed (unlike the one-handed system used in conjunction with ASL and some other sign languages) and is a series of hand configurations representing the letters of the alphabet (see illustration on next page). It is used by signers for spelling English names and places, or words for which there is no equivalent sign.

BSL signs which are not part of the fingerspelling system are made up of a different set of hand configurations from those of the manual alphabet, and involve a variety of movements and locations on the body. The activity of the hands is accompanied by various kinds of non-manual activity, such as facial expression and head movement. Just as the words of spoken language can be described as being made up of individual sounds or 'phonemes', signs can be described as being made up of various components, such as places on the body where the sign is made, hand shape and arrangement, and movement. The description of individual signs will be discussed in detail in chapter 3.

As I suggested above, there is no one to one correspondence between the meanings of BSL signs and English words. Some signs may have more than one possible English translation, and some English words may have more than one possible BSL translation. One BSL sign, made with a shaking motion of the right hand in front of the body, palm inwards, may mean 'pain', 'expensive' or 'Brighton', depending on the context (see illustration on p. 10).

The British manual alphabet

PAIN, EXPENSIVE or BRIGHTON

Conversely, the English verb 'read' may be translated into one BSL sign if the object is a book, and into another if it is a notice:

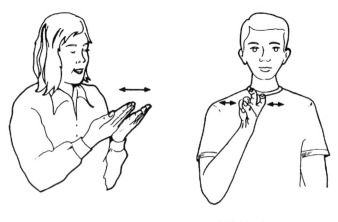

READ (a book)   *READ (a notice)*

In addition, the syntax of BSL, or the way the signs are put together, is different from the way in which words are combined in English. In English, for example, it is normal for the order of the words to be subject-verb-object, as in the sentence 'I saw the boy'. In BSL, however, this order may not necessarily be followed, and a subject and object may not always appear overtly in the way that usually happens in English. The syntax of BSL will be discussed in detail in chapter 4.

Despite the fact that BSL has its own structure, which is distinct from that of English, it is of course used within a hearing community of which the majority language is English. As a result there is some influence from English on BSL vocabulary, and on BSL syntax in certain situations. As examples of English influence on the vocabulary, the signs for 'mother' and 'father' are finger-spelled 'm' and 'f' repeated, and the sign for 'England' is finger-spelled 'e' with a rubbing motion of the fingers added. The syntax of BSL is affected particularly in formal, public situations, where the order of signs tends to approximate to that of English words. (For further details see chapter 6.)

Not only is BSL distinct from English, but other sign languages are also distinct from the spoken language of the corresponding hearing community. We may recall that ASL is different from BSL (in fact the two sign languages are usually considered mutually unintelligible, although a small proportion of the vocabulary may be shared), despite the fact that they are both used within English speaking communities. ASL is no more similar to English than is BSL. Similarly, Swedish Sign Language is distinct from Swedish as is Norwegian Sign Language from Norwegian. It is interesting to note that the difference between Swedish and Norwegian sign languages is reported to be greater than that between the Swedish and Norwegian spoken languages, which are mutually intelligible (Martinsen, personal communication).

Is BSL iconic (or pictorial)?

People asking this question usually want to know if there is a direct, depictive relationship between signs and what they represent. According to Hockett (1958, p. 577), iconicity involves 'some element of geometrical similarity' between a sign or its equivalent and its meaning, whereas arbitrariness is the absence of iconicity. Given that iconicity is often contrasted with arbitrariness, and also that arbitrariness is generally considered an important characteristic of language (see below for further discussion), a question about the presence of iconicity in BSL takes on particular significance.

One might expect a language in a visual medium to exhibit

more iconicity than one in an auditory medium, in that objects in the external world tend to have more visual than auditory associations. Spoken languages are recognized to have some onomatopoeic words, like 'peewit' in English, which represents the sound made by the bird, or 'splash' which represents the sound of water, but there is a limit to the number of entities or actions which have salient auditory characteristics. Many entities and actions have salient visual characteristics, however. In the following examples of BSL signs, there is a direct relation between the sign and a visual characteristic of what it represents:

HOUSE: hands outline roof and walls

COME: index finger moves towards the signer

NEAR: one index finger is held upright near the other

These signs provide a direct representation of shape, movement and spatial relationship respectively, each being visual characteristics easily associated with the meaning of one of the signs. It is difficult, on the other hand, to imagine any characteristic sounds which might be associated with any of these meanings.

It will of course be realized that iconicity is only possible in signs with meanings that lend themselves to visual characterization. Although visual characterization of concrete objects, movement and spatial relationships may be generally easier than auditory characterization, signs representing abstract ideas, for example, are much less likely to be iconic. There is a danger in assuming that because BSL makes use of iconicity, this is its only resource, and that it cannot be used to represent non-visual meanings. Some systems make use only of iconicity (e.g. mime and ad hoc systems) but these will be limited in what they can communicate. However, there seems to be no reason why BSL should not exploit both iconic and arbitrary relationships between signs and their meanings. We can postulate three categories of sign in BSL: (i) arbitrary; (ii) indexic; and (iii) iconic. (cf Peirce's (1932) tripartite categorization of signs, where our first would be similar to his 'symbol' and the other two the same as his categories of index and icon.)

(i) Arbitrary signs exhibit no obvious relation between the sign and its meaning. Both concrete entities and abstract ideas may have arbitrary signs, as the following descriptions of signs show:

SISTER: bent index finger touching nose

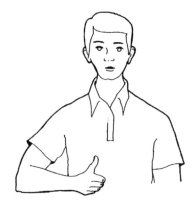

GOOD: fist held with thumb upwards

TRUE: right hand, flat palm, contacts left hand, flat palm upwards, so that right hand is above left and the hands at right angles and perpendicular to one another

    (ii) Indexic signs involve pointing directly at their referent, or at a point in space representing that referent. 'I' and 'you' are signed by pointing to the signer and the addressee respectively, and 'he' and 'she' are signed by pointing directly to a third person if present, or by pointing to a location in space which refers to a third person. Some parts of the body are also signed indexically: 'foot', for example, is signed by pointing to the signer's foot.

(iii) Iconic signs involve depiction which can be either 'virtual' or 'substitutive' (cf Mandel, 1977a). In virtual depiction, the hand traces a picture in space, as in 'football', where the hands outline the shape of a football.

FOOTBALL

In substitutive depiction, the hands are formed into the shape of the object itself, or an object typically involved in the action. In the sign for 'tree', for example, the forearm is held up and the fingers spread to represent a tree's trunk and branches; 'stand' is also an example of substitutive depiction in that the index and middle fingers are held in a 'V' shape, pointing downwards, as in the shape of two legs standing.

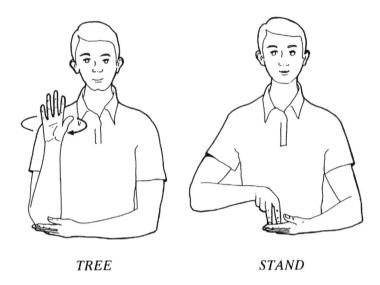

TREE   STAND

It is important to realize that while iconicity means non-arbitrar-
iness, it does not necessarily mean non-conventionality. This is
because where there is an iconic relation between a sign and its
referent, the details of this relationship do not seem to be universally determined. The BSL sign for 'tree' was given as an example
of an iconic sign, involving substitutive depiction. Now the signs
for 'tree' in both Danish and Chinese Sign Language can also be
said to be iconic, but they are different from one another as well as
from the BSL sign. In Chinese Sign Language there is substitutive
depiction of 'tree' as in BSL, but the index finger and thumb of
each hand are placed together in a circle representing the diameter
of a tree trunk. In Danish Sign Language 'tree' is signed with
virtual depiction in that the hands trace the outline of a tree,
from top to bottom (see Bellugi and Klima, 1976, p. 523). These
examples show that iconicity does not mean determinism of form,
but that forms are conventional for a given language community.
(This point is often made for onomatopoeic forms like 'cock-a-
doodle-do' and French 'cocorico' in spoken language, cf e.g.
Mandel, 1977a, p. 61.)
    Another point about iconicity is that it should not be equated
with transparency. The fact that there is a non-arbitrary relationship between a sign and its referent does not mean that the sign
can be understood without prior knowledge of its meaning. Klima

and Bellugi (1979) distinguish between transparency and translucency of signs: a sign is transparent if its meaning can be guessed
without prior knowledge, and it is translucent if a relation between
the sign and its meaning can be discerned once the meaning is
known. Klima and Bellugi tested the transparency and translucency of 90 ASL signs by showing these signs to a group of people
who did not already know their meaning, and to a group who did.
The experiment with the first group was to test how many of
the signs were transparent, that is, how many would be guessed
correctly. They found that 81 out of 90 signs were not guessed by
any of the ten subjects, thus indicating a rather low degree of
transparency for these signs. However, when testing translucency
in the same signs by showing them to a second group, they found
that for more than half of the signs presented there was overall
agreement on the basis for the relation between the signs and
their meaning. (I obtained similar results from a pilot test using
BSL signs.)

Having discussed the nature of iconicity in sign language, we
may ask what its significance is for users. There is some evidence
that it may be useful to hearing sign language learners, who seem
to find it easier to remember signs if they can perceive an iconic
relation between the sign and its referent (cf Mandel, 1977b). This
has led to certain folk etymologies of signs used in sign language
classes, like the idea that 'morning' in BSL (fingertips touch left
side of chest then right) comes from the idea of drawing the
curtains back. It is true that deaf people seem to use iconic principles in inventing some new signs, but the iconic relation between
the sign and its referent is often not perceived by deaf people
once it has become established. Also, some research on ASL has
shown that there is a tendency for signs to become more arbitrary
and less iconic over time (cf Frishberg, 1975).

As far as native acquisition of sign language is concerned, some
researchers have suggested that the first signs tend to be learned
earlier than the first words in hearing children because of the
greater iconicity of signs (cf e.g. Brown, 1977). However, as others
(e.g. Woll and Lawson, 1981) point out, children may be too
young to perceive the iconic relation, as in the case of the BSL
sign for 'milk' which comes from the motion of milking a cow.
Brennan (personal communication) noted that a two and a half
year old produced the iconic sign for 'tree' (see above) with the
forearm horizontal rather than vertical, thus losing the resem-

blance to an upright tree. In any case, Bonvillian (1983) found
that only about a third of the signs learned by very young children
were recognizably iconic.

Further psycholinguistic evidence against overestimating the
significance of iconicity in sign language comes from the findings
by Klima and Bellugi (1979) that iconicity did not have a role in
deaf signers' recall of ASL signs: instead the abstract formational
components of signs seemed to be important in memory processes.
(The nature of these abstract formational components in BSL will
be discussed in chapter 3.)

So while the presence of iconicity in BSL can be recognized, its
significance should not be overestimated. This is for the following
reasons: arbitrariness is also found in the language; iconicity in
BSL does not preclude some degree of conventionality; and
psycholinguistic evidence suggests that iconicity does not appear
to play a significant role for native signers in their acquisition and
use of sign language.

Is BSL a language?

So far we have assumed that BSL is a language, if only in the use
of the term 'language' to describe it. However, we should give
some consideration to this question, as it is often asked explicitly
or implicitly (as in the questions discussed above). It is a very
difficult question to answer, partly because linguists are still far
from being in agreement about what the defining characteristics
of language are. A definition such as 'a system of communication'
is not sufficient because we presumably want to distinguish
language from traffic signals or bee-dancing. The definition of
language that we choose will depend on our criteria for language.
The following two questions will lead to different answers as to
what language is: (i) What is language like? (ii) What can language
do? The first question involves emphasis on the structural properties of language, and the second on its functional properties.

The first question has most commonly been asked by linguists,
who have been concerned both to discover properties that are
common to all languages (cf e.g. Greenberg, 1966) and to determine what differentiates human language from animal communication systems (cf e.g. Hockett, 1960). The latter approach will

be most useful for our purpose of distinguishing language from non-language.

Lyons (1981) draws attention to the particular flexibility and versatility of languages, and suggests, in line with the work of many others, that this is made possible by certain important structural properties, in particular, *arbitrariness*, *duality*, *discreteness* and *productivity*. We may consider whether these properties are reflected in BSL.

Arbitrariness was described earlier as contrasting with iconicity. Linguists of the twentieth century place particular emphasis on the arbitrariness of language, no doubt largely because of the influential work of the Swiss linguist, de Saussure. Saussure's idea of 'l'arbitraire du signe' drew attention to the arbitrary relationship between a word or 'signifier' and what it represents, the 'signified'. As Saussure (1959) points out, the word 'tree' or 'arbre' (in French) is a purely arbitrary form which happens to have been selected to represent the meaning, 'tree'.

We may make several observations about this view of arbitrariness: first, it was not designed to encompass sign languages, whose visual medium, as has been pointed out, may lend itself more to non-arbitrary representation; second, linguists before the time of Saussure were divided as to whether language was governed by nature or convention (cf Robins, 1967, p. 17), the latter now usually being associated with arbitrariness; third, arbitrariness was discussed by Saussure with reference to the relationship between words and their meanings and not, for example, with reference to syntax (the way words are put together).

Lyons (1977) points out that a definition of 'arbitrary' as the absence of iconicity is rather narrow. He says:

> It is legitimate, however, to use the term 'arbitrary' to describe any feature that cannot be said to derive from the properties of the channel along which language is normally transmitted, from the physiological and psychological mechanisms employed in the production or reception of language or from the functions language is called upon to perform (pp. 70–71).

Language would doubtless appear less arbitrary if the term were defined in the broader sense suggested by Lyons. Bolinger (1975, 1980) suggests that language has both arbitrary and non-arbitrary aspects. He shows that whereas sound systems tend to be arbitrary, syntax may not.

Lyons (1977) suggests, nevertheless, that arbitrariness in the narrow sense (i.e. absence of iconicity) may well be an important characteristic of language. We have seen that BSL makes use of both arbitrariness and iconicity in individual signs, and I see no reason why the two properties should be mutually exclusive in a language. Frishberg (1975) has suggested that there may be an ideal balance of arbitrariness and iconicity in language.

A final point about arbitrariness is that it is often associated with conventionality in language (as opposed to 'naturalness'). As we saw earlier, iconicity in BSL does not imply complete freedom from conventionality since the actual form of an iconic sign is culturally determined, and iconic signs tend to be translucent rather than transparent. So in so far as conventionality is an important characteristic of language, it is certainly exhibited by BSL.

The next property of language to be considered, *duality*, is defined by Lyons (1981, p. 20) as 'the property of having two levels of structure, such that the units of the primary level are composed of elements of the secondary level and each of the two levels has its own principles of organization'. In spoken language, meaningful units such as words make up the primary level, and are composed of secondary level units of sounds, which in themselves do not have meaning. So, to give an example, the word 'sister' has meaning on the primary level, though its individual sounds do not. In BSL, the sign for 'sister' (see above, p. 13) has a similar meaning to the corresponding English word on the primary level, but the parts which make it up, the bent index finger touching the nose, do not themselves have meaning, and so can be considered component parts on the secondary level like sounds. Thus BSL can be considered to exhibit duality.

The property of *discreteness* is characteristic of the secondary level of language, which means sounds in spoken languages, formational components in signs. We usually consider the sounds of spoken language to be discrete, or separately identifiable, so that we consider [b] and [p], for example, to be separate sounds in English. The difference between them is important for distinguishing words like 'bit' and 'pit' from one another. In actual speech though, the distinction between [b] and [p] is relative rather than absolute, since it depends on when our vocal cords start vibrating after the closure of the mouth and lips (ignoring the difference in aspiration which we find in English). The onset of vocal cord vibration is earlier for [b], later for [p], so that one could produce a sound somewhere between [b] and [p]. However, this sound does not generally occur in English: English maintains the discreteness of [b] and [p] from the point of view of the sound system, even though the vocal signal is continuous (the opposite of discrete). Instead of using vocal signals, BSL uses the visual-spatial medium, which is clearly continuous from a physical point of view. However, it too can be divided up into discrete parts for the analysis of contrasts between signs. To give an example, the signer's chest and his or her lower trunk are spatially contiguous, but the signs for 'sorry' and 'delicious' are differentiated by the fact that the first is made on the chest, and the other on the lower trunk (Brennan, Colville and Lawson, 1980, p. 71). Both signs are made with a flat hand in circular motion.

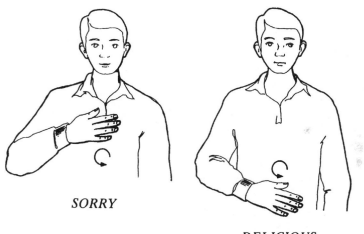

SORRY

DELICIOUS

The contrast between these examples illustrates that discreteness is a property of BSL. It is worth pointing out here that mime is different from sign language in that it does not appear to exhibit discreteness (cf Klima and Bellugi, 1979). The property of discreteness in BSL will be further illustrated in chapter 3.

The final structural property of language that we shall consider, is its potential to be used for constructing utterances that have never been produced before: this is known as *productivity*. Limited signal systems do not have this property. Traffic lights, for example, are able to signal 'stop', 'go', 'get ready to stop' and 'get ready to go', but not, for example, 'you will be fined if you cross a red light', or 'there was an accident here this morning'. The potential of language to produce an unlimited number of new utterances comes from the fact that although it has a finite number of elements and units, grammatical rules specifying their combination allow an infinite number of constructions of units. It is important to note here that the notion 'grammatical rule' is to be understood in the sense of patterns followed by speakers using their own language, rather than in the prescriptive sense of rules which have to be obeyed (and are often not). An example of a grammatical rule in English would be that definite articles occur before the noun rather than after it, allowing a phrase such as 'the book' but not 'book the'. Such rules are language specific: in Swedish, for example, the definite article is placed after the noun, not before it. An example of the kind of prescriptive rule we are not concerned with here would be the following: 'Do not end a sentence with a preposition'. Many English speakers have been taught this rule explicitly at school, but few follow it, at least in speech. The kind of rule we are concerned with does not have to be learned consciously by native speakers, but is simply followed. In BSL signers are clearly using rules in a productive way because they are continually producing new utterances, and there does not seem to be a limit as to what they can talk about. Research on grammatical rules in BSL is only just beginning, but it should be emphasized that the approach is descriptive rather than prescriptive. We are seeking to discover what grammatical rules are being followed by native signers, not telling them what rules they should follow. An example of a grammatical rule in BSL is that Yes–No questions are formed by raising the eyebrows while signing what would otherwise be an affirmative statement. So, for example, raising the eyebrows while producing the sign for 'good' (see illustration on p. 14) has the effect of asking whether someone or something is good rather than stating that this is the case. (See chapter 4 for more information on grammatical rules in BSL.) Although research is only just beginning in this area, BSL certainly seems to have the characteristic of productivity in that it is rule-governed (cf Lyons, 1981, p. 23).

So far we have considered whether BSL manifests the structural properties characteristic of language, but, as I indicated earlier, language can be described in terms of its functional as well as its structural properties. Various schemes for the functions of language have been suggested (see Robinson, 1972 for discussion), but one of the best known is that produced by Jakobson (1960). Jakobson suggests that language is used for the following communicative functions: referential, conative, emotive, phatic, metalinguistic and poetic. The referential function has to do with the conveying of information, as one might, for example, in describing the events of one's daily life. This use of language for referential or descriptive purposes is common for BSL: deaf people meeting in clubs spend a considerable amount of time telling one another about various things which have happened to them recently. The conative (or instrumental) function of language is its use in getting other people to do things: BSL is used to order food and drinks in a deaf club, or to keep children under control. The emotive (or expressive) function has to do with conveying the speaker's (or the signer's) feelings: in BSL feelings are conveyed especially by facial expression and body stance. The phatic function refers to the use of language to signal contact between people, without necessarily conveying information referentially. Greetings fulfil this function, and in BSL there are signs conventionally made when initiating encounters. The sign for 'good', made with movement towards the addressee (or with a sweeping movement encompassing a group of addressees) is equivalent to 'hello'. The metalinguistic function of language refers to the use of language to talk about language itself: BSL users often do not recognize BSL as a language, but will nevertheless use it to discuss the difference between signs in different regions, or to correct a hearing person's error. The last function, the poetic, refers to the use of language for aesthetic or literary purposes. Not very much research has been done on this in BSL, although Klima and Bellugi (1979) report the exploitation of ASL for the purpose of wit and poetry. BSL is certainly used for jokes and story-telling, and there is at least one BSL poet, Dorothy Miles, whose poetry has been signed on television. The poetic function of languages with low social status is not generally so widely recognized as in the case of the 'literary' languages. However, there are indications that the status of BSL is improving, so we may expect to see more public manifestation of its poetic function.

I have been trying to answer the question of whether BSL is a language, and have shown that it manifests at least some of the structural and functional properties of language which are considered criterial. However, I have not dealt with the question of whether the medium of BSL disqualifies it as a language. Hockett (1960) gives a 'vocal-auditory channel' as his first design feature of language. Language does of course exist in the written medium, but writing is usually considered a secondary manifestation in relation to speech. There are several reasons for this, for example, that people generally learn to speak before they learn to write, and that speech developed before writing in human history. Nevertheless, the existence of both speech and writing demonstrates what Lyons (1981, p. 11) calls the 'medium-transferability' of language, and he suggests that too little attention has been paid to this property. Of course there is no a priori reason why the primary medium of language should be speech, and there are some proponents of the theory that language actually originated in the visual-gestural medium (cf Hewes, 1973). Reasons given for subsequent use of the vocal medium include the fact that the visual medium is not available at night, and that communication with the hands interferes with their use for other purposes. However, these are practical rather than linguistic reasons for the advantages of one medium over another, and there is an obvious practical reason why the vocal medium is not suitable for deaf people. In any case, the visual medium of sign language certainly has some advantages which the spoken medium lacks. For example, sign language can be communicated over longer distance than spoken language (without amplification) and can be used in noisy conditions (such as factories, discotheques) or where there are barriers to sound (e.g. train windows).

But does sign language have medium-transferability? (Recall that BSL is not a secondary representation of English.) I think the answer to this is, potentially, 'yes', though the potential is not fully realized. I would argue that BSL is like a spoken language used in a developing country, which does not have a written form. The speakers of such languages are not able to write them down, but there is a potential for a written form, and in such cases written forms are often produced by missionaries or linguists arriving in the area, equipped with the International Phonetic Alphabet or equivalent. Phonetic alphabets are obviously not appropriate for sign language, but notation systems are being developed by linguists (see chapters 3 and 8), and one of these, 'Sign Writing' (see chapter 8, p. 189) has a version designed for use by deaf people writing their own sign language down, and can be either printed or handwritten. So far this system has been used to produce a newspaper in ASL, and is supposed to be usable for all sign languages (see Sutton, 1981). It has not yet been used by signers of BSL as far as I know, but I see no reason why it should not be. In any case, it seems to me that medium-transferability must be possible if a language has the property of discreteness, which does seem to be the case with BSL as well as ASL. It is also worth mentioning in this connection that research is currently being conducted on transferring ASL to point-light displays for eventual transmission by telephone (cf Tartter and Fischer, 1983).

A final point to mention in connection with the question as to whether BSL is a language, is the danger of approaching a sign language with oral preconceptions, i.e. of looking for exact parallels with spoken language, and concluding that it is not really a language if the parallels are not there. This kind of approach may not only lead one to miss some important aspects of BSL structure, but it may also lead one to lose sight of the important connections between structure and function in language. If one carefully maintains the connection, however, the link between structure and function in BSL may be analysed in two directions. Going from function to structure we may ask: how are certain important grammatical functions, such as time-marking and negation, carried out in BSL? In the other direction (structure to function) we may isolate certain structural features of BSL, like mouth movement and facial expression, and try to work out what function they perform. An attempt to describe BSL structure in relation to its function should help to make progress in our discovery of what characteristics are fundamental to language, regardless of their medium, and which are medium-specific. Thus we may come closer to answering not only the question 'Is BSL a language?' but also the question 'What is language?'

Summary

In this chapter I have tried to give a general introduction to BSL by discussing questions commonly asked about it. We have seen that sign language is not universal, but that BSL is distinct from sign languages in other countries, such as American or Chinese Sign Language. We have also seen that it is not based on English, and that although it exhibits some iconicity it also makes use of

What is BSL?

arbitrariness and conventionality. Finally, BSL seems to be a language according to many of the structural and functional properties found in languages as we know them, but we are still uncertain about what the defining characteristics of language are and hope that further research on BSL will shed light on this question.

2

The origin and use of BSL

In this chapter I plan to give a general view of the historical and social factors which have affected the development of BSL and the way in which it is now used. Whereas chapters 3 and 4 will deal specifically with the structure of BSL as a language, this chapter will focus on the use of BSL in its historical and social setting.

On p. 1, I defined BSL as a visual-gestural language used by many deaf people in Britain as their native language. I did not say what I meant by deaf people, but it may have been reasonably assumed that I was referring to people with some degree of hearing loss. However, it would probably be more accurate to describe BSL as the language of the 'deaf community' in Britain rather than of 'deaf people', since there are many deaf people who do not use BSL, and many people who use BSL who are not deaf. Deaf people who do not use BSL include many of those who became deaf after learning to speak, especially those who became deaf as adults, and some of those who were born deaf, but have never had an opportunity to learn BSL through lack of contact with the deaf community. Examples of people who use BSL but who are not deaf include those whose parents are deaf, or those who have learned BSL as a second language to English, through contact with the deaf community.

So what is the deaf community? All those whose writings on the deaf community that I have read (Padden, 1980, Markowicz and Woodward, 1975, Lawson, 1981) seem to agree that sign language is its defining characteristic, whether ASL in the case of the American deaf community, or BSL in the case of the British deaf community. The close link between the notions of language and community is also alluded to in the term 'speech community', which is defined by Gumperz (1972, p. 219) as 'any human aggre-

gate characterized by regular and frequent interaction by means
of a shared body of verbal signs and set off from similar aggregates
by significant differences in language usage'. I shall be using the
term 'deaf community' to mean the deaf sign language community,
which in Britain refers to users of BSL.

As we saw in chapter 1 (p. 7), BSL was not invented as an
artificial sysem, but is assumed to have developed spontaneously
like spoken language. When a communication system is needed
between two or more people, it will develop quite naturally even
if its 'inventors' are not exposed to a pre-existing language. This
has been shown quite dramatically in the research of Feldman et
al. (1978), where some deaf children who were not signed to by
adults, developed their own sign systems.

If language develops primarily out of a need for communication
between two or more people, it seems reasonable to assume that
BSL developed when deaf people came together in groups. Some
kind of 'home sign' system may have been used in deaf families,
though it is worth bearing in mind that not more than about 10
per cent of deaf children have deaf parents (cf Conrad, 1981).
Deaf children with deaf parents in early times may have developed
a family sign system which, unless they were in contact with other
deaf families, may have been different from any other; and deaf
children with hearing parents may have evolved some more
limited visual system of communication for the family. However
we can only speculate about such systems since I know of no
written records that have been kept of any, and cine-film tech-
nology has not been available for very long.

Although there would have been individual isolated deaf families from an early date, the real beginning of the deaf community
must have been in the first institutions for deaf people, which
were schools and missions to the deaf: both of these became
established in the nineteenth century. Because the deaf in Britain
have never lived in isolation like some cultural minorities, but
have been geographically scattered, institutions for deaf people
would have been the main meeting point for them. Since such
institutions did not become established until the last century, we
cannot speak with certainty of the existence of BSL before then.
This makes it a rather new language, especially compared with
the well established European languages like English and French,
and may lead one to question whether BSL should in fact be
described as a pidgin or a creole, as are some newly emergent

spoken languages. This question will be further discussed in chapter 6. Meanwhile, since schools for the deaf and social centres for the deaf, which have developed from the earlier missions, are still the main focus for the use of BSL and the factors which condition its status, it may be useful here to sketch their history briefly.

Education for deaf children in Britain did not become free and compulsory until 1893 (1891 in Scotland) with the passing of the Education (Blind and Deaf Children) Act (see Hodgson, 1953). However, the first school for the deaf was started in the eighteenth century, and interest in deaf education in Britain seems to have begun in the seventeenth century. The writings and records of these early educationalists are the first indication we have of the use of any kind of sign language in Britain. According to Hodgson (1953, p. 95), John Bulwer was 'the first English writer on the problem of deafness', and in 1644 Bulwer published a book called *Chirologia: Or the Naturall Language of the Hand . . .* which dealt with the use and value of manual gestures for speech, oratory and acting (cf Wright, 1969, p. 146). His gestures do not seem to be based on the sign language of the deaf themselves, though he does refer to a manual alphabet used by the deaf. According to Hodgson, Bulwer was the first to advocate a school for the deaf, and like most people interested in the education of the deaf in Britain from this time onwards, he was really more interested in devising ways of teaching the deaf to speak than in describing or using any sign language they might have of their own. Bulwer is also known for his *Philocophus, or the Deaf and Dumb Man's Friend . . .*, which is a pioneering work on the art of speech-reading.

George Dalgarno, a teacher who invented a finger alphabet for teaching the deaf (see Hodgson, 1953, pp. 91–2), also took a more theoretical interest in language, recognizing that language is not necessarily to be equated with speech. He says, 'Neither is there any reason in nature why the mind should more easily apprehend the image of things impressed upon sounds than upon characters; when there is nothing either natural or symbolic in one or the other' (quoted in Hodgson, 1953, p. 92). In these ideas, however, he was ahead of his time, since teachers of the deaf from this time right up to the twentieth century have tended to concentrate on speech teaching in particular, rather than on language teaching in general.

Bulwer and Dalgarno were theoreticians of deaf education
rather than practitioners, but Dalgarno's alphabet was used by
one of the first known English teachers of the deaf, John Wallis,
who began teaching a deaf pupil in 1661. According to Hodgson
(1953, p. 99), 'He seems to have begun his teaching with natural
signs (gestures) which he learned from his pupil'. It is interesting
that Wallis used the pupil's own signs, rather than inventing any
for him, and this raises the question of whether the pupil already
used any kind of sign language himself. Unfortunately we have
no information about this. Although Wallis, like Dalgarno, recognized that ideas might be expressed in a visual as well as a spoken
medium (see Seigel, 1969, p. 99, and Wallis, 1670), his main aim
was nevertheless to teach speech, so that he would have used
signs primarily as a means to this end. William Holder, a contemporary of Wallis and also his rival as a teacher of the deaf, had a
similar aim, and he is reported to have 'used a leather strap to
illustrate the position of the tongue in the articulation of various
sounds' (Wright, 1969, p. 148). Like Wallis, Holder also used
Dalgarno's alphabet as a teaching aid, although I know of no
record of its use after this time. An early version of the two-
handed alphabet which is widely used in the British deaf
community today, and even known by some hearing people, first
appeared in an anonymous pamphlet with the title *Digiti-Lingua*,
in 1698.

A two-handed alphabet seems to have been used to some extent
in deaf education by Henry Baker, a teacher of the deaf in the
eighteenth century (cf Hodgson, 1953, p. 120), but he was very
secretive about his methods. Secrecy seems to have been characteristic of eighteenth century education, possibly because of the
prevailing attitude to deafness as something which could be 'cured'
if only a technique could be found. This naturally led to charlat-
anism and profiteering. Seigel (1969) argues that the British attitude to deafness in the eighteenth century was very different from
that prevailing in France, where the ideas of the Enlightenment,
and the associated new theories concerning language and symbolic
communication, received immediate application in a new
approach to deafness and sign language. In Britain, however,
Seigel says that educators of the deaf remained isolated from the
new intellectual climate and were 'basically utilitarian' (Seigel,
1969, p. 97). He says that 'they overemphasized the "correcting"
of the obvious manifestations of deafness, and they disregarded

the complexities of language as an intricate and highly formal system of symbolic communication' (p. 97). It was probably due to this difference of attitude that sign language was systematically introduced into deaf education in France in a way that it was not in Britain (as we shall see).

Deaf education in Britain in the latter part of the eighteenth century and the earlier part of the nineteenth century was dominated by the secret methods of the Braidwood family, who established various schools for the deaf. The first of these was set up by Thomas Braidwood in 1760, in Edinburgh, and was known as the 'Braidwood Academy'. We know little of Braidwood's methods because of the secrecy surrounding them, although Hodgson states that with his first pupil 'he made no use of manual signs of any sort, because he had never heard of them' (Hodgson, 1953, p. 140). While it seems plausible that Braidwood had no experience of manual signs when he began working with individual pupils, it seems likely that once there were several forming a small community, they would have used signs among themselves. Perhaps the teachers learned to sign from the pupils themselves, for McLoughlin (1980, p. 18) states that the Braidwood schools used a 'combined method of speech, lip-reading and natural signs'.

In 1783 the Braidwood Academy was moved from Edinburgh to London, where Thomas Braidwood was joined by his two nephews, Joseph Watson and John Braidwood, trained in the secret methods. Like the Edinburgh Academy, this school was open only to those who could afford it, but in 1792 a Society was formed to undertake the education of the 'indigent deaf' (cf Hodgson, 1953, p. 148). This led to the 'asylum system' of deaf education, whereby schools for poor deaf children were supported by charity. The first asylum, in London, was run by Braidwood's nephew Watson, who carried on the Braidwood method. After 1806, when Thomas Braidwood died, Watson clearly felt released from his bond of secrecy, since in 1809 he published his *Instruction of the Deaf and Dumb*. In this Watson reveals knowledge of and interest in sign language, suggesting that all teachers of the deaf should be able to understand it. He explicity disagrees with the French method of Abbé de l'Epée (1712–89) who introduced 'signes méthodiques' to teach French to deaf pupils, using these 'methodical signs' in combination with the 'signes naturels' he saw them using. He suggests that instead of the teacher manipulating the sign language, signs should be used to introduce pupils to speech. In his writing Watson was clearly uncertain about the linguistic status of sign language, but he could possibly be interpreted as advocating what in modern terms would be bilingualism in BSL and English rather than Total Communication (see chapter 7, p. 174 for discussion of this approach).

Epée's system of 'methodical signs' had no chance of being tried in Britain until the death of the last Braidwood, Thomas, who was head of one of the asylum-type schools for the deaf in Birmingham. Thomas Braidwood was replaced by a Swiss man, Louis du Puget, who introduced Epée's 'silent method' which involved the use of signs. This was the beginning of an interlude in the exclusion of signs from the formal education of the deaf, and it lasted until the late nineteenth century. During this time the use of signs would have become common in British deaf schools, both inside and outside the classroom.

However, there was little direct contact between users of Epée's original system and users of signs in British schools because the Braidwoods had ignored it in the eighteenth century, and now that it became influential in the nineteenth century in Britain, it was on the wane in the rest of Europe, where the German or 'oral' method as advocated by Heinicke was becoming influential. It is probably partly because of the separate educational histories of France and Britain that BSL developed quite separately from French Sign Language. ASL, on the other hand, is sometimes described as descended from French Sign Language, because of contact in 1815 between Thomas Gallaudet, the American teacher of the deaf, and Sicard, Epée's successor in France. It is interesting to note that Gallaudet turned to the French for advice on deaf education when he was rebuffed by the Braidwoods in Britain (see Hodgson, 1953, Wright, 1969).

The opposing educational methods of Epée and Heinicke had been discussed in a correspondence between them in the late eighteenth century, which was the beginning of what is known as the oral–manual controversy. While Epée's manual system was more influential in his and Heinicke's lifetimes, Heinicke's oral method was promoted later, in the nineteenth century, by some of Heinicke's more ardent followers. Two of these, Gerrit van Asch and William van Praagh, came to England in the 1860s to help re-establish oralism, and in 1872 the Association for the Oral Instruction of the Deaf and Dumb was established. The aims of this association were given international recognition at the

International Conference of Teachers of the Deaf in Milan in 1880, where it was resolved that:

> Considering the incontestable superiority of speech over signs in restoring the deaf mute to society, and in giving him a more perfect knowledge of language . . . the oral method ought to be preferred to that of signs for the education and instruction of the deaf and dumb (quoted in Wright, 1969, p. 177).

After this the oral method became the preferred method of instruction everywhere except the United States, where both oral and manual methods were used.

By 1893, as stated on p. 29, deaf education in Britain had become free and compulsory. The asylum system of deaf education was ended in that existing schools were to be funded by grants and rates, and new schools were to be built where necessary by the local School Boards. Deaf schools would thus become even more of a focus for the deaf community in that, in theory at least, every deaf child could be educated in a special school. The system of deaf education remained quite separate from that of hearing children until 1944 when the two were integrated to some extent by the Education Act of 1944 (see Wright, 1969, p. 180).

This overview of the development of deaf education in Britain has aimed to show how the establishment of schools must have satisfied an important precondition for the development of BSL: a community of deaf people interacting with one another. We know indirectly from some educators' comments that some kind of signing was used between deaf pupils, but we know little of its nature, since the main interest of most educators was the development of speech. We have also seen how attitudes towards signing as part of formal education were overwhelmingly negative, and this should help to illuminate our discussion later in this chapter of the issues surrounding the use of BSL in the twentieth century.

We shall now turn to the development of the missions to the deaf, which, in addition to the schools, were the other important focus for the deaf community. Many missions to the deaf were established in the nineteenth century, the first being set up in Scotland (in Edinburgh and Glasgow) in the early part of the century, and then several being established in the North and Midlands in the middle of the century. These early missions were mostly the result of local initiative, often from deaf people themselves, and were often attached to schools for the deaf as a way of providing for the spiritual and educational needs of former pupils of the schools. They depended for their support on local charity, and according to Lysons (1979), were inspired by three motives: 'Evangelism, Mutual Aid and Philanthropy', the first two being the more important. Although the primary emphasis was on religious instruction, the facilities needed for this, such as a regular meeting place for local deaf people, also served general social and recreational purposes, thus acting as a natural focus for a local deaf community. The religious instruction would often be carried out by sympathetic local churchmen (cf Lysons, 1978).

In addition to these local initiatives, there were attempts later in the century to provide for the spiritual welfare of the deaf by establishing diocesan missions where necessary under the auspices of the Church of England. Such missions were set up mostly in rural areas where no local mission had been established, since, as Lysons (1979, p. 34) points out, 'Only in populous areas would the deaf be sufficiently numerous to make effective local provision either by school or mission feasible'. The effect of the Church of England's attempt to reach all deaf people by 'filling in the gaps' in this way was to complete a network of missions to the deaf, from which the present centres for the deaf have developed. Nowadays there are centres for the deaf in most fairly large towns, and often these centres have their own premises, which may consist, still, of a chapel for services as well as a large hall for social and sporting events, and perhaps also offices and a bar. Since 1960 local authorities have been financially responsible for the welfare of deaf people and have provided services either instead of the voluntary societies or through their agency. In some places the services provided by the local authority, such as case work, are kept distinct from those provided by the voluntary society, such as religious services in sign language.

Thus the missions to the deaf and the schools were the two main focuses for the newly formed deaf community and its sign language. Whereas in the schools the official attitude to sign language was generally negative, in the missions sign language was accepted and promoted as a means of religious instruction. So whereas in the schools sign language would have been used mostly in informal situations outside the classroom, in the missions sign language had a formal usage, in church services, as well as an informal, social usage. The difference between the schools and the missions in their attitude to sign language which was evident in the nineteenth century is still reflected in the twentieth century, as we shall see.

Having looked at the historical development of the schools and centres for the deaf and their role in the establishment of the deaf community and BSL, I shall now describe the current use and status of BSL, first in deaf education and then in adult deaf life. Now that there is no longer a close link between the schools and the centres, as there was between the schools and at least some missions, the school is the focus for the community of deaf children, while the centre is the focus for the community of deaf adults. Since many schools for the deaf are residential, only those children who go home for the weekend are generally able to go to their local deaf centre, and most children do not become fully fledged members of their local deaf centre until they leave school. This separation between the school and centre community is reflected in a difference in the type of sign language used in the two communities, so that leaving school and entering the adult deaf community also means acquiring a new sign language variety.

Those schools for the deaf which are residential can be considered communities in the sense that the pupils spend almost all of their time together. Those children who have deaf parents will know how to sign when they begin school, whereas those who have hearing parents will learn from their peers, and the resulting sign language variety will probably be similar to the adult variety, though with features that are peculiar to the school itself. Adult signers can usually tell not only where a deaf person comes from but also where he or she went to school. In a pilot study of variation in signs for numerals, I found that a particular variant of the sign for 'six', right index finger on left fist, was only produced by people who had been to schools in North West England, and who were over 40 (Deuchar, 1981). Although signing is supposed to be forbidden in some schools, I would guess that all residential schools have some signing system which is used by the children, even if it is only used secretly. Unfortunately almost no research has been done on signing among the pupils of schools, probably because of negative attitudes to sign language and, indirectly, towards those who do research on it.

As has been suggested, the negative attitude to sign language which prevailed in educational policy from the time British schools for the deaf began, has survived into the twentieth century, and been reinforced by the resolution of the Conference of Milan (see p. 33), so that oralism is the predominant trend. Oralism today is better informed by modern linguistic theory than were the seventeenth and eighteenth century teachers of the deaf, which means that it is not restricted to speech teaching, but 'involves the use of speech and lipreading, the use of auditory aids and the written word' (Denmark, 1976, p. 76). Its main aim is to teach English and other subjects in the way described without manual aids. This means that sign language is banned from the classrooms of some oralist schools; many teachers of the deaf are not competent in it, and see English as the only acceptable means of communication; thus a negative attitude is conveyed towards the sign language which is the first language of many deaf children and is used by almost all of them outside the classroom. Many oralists think not only that signing or 'manual communication' interferes with the acquisition of English, but also that it is unsystematic and non-linguistic. The following statement by a pure oralist is fairly representative: 'The signs in general use do not follow a system of rules and therefore cannot be regarded as a language' (Watson, 1976, p. 6). Nevertheless, it must be acknowledged that this kind of statement is becoming less frequent as more research is being done on BSL. Until recently the term 'BSL' was not used at all in discussions on the appropriateness of sign language in deaf education, but it is interesting to note that the term is used in a 1981 proposed policy statement (later rejected) of the British Association of Teachers of the Deaf (BATOD). Here, 'British Sign Language' is described as 'A mode of manual visual communication incorporating the national or regional signs used in Britain within a specific structure. It is recognised as a language in its own right, distinct from English' (Teacher of the Deaf Association Magazine, September 1981, p. 8). As for the fear that the use of BSL might interfere with the acquisition of English, this does not seem to be supported by the evidence, but this issue will be further discussed in chapter 7.

Schools for the deaf differ in the extent to which they adhere to pure oralism in the classroom, and the extent to which they forbid signing outside the classroom. Policy varies, from a total ban on signing both in and outside the classroom to an acceptance of signs outside formal lessons, to the use of signs to support speech both in and outside the classroom. The latter is sometimes called 'Total Communication', this term sometimes being used in the broad sense of a philosophy according to which any method of communication which works is to be used (cf Denton, 1976) and sometimes in a narrow sense, referring to a 'combined' or 'simultaneous' method of communication. When signs are used simultaneously with speech, the resulting sign variety is sometimes called 'Signed English', because the order of the signs reflects the structure of English. This variety will be further discussed in chapter 6. In some schools the methods used are uniform throughout the school, whereas in others, especially the 'pure oralist' ones, signing may be allowed in classes of lesser ability. In these schools the idea that sign language is for less capable children naturally reinforces the low status of sign language in general.

There are a few other methods used in some schools which deviate from pure oralism, but which do not involve the use of BSL. One of these is the Paget Gorman Sign System, and the other is Cued Speech. The Paget Gorman Sign System, which was mentioned in chapter 1 (p. 7) was artificially developed by two people, Sir Richard Paget and Pierre Gorman, between 1934 and 1971. Their aim was to devise a manual representation of English where signs chosen for their iconicity corresponded to (though they did not represent the sounds of) English words, and where there were signs for affixes like '-ly', '-er' and '-ed'. The idea was for the full grammatical structure of English to be represented on the hands, and for this system to be a means of teaching English that would be gradually phased out. Some teachers consider it preferable to BSL either because they do not consider BSL to be a language, or because they recognize that the structure of BSL is not the same as the structure of English, so that it has to be adapted if there is to be simultaneous speech and signing. For further details of PGSS see Craig (1973) or Griffiths (1980).

Cued Speech has been viewed as a compromise between the oral and manual approaches, though it does not use signs to represent ideas, but rather a system of hand positions and configurations which are designed to disambiguate sounds which appear similar on the lips, like 'p' and 'm' for example. For further details see Cornett (1967).

The oral–manual controversy which began in the eighteenth century (see p. 32) still continues today in intense discussion of the appropriate methods to be used in the education of the deaf. The discussion is sometimes polarized as an argument between 'oralists' and 'manualists', or those who advocate the use of speech versus the use of sign language in deaf education. This is in fact a simplification of the real situation (and for a useful summary of the opposing views in tabular form, see Freeman et al., 1981, p. 3). Oralists do indeed advocate the use of speech, or rather English, in its various forms as a main means of instruction, though some would allow the supplementary use of signing if necessary. Whereas the term 'oralist' is used both by advocates and opponents of oralism, the term 'manualist' tends to be used only by oralists. This is probably because oralists see their 'opponents' as advocating the use of sign language to the detriment or even exclusion of speech, whereas as far as I know, none of those who support the use of sign language would advocate the exclusion of speech, and those who do use sign language in the classroom tend to use Signed English, with speech, rather than BSL (see chapter 6 for further discussion of these sign varieties), and to advocate 'Total Communication'. Although oralism was approved in 1880 by the Conference of Milan, its relative lack of success for a large number of deaf children has led to continual discussion of alternatives, and in 1964 a government enquiry was set up 'to consider the place, if any, of finger spelling and signing in the education of the deaf'. The results of this, known as the 'Lewis Report', represented opposing opinions rather than research findings, though the committee proposed that research should be done. The lack of research on BSL at that time is reflected in the claim in the report that 'signing as commonly used at present among the deaf adults and, even more, signing as it develops spontaneously among deaf children, are non-linguistic media of communication' (Department of Education and Science, 1968, p. 90). This statement is based on the opinion of the committee members and those who submitted evidence to them, none of whom were linguists, but it is significant in that it conveys the negative attitudes to signing prevalent even among deaf people. Through their mainly oral education and the attitudes of hearing people, deaf people themselves have come to believe that their most natural and easy means of communication is not a language. The committee have unfortunately made the mistake of equating 'language' with English: their statement would be quite reasonable if 'non-linguistic' were replaced with 'non-English'. This attitude to sign language as ungrammatical or non-linguistic is similar to attitudes to non-standard dialects of English, as expressed in the view that only standard English is suitable to be used in the classroom: such attitudes reflect the idea that a language must be taught to be a proper language. Thus we have a vicious circle in that BSL cannot be used in education because it is not a proper language, and it is not a proper language because it is not used in education. Nevertheless, some progress was made between 1968 and 1980, since as I said on page 36, a BATOD statement in 1981 recognized BSL as a language in its own right.

A final comment on the oral–manual controversy is that it has to be considered in the light of the educational aims professed by those involved in it. The Lewis report states that the aims in educating deaf children should be 'to enable them to realise their full potential and so far as possible take their place in society in due course' (Department of Education and Science, 1968, p. 88). Some educators of the deaf see BSL as contributing to the first aim, because of its cognitive and social value, but as interfering with the second, since they think that the use of BSL may isolate deaf people from the hearing majority. The achievement of bilingualism in BSL and English as a way of fulfilling both aims is rarely discussed, perhaps because we are accustomed to monolingualism in Britain. However, this will be further discussed in the context of the acquisition of BSL.

As suggested earlier (p. 34), the role of sign language in the nineteenth century schools for the deaf was different from that in the missions, and this difference has been even more pronounced in the twentieth century, when oralism became the prevailing trend in schools. Whereas teachers of the deaf often are not competent in sign language, and it is rarely a required component of their training, competence in sign language is a prerequisite for becoming a social worker with the deaf (the social worker being the contemporary equivalent of the missionary). A social worker with the deaf finds sign language essential to communicate with his or her clients, many of whom may be 'failures' from the oral system of education, and also to interpret for them in their dealings with the hearing world, as in visits to the doctor, job interviews, etc. Social workers will tend to come into contact with deaf people particularly through the deaf centres, where they can be identified, and at these centres BSL is the accepted means of communication. Although some deaf who attend cannot sign, they are in the minority, and competence in BSL would seem to be a prerequisite to full integration in a deaf club based at a deaf

centre. Because of the attitude towards sign language in many
schools for the deaf, and the idea that those who can succeed
orally will not need sign language, orally competent deaf people
who are well integrated with the hearing world will tend not to
frequent the deaf centres, as they see them as a place for failures,
stigmatized by their use of sign language. The fact that the 'oral'
deaf do not usually attend deaf centres reinforces the position of
BSL there, and it is almost the only place where those for whom
BSL is their main language can enjoy relaxed communication,
since obtrusive use of BSL in public is usually avoided. Another
factor which reinforces the status of BSL in deaf centres is the
use of sign language in services for the deaf. However, it is usually
Signed English (or signs with speech, see chapter 6) which is used,
indirectly conveying the attitude that whereas manual communication is appropriate for deaf people, in formal settings it should be
as close to English as possible. Social workers and chaplains of
the deaf tend to have an instrumental attitude to sign language in
that, whereas they see it as indispensable for communication, they
agree with many teachers of the deaf that it is not a language of
the same status as English.

   This attitude is sometimes expressed in the desire to 'improve'
sign language as well as to promote it, and is reflected in the
activities of a Committee for the Study of Sign Language in the
1960s. This was established in 1964 under the auspices of the
College of Deaf Welfare, and its aims, insofar as they can be
determined from their unpublished records, were: (1) standardization; (2) improvement; (3) codification and extension of the sign
language vocabulary; and (4) promotion of the teaching of sign
language. The committee aimed to develop a system ('the Basic
Sign Language') which could be introduced into schools, but their
work came to an end abruptly, partly because of the closure of
the College of Deaf Welfare. Nevertheless, the minutes of their
meetings are an interesting indication of prevailing attitudes to
sign language even among those who promoted it, particularly the
idea that sign language must be similar to English to be grammatical. For example, despite the fact that not all languages in the
world mark tense on verbs, it is stated in the report of a meeting
held on 18 May 1966 that 'in an endeavour to make an attempt
at grammatical structure for the Basic Sign Language, the
Committee should consider in particular the tenses of verbs'. The
Committee aimed to develop a way of marking tense on verbs

similar to that in English despite the fact that they described how
time is marked in sign language. (For a discussion of the notions
of tense and time, see chapter 4, p. 94.)

So far, I have used the term 'sign language' or 'BSL' with
reference to the language used informally among deaf pupils in
schools, and by adult deaf people. One might wonder whether
there is sufficient standardization to refer to 'BSL' as an entity.
Since there is a lack of research on signing among school children
(see p. 35), it is not possible to be certain about the degree of
similarity between systems used in different schools, which are
geographically scattered. Nevertheless, one might expect school
sign systems to be somewhat similar to adult BSL because of the
presence in schools of deaf children with deaf parents who use
BSL. So is adult BSL standardized, or are there different systems
used in different parts of the country? Unlike English, BSL does
not have a written, accepted standard form, but in the absence of
more detailed research, one can say that a similar system does
seem to be used throughout the country. There is regional variation and variation related to other factors (see chapter 6 and
Deuchar, 1981) as in all languages, but this does not appear to
interfere with comprehension. The degree of standardization there
is may be due to considerable contact between the deaf centres
for sporting and social events, and national congresses of the
British Deaf Association. Gorman (1960, p. 215) suggests that
welfare workers play an important role in the standardization of
sign language through their mobility; this may be true of those
welfare workers who are native signers, but it needs studying
further.

We now turn to the role of the British Deaf Association (BDA)
in the promotion of BSL in the deaf community over a long period
of time. The BDA was founded in 1890 (as the British Deaf and
Dumb Association: the name was changed in 1970) in protest
against the fact that no deaf witnesses were heard by a Royal
Commission which recommended the use of the oral method in
British deaf education after the conference of Milan. Since that
time the BDA has taken up all aspects of deaf welfare and in the
area of deaf education has constantly advocated the use of manual
methods as well as oral methods. In 1960 the BDA produced a
manual of sign language vocabulary (Goodridge, 1960). Nevertheless, like teachers and social workers with the deaf, until recently
the BDA has not recognized BSL as a language in its own right.

In 1970, in a report commenting on the Lewis Report, the BDA, while arguing for the use of manual methods in deaf education, says that 'It was agreed that there was no complete grammatical sign language in the full meaning of the words in common use today' (p. 6) and that 'Where communication was carried on by signs alone this consisted of stringing signs together to convey ideas but in no way did it constitute a genuine form of language with an acceptable grammatical basis' (p. 7). However, by the late 1970s the BDA was publishing articles on BSL in its bi-monthly publication, the *British Deaf News*. These articles recognize BSL as a language in its own right and report on the results of recent linguistic research. The BDA has also had talks on BSL at some of its recent conferences.

The activities of the BDA in the 1970s also included the establishment of a Communication Skills Programme, supported by a grant from the Department of Health and Social Security. Among its aims were to promote the publicity, study and teaching of sign language and to set up a registry of interpreters, which would provide better training and professional status for sign language interpreters. In 1980 the Council for the Advancement of Communication with Deaf People was set up to pursue similar aims, as the Programme came to an end in 1981. This Council includes representatives of the major organizations concerned with the welfare and education of the deaf, and so should co-ordinate efforts and promote more co-operation between 'oralist' educators and 'manualist' welfare workers than has hitherto existed. For further details see Simpson (1981).

In 1981, as a result of the appointment of a new general secretary, the BDA underwent considerable change. It became primarily a 'consumers' organization', with deaf people more centrally involved than before. In addition to continuing its efforts for the use of manual as well as oral methods in schools, or 'Total Communication', a campaign was launched 'to improve the status of British Sign Language' (*British Deaf News* 1981, vol. 13 no. 6, p. 205). This was a clear indication that the status of BSL as a language in its own right had been fully recognized by the BDA, so that the organization was now free to promote the use of BSL in the deaf community as a whole, and no longer had to apologize for the 'inadequacies' of BSL, as it had as recently as 1970. Nor did the BDA have to limit its concerns any longer to the use of BSL in a modified form, as an aid to the teaching of English.

(One indication of initial success in improving the status of BSL is that BDA interpreters were first involved in political conferences in 1981, including the Labour Party Conference, where part of the party leader's speech was shown in sign language on television at peak viewing time, thus introducing many hearing people to BSL for the first time.) In 1982 the BDA organized a 'British Deaf Awareness Week', during which they launched a 'BDA Manifesto', of which one of the main points is as follows: 'The BDA asks the Government to recognise British Sign Language as a real language of a group of British people, especially when making laws' (*British Deaf News* 1982, vol. 13 no. 11, p. 419).

Two other members of the new Council for the Advancement of Communication with Deaf People may be singled out for their contribution to the use and status of BSL. One is the Royal National Institute for the Deaf (RNID), which has existed since 1924, and acts as a very useful resource centre for information relating to deafness, including sign language. It has an excellent library open to all, and has been instrumental in arranging conferences for the discussion of the methods of communication in deaf education (see Royal National Institute for the Deaf, 1976a, 1976b). A much more recent and smaller organization is the National Union of the Deaf (NUD), which was set up in 1976. The NUD is noteworthy for the fact that it was set up entirely through the initiative of deaf people, as a pressure group to promote the interests of the deaf. Through its regular newsletter and other activities it has campaigned for acceptance and recognition of BSL, and has also provided a useful forum for information and discussion on BSL by deaf people themselves. Like many speakers of non-standard or non-legitimized languages, many deaf people never thought of their primary means of communication as a language with its own grammatical rules, but the NUD newsletter has published the views of deaf people and provided information in an accessible form.

Another recent pressure group which has had an impact on the status of BSL is the Deaf Broadcasting Campaign (DBC), which began in the late 1970s following the first television programme designed especially for deaf people and using signs ('Signs of Life', BBC 2, 1979). Their aim was to promote the use of subtitling and sign language on television, and they have had some success in both areas. Sign language interpreting of the news has been tried experimentally on certain local television stations, and in autumn 1981 and 1982 there was a BBC 'magazine' programme 'See Hear!' for deaf people, with sign language used throughout as well as speech and subtitles. I understand that the BBC also hopes to develop a television course for teaching sign language to beginners. Thus there are indications that the status of BSL is likely to improve even further in the future, both in deaf and hearing society. The use of BSL on television may also contribute to its standardization.

It seems likely that the establishment of the term 'BSL' in reference to the sign language of the deaf community in the late 1970s, and the recognition among people connected with the deaf community (both welfare and education) that BSL can be seen as a language in its own right, is at least partly due to recent interest in BSL by linguists and psychologists. This has led to the expenditure of public money on BSL research, in the form of grants to institutions of higher education. When I began a nine month period of data collection in a deaf club in 1976 for my doctoral thesis on BSL (Deuchar, 1978a), I knew of no one else in linguistics who had conducted a research project on BSL. My terms of reference had to be linguistic research on ASL, which had become established as a legitimate area of research by the early 1970s. However, in 1978, when my thesis was completed, there began a three year research project at Bristol University on 'Sign Language Learning and Use', which involved data collection in deaf clubs and interpreter testing. The project had three full time members of staff, a psychologist, an interpreter and a linguist, and also employed deaf people as research assistants. Then in 1979 a 'British Sign Language' Project began at Moray House College of Education, Edinburgh, with the aim of analysing the grammatical structure of BSL. This project was staffed by a linguist, an interpreter, and a full time deaf research associate. In 1982 began a continuation project, 'The Structure and Function of British Sign Language'. Other projects on smaller scales have begun elsewhere, but the projects based in Bristol and Edinburgh are notable for being conducted by team research which has actively involved the deaf community. Thus deaf people have simultaneously learned more about their own language, and gaining confidence in their language, they have achieved more confidence as a group. The effects of the research on the wider community have been increased by the organization of workshops for anyone working on BSL or interested in doing so, with significant participation of deaf people. The first workshop met in 1979 to discuss a notation system which could be used in BSL research. This led to a report compiled by the Bristol group, *Coding British Sign Language*, and after another workshop this was revised and extended by the Edinburgh group as *Words in Hand* (Brennan et al., 1980).

Conferences on sign language research, attended by those not directly involved in research as well as those reporting on it, have also been a way of disseminating information about BSL and contributing to its status internationally as well as nationally. The First International Symposium on Sign Language Research, held at Stockholm in 1979, included five papers on BSL (published in Ahlgren and Bergman (eds), 1980). Then in 1980 the first national conference on sign language research was held in Britain at Lancaster and attended by over a hundred people including teachers of the deaf, social workers, and representatives of the deaf community. The proceedings of this were published as *Perspectives on British Sign Language and Deafness* (Woll et al., 1981), the first book published to have 'British Sign Language' in its title. Then the Second International Symposium on Sign Language Research was held in Bristol in 1981, and BSL research was again well represented (see Kyle and Woll, 1983, for the proceedings). Research papers on BSL have also been presented at conferences with a more general theme of language or linguistics, thus promoting the status of BSL among those professionally concerned with language, though not necessarily with deafness. For example, papers on BSL have been presented at meetings of the Linguistics Association of Great Britain, and Woll and Lawson (1981) gave a paper at a conference on minority languages, thus establishing the status of BSL as one of the minority languages of Britain.

Summary

In this chapter I have tried to give an overview, intended mainly for those unfamiliar with the deaf community in Britain, of the historical and social conditions under which BSL has developed. The establishment of schools for the deaf and missions to the deaf in the nineteenth century may well have been the first focus for the deaf community, and thus the first opportunity for BSL to begin to develop. BSL has developed as a kind of underground language with considerable social stigma, both because of the attitude in the schools that it was not a proper language, and because of the attitude originating in the missions that, though useful as a kind of crutch to the deaf, it could not be considered on a par with spoken languages unless something was done to improve it. We have seen that both these attitudes have been modified recently with more awareness of the nature of BSL as a language both in and outside the deaf community. At least some of this change of attitude seems to have been informed by the existence and results of linguistic research on BSL, and it is to this that we turn in the next chapter.

3
The structure of BSL signs

Having given a general introduction to what BSL is and to its historical and social background, I shall now begin a more technical, linguistic analysis of BSL. This chapter will be concerned with the analysis of BSL at the level of the individual sign, which we can consider to be more or less equivalent to the word in spoken language. The next chapter will then deal with analysis above the level of the sign, or what happens when signs are combined together.

This chapter, then, will deal with the 'phonology' of sign language. The term 'phonology' is generally used to refer to 'the sound systems of languages' (cf Crystal, 1980a, p. 268), but despite its apparent inappropriateness for a language that does not use sound, it will be used here to refer to the system of visual components making up signs. This system can be considered equivalent to the sound systems in spoken languages.

Phonological analysis of a spoken language could be said to involve the following: establishing the inventory of possible sound elements in that language, formulating the rules or constraints governing their combination into larger structures (e.g. words), and studying the processes of change or modification that can be undergone by those sound elements.

To illustrate briefly from the phonology of English, we know that certain sounds are possible in English, while others are not. For example, the sound [ɬ] which occurs in the Welsh pronunciation of the name 'Llewellyn' and which we call a 'lateral fricative', cannot occur in English. The English pronunciation of the name substitutes a possible English sound, [l]. Some English sounds do not, conversely, occur in other languages. The dental fricatives [θ] and [ð] or 'th' sounds, for example, do not occur in French or German.

Once we have established the list of possible sounds in a language, we can work out the constraints on their combination. In English, [s], at the beginning of a word or syllable cannot be followed by [r], though it can be followed by [t] or [tr], as in 'stop' and 'strip'. In Japanese neither of these sequences would be possible as a consonant must always be followed by a vowel (cf names like 'Yamaha', 'Suzuki') or an identical consonant, as in 'Nippon', the formal Japanese name for Japan.

The sounds of a language can also be modified under certain circumstances. The term 'phonological processes' is often used to refer to various kinds of change. In English, vowels are often 'reduced' or 'centralized' when unstressed. For example, the vowel of the word 'the' is not normally stressed except for particular emphasis (e.g. '*the* person' vs 'the person'). Unstressed it is a central 'schwa' vowel, [ə], while stressed it is a high front vowel, [i].

We shall now consider briefly how these three aspects of phonology (inventory of *elements*, *constraints* on structure, and phonological *processes*) might apply to BSL. A more detailed consideration, especially of the inventory of elements, will follow later in the chapter.

I have implied that the *elements* of BSL will be comparable to the sound elements of spoken language. This is true in so far as we can isolate elements of signs that can be combined with one another in various ways to form words. However, the characteristics of the visual as opposed to the auditory medium will determine the distinct nature of the elements of a sign language as compared with the elements of a spoken language. In spoken language, sounds can come only from the mouth, and are often analysed as sequential entities. The word 'pet', for example, may be analysed as a sequence of [p], [e] and [t]. In sign languages, however, where visible activity is not restricted to one part of the body, sequential analysis is more difficult. Not only can we recognize distinct parts of configurations of the body as being involved in activity, but we can also recognize distinct types of activity or movement. The body part acting, and the type of activity performed, will be perceived simultaneously, so it seems that the inventory of elements for BSL must include elements which act (or 'articulators') as well as elements of activity (or 'articulation'). Elements which act might include the following: head, eyes, eyebrows, mouth, and hands in various shapes, such as closed fist, open hand with fingers spread, index finger extended from fist, etc. Elements of activity might then include, for example nodding or shaking (for the head), widening or narrowing (for the eyes), raising or 'knitting' (for the eyebrows), opening or closing (for the mouth) and movement away from and towards the signer (for the hands). However, as we shall see, the phonological analysis of BSL is only in its very early stages, and so far most attention has been paid to phonological elements related to hand activity.

As far as *constraints* on the structure of BSL signs are concerned, we can identify a constraint on hand activity which was formulated for ASL by Battison (1974) and is known as the 'Symmetry Condition'. According to this condition, if both hands move in a two-handed sign, they must both have the same hand-shape and the same movement. This condition seems to apply to BSL and is exemplified in signs like that for 'sign', where flat spread hands, facing one another, move in a circular, alternating movement. Constraints on the structure of signs will be discussed in more detail later in this chapter.

Finally, the elements of signs can undergo phonological *processes*. A handshape, for example, can be modified according to the preceding or following signs, and one hand may be deleted in two handed signs. These processes will be further exemplified later.

So far I have tried to illustrate how the notion of phonology can be applied to BSL in analysing the structure of individual signs. Before proceeding with a more detailed analysis, it is important to point out that the type of phonological analysis achieved will depend to a large extent on one's goals and methodology.

Sommerstein (1977) differentiates between the goals of classical phonology and generative phonology. He suggests, roughly, that whereas the former seeks to establish which phonological elements are used by a language to distinguish one utterance from another, the latter seeks to determine the principles governing the pronunciation of a language, and how these relate to the organization of the language as a whole. The classical approach might be described as more concrete and practical, and the generative approach more abstract and theoretical. As Sommerstein points out, generative phonology is the more modern approach, though classical phonology (or 'classical phonemics') still has considerable influence.

The different goals have entailed different kinds of methods. The classical approach has concentrated on actual speech data, while the generative approach has tried to formulate phonological rules which will form a component of the grammar of the language. The classical approach became established in the first half of this century, and its emphasis on the purely observable data (i.e. speech sounds) was in keeping with the empiricism of the current philosophical climate. Its methods were particularly applicable to previously unanalysed languages (such as American Indian and African languages) because of the fact that it did not presuppose knowledge of the grammar of the language. Also, since data were recorded by the phonetic transcription of utterances, it was particularly useful in the analysis of the sound systems of languages of non-literate communities, for which a writing system might later be developed. The procedure was to isolate all the sounds or 'phones' of the language, on the basis of phonetic transcriptions, and then to work out which of these phones functioned to distinguish utterances from one another. Phones or groups of phones with distinctive function would then be grouped as phonemes. Phonemes were identified by the 'pair test' whereby native speakers were asked to say whether two utterances with a minimal difference of sound were the same or different. To show how this works we can imagine that native speakers of English, for example, would identify 'rice' and 'lice' as different words, thus indicating that [r] and [l] function as phonemes in English to distinguish words. In Japanese, however, there are no pairs of words distinguished by a contrast between [r] and [l], so these are not separate phonemes in Japanese.

Two important criteria were used to group sounds or phones into phonemes: those of complementary distribution and free variation. If two phones were in complementary distribution, they never occurred in the same phonetic environment and thus could not be said to contrast: they therefore could not be separate phonemes. They could also not be considered to be separate phonemes if they were in free variation: that is, if one sound could be substituted for another freely without changing the word. In English, for example, the [l] in 'pill' is phonetically different from the [l] in 'lip' but the two are in complementary distribution, which means that they never occur in the same phonetic environment, so are assigned to the same phoneme. Also in English, several kinds of 'r' are in free variation but they are assigned to the same phoneme because they never function to distinguish one word from another.

This procedure of identifying phonemes entailed the recognition of two stages in the analysis: the phonetic and the phonemic. While phonetic analysis was a relatively arbitrary initial segmentation of the raw speech data, phonemic analysis identified those elements of the language which were significant for their function in distinguishing one word from another. The phonemic analysis provided the basis for the phonological inventory of the language. The next steps were then to determine the constraints on combination of the phonemes, and what phonological processes they could undergo.

The classical phonemic approach relied on the assumption that the phonological analysis of the language could be done on the basis of phonetic evidence alone, and without recourse to grammatical information. This assumption is rejected by generative phonologists who, as I said before, see the phonology of a language as one component of its grammar. The phonological component of a generative grammar consists of rules which relate a set of 'underlying representations' and a set of 'phonetic representations'. The underlying representations are produced according to the syntactic and morphological rules of the grammar, and are equivalent to sequences of phonemes. Since the main purpose of this approach is to determine the pronunciation of lexical items with reference to the grammar, the notion of functional contrast, and the use of minimal pairs, is less important (cf Sommerstein, 1977, p. 5). Also, the phoneme is no longer the basic unit of phonological description: it is replaced with features, which are smaller units in terms of which phonemes can be described. Generative phonology and feature theory will not be further discussed here, however, as they have not yet been applied to sign language research with any great success (but see Wilbur, 1979, chapter 2). I have mentioned them briefly because of their importance in current phonological theory as applied to spoken languages, but the first phonological analyses of sign language have been heavily influenced by the classical phonemic approach.

It is probably true to say that no phonological analysis of BSL has yet been done purely in order to establish the phonological system of the language. Interest has tended to focus more on syntax (see chapter 4), but phonological information has been gained through the practical exercise of establishing a notation system. Like the African and American Indian languages mentioned earlier, BSL is a language previously unknown to linguists, and is also unwritten, but unlike them, it cannot be transcribed using an existing phonetic notation system. So the devising of a transcription system for BSL was a high priority for BSL researchers. For rough and rapid transcription it was possible to follow the American practice of using English glosses in capital letters as convenient mnemonics to represent individual signs (and we follow it here), e.g. BOOK, SIGN, to represent the signs for 'book' and 'sign' respectively. English glosses have limitations in that (a) they imply a one to one correspondence between word and sign which clearly does not exist (see chapter 1, p. 8) and (b) they give no information about how the sign is made, but assume that the sign can be identified by the gloss reader on the basis of prior knowledge of the sign. So a 'phonetic' or 'phonemic' notation is clearly needed to supplement English glosses. Again, American ASL researchers have provided a precedent in the use of a notation system devised by William Stokoe, an important pioneer in the phonological analysis of ASL. It is interesting to note that Stokoe (1960, 1978) described his notation system in conjunction with his description of ASL structure, which reminds one of the close link between transcription and analysis that was characteristic of the classical phonemicists, and shows that Stokoe was clearly working under the influence of their approach. We may also note that his notation system was used for an important dictionary of ASL (Stokoe, Casterline and Croneberg, 1976), the first of its kind in which signs could be looked up according to their formation components rather than according to the alphabetic order of their English translations.

As I said, a notation system for BSL had to be established for practical purposes. Deuchar (1978a, 1978b) used an adapted version of Stokoe's system, but this was further refined and developed as the result of national workshops on BSL notation, in May 1979 and November 1979. These workshops were set up after the establishment of BSL research projects in Bristol and Edinburgh, and the aim was to establish a relatively uniform notation system for general use. Two printed reports resulted from the workshops, *Coding British Sign Language*, produced by the Bristol group, and *Words in Hand* (Brennan et al., 1980), produced by the Edinburgh group. *Words in Hand* developed out of the workshops, but is subtitled 'A Structural Analysis of the Signs of British Sign Langage', and represents a considerable amount of work done by the Edinburgh group on the phonological analysis of BSL, as well as its notation system. Thus as in the case of ASL research, phonological analysis has gone hand in hand with the development of a notation system. Because of the lack of knowledge about the linguistic structure of the language as a whole, phonological analysis has also taken place almost without reference to the grammar of the language, relying, as did the classical phonemicists, on the 'raw phonetic data', or visible activity, alone.

As I said before, the classical phonemic approach relied on a phonetic transcription of the data, which could then be analysed phonemically. In the development of a notation system for BSL there has been some confusion about whether it is supposed to be a phonetic or a phonemic transcription. Although many researchers have recognized the importance of a prior phonetic transcription, just developing this involves making assumptions about what will be significant phonologically. The problems this raises will be discussed later, but meanwhile I will outline the main characteristics of the BSL notation system described in Brennan et al. (1980). At the same time this will give an idea of what is now known about the phonetic/phonological structure of BSL.

It will be recalled that the BSL notation system is based on that developed by Stokoe for ASL. Stokoe's system depends on a concept of the sign being a product of simultaneous components. He says (Stokoe, 1978, p. 37):

> The sign morpheme, . . . unlike the morpheme or word of a spoken language, is seen as simultaneously not sequentially produced. Analysis of the sign morpheme then cannot be segmentation in time but must be aspectual. The aspects of a sign that appear to have the same order of importance and the same part in language structure as the segmental phonemes of speech are the aspects of configuration, place and action.

A little later Stokoe says (p. 38): 'the *aspects* position, configuration, and action may only be described in terms of contrast with each other'. Here we may note that a fairly intuitive analysis of the sign into three aspects is claimed to be phonological in the sense of representing three parameters on which significant contrasts can be made. Stokoe uses the term 'chereme' for these aspects, which reminds us of its supposed equivalence to 'phoneme'.

Stokoe uses the terms 'tab' for position or 'where sign activity occurs'; 'dez' for configuration or 'what acts', and 'sig' for motion or 'the action' (cf Stokoe, 1978, p. 39). We should note that his system was originally designed to deal only with hand activity, and the BSL system has the same limitation of scope. Later we shall discuss the role of non-manual activity, and whether it can be dealt with by the existing notation system. The existing system is also limited to the individual sign, which is not a problem for our phonological analysis, but needs consideration when we deal with chunks of signs in combination.

The possibility of applying the notions tab, dez and sig to BSL signs can be demonstrated by analysing the following signs: I, THINK, KNOW and CLEVER.

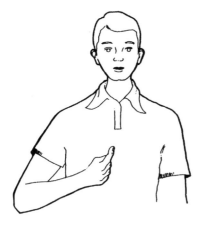

I
tab: chest
dez: index finger extended
*   from closed fist*
sig: contact with tab

THINK
tab: forehead
dez: index finger extended
*   from closed fist*
sig: contact with tab

KNOW
tab: forehead
dez: thumb extended from
    closed fist
sig: contact with tab

CLEVER
tab: forehead
dez: thumb from closed fist
sig: movement from right to
    left in contact with tab

The above examples show how BSL signs can be analysed into tab, dez and sig, and how these contrast with one another. The signs I and THINK can be considered a minimal pair because they only contrast in tab; THINK and KNOW are a minimal pair contrasting in dez; and KNOW and CLEVER contrast in sig. Thus Stokoe's tab, dez, and sig can be used to identify components of BSL signs as well as to contrast them with one another.

    The above examples involved the use of only one hand. However, there are two-handed signs, of two types: (1) where both hands move and (2) where the left or non-dominant hand remains stationary, and the dominant hand acts upon it. In type (1) both hands are considered to form a double dez; and in type (2) the stationary, non-dominant hand is considered to be the tab while the other is dez. Examples of both types, with analysis of their components, are the following:

GIVE (1)
tab: neutral space in front of
    signer
dez: open flat hands with
    fingers together
sig: movement away from
    signer

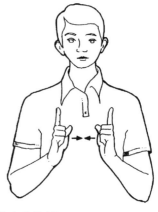

MEET (1)
tab: neutral space in front of
    signer
dez: index fingers extended
    from fist
sig: dezes contact one another

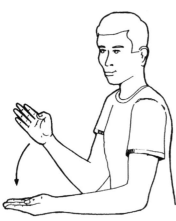

TRUE (2)
tab: non-dominant flat hand
dez: dominant flat hand
sig: contact with tab

RIGHT (2)
tab: non-dominant flat hand
dez: thumb extended from
    closed fist
sig: contact with tab

As the type (2) examples show, the non-dominant hand tab may or may not be the same shape as the dez. Constraints on the structure of signs involving two hands will be discussed later.

Just as there may be more than one dez (in the case of two hands moving), there may be more than one sig, either simultaneously or sequentially. CLEVER (see p. 55) actually has two simultaneous sigs: contact with the tab and movement across it. The following is an example of a sign with two sequential sigs:

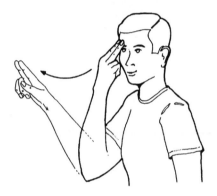

NAME
tab: forehead
dez: index and middle finger extended from fist
sig: contact with tab, then movement away

If a sign has more than one tab, it is usually considered to be a compound sign (the reasons for this will be discussed later). The following is an example of a sign with more than one tab:

BELIEVE
tab 1: forehead
dez 1: index finger extended from fist
sig 1: contact with tab

tab 2: non-dominant flat hand
dez 2: flat hand
sig 2: contact

So far we have used verbal descriptions for tab, dez and sig, but Stokoe devised symbols for each. Stokoe et al. (1976, p. viii) explain their notation system as follows:

> If we use 'T', 'D' and 's' as cover symbols for any possible tab, dez, and sig, we can write a sign thus: TD^S. This formula or convention for writing a sign indicates that at or in some place (T), visibly distinguished from all other sign language places, a hand configuration (D), distinctly different from all others used in sign language, performs an action (s), visibly unlike all other such actions.

Stokoe's system also allows for a double dez, indicated by the formula TDD^S, and for one or more sigs, indicated by formulae such as TD$_S^S$ (simultaneous sigs) and TD^{SS} (sequential sigs).

Before illustrating how BSL signs can be notated using this formula, we need to list the set of possible tabs, dezes and sigs for BSL, together with their symbols. We should note that just as spoken languages do not have identical inventories of sound elements, sign languages will also differ as to the elements they use. Thus BSL does not use all of the elements used in ASL, and vice versa.

The notation system developed for BSL and described by Brennan et al. (1980) followed Stokoe in trying to isolate elements which functioned to differentiate signs from one another, and the minimal pair test is used frequently for this purpose. What follows will not be an exhaustive list of all the possible tabs, dezes and sigs for BSL, but those which seem to have the most important contrastive function.

Tab

The considerable mobility of the hands means that signs can be made in various places in relation to the signer's body. Brennan et al. (1980, p. 49) list the following five major places: 'the head (including the neck), the trunk, the arms, the hands and the area of space in front of the signer's body'. Very few signs are made outside this general area, probably for reasons of ease of articulation (e.g. touching the knees with the hands might involve bending) and visibility (e.g. signs made on the back would not normally be visible).

The following is the list of what seem to be the main body tabs in BSL with their symbols (hand tabs will be identified in conjunction with the dez list):

Ø	neutral space in front of body
Ȏ	whole face
Ā	top of head
⌒	upper face
ʊ	eyes
ᴜ	nose
ᴗ	lower face
ᴖ	mouth/lips
)	cheek
Ɔ	ear

π   neck

[ ]   central trunk

⌐ ⌐   upper trunk

∟ ⌐   lower trunk

\   shoulder and upper arm

∕   forearm/elbow

D   back of wrist

The symbols used are taken from Stokoe et al. (1976), except where new ones have been found necessary for BSL. The new tabs added for BSL are top of head (∩), eyes (ʊ), mouth/ lips (◡), ear (⊃), upper trunk (⌐ ⌐) and lower trunk (∟ ⌐). These tabs were added because they appear to function contrastively in minimal pairs (see Brennan et al., 1980). For example, it seems that we need the tab 'lower trunk' in order to distinguish the signs SORRY (made on the chest) and DELICIOUS (made on the lower trunk): see illustrations in chapter 1, p. 21. Our need for extra symbols for BSL illustrates the fact that languages do not have identical phonological inventories. As a further illustration of this we may note that Klima and Bellugi (1979, p. 135) discovered that Chinese sign language has an under arm tab. This is not used in either ASL or BSL. The ASL tab, wrist face up (ɑ) has not been listed here, as it seems to be used in very few signs. Brennan et al. (p. 77) list it for BSL, but say that its status is questionable. Other tabs listed in Brennan et al. that I have not included here are: 'under chin' (⩔), 'lower arm' (∕) distinct from 'elbow' (∕), 'hip' (⊬), 'upper leg' (∣), and 'lower leg' (∣). 'Under chin' and 'elbow' seem to be used distinctively for very few signs, and 'hip', 'upper leg' and 'lower leg', being outside the normal signing area, are used for only a few indexical or iconic signs. (For example, the sign FOOT is made by pointing to the foot, and the sign DOG is made by slapping the upper leg, as when summoning a dog.)

Dez

As we have seen, the hand or hands can be held in various shapes or configurations. These have symbols like the tabs. However, whereas the symbols for the body tabs in the Stokoe system are relatively iconic, those for the hand configurations are alphabetical letters (with or without diacritics) referring to the handshape used to represent a given letter in the American one-handed finger-spelling alphabet. In spite of the fact that the American alphabet is not widely known in Britain, it is convenient to use the same system of notating the dezes of British signs for the following reasons: (a) the British fingerspelling alphabet is two-handed, so that letters cannot be used to refer to one hand configurations; (b) many of the American hand configurations are in fact used in BSL; and (c) it is convenient to have a system which can be understood internationally. The following is a list of the dezes which seem to be important in BSL, each with its symbol and an illustration.

A *(closed fist)*

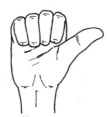

À *(thumb extended from closed fist)*

B *(flat hand, fingers together, thumb may or may not be extended*

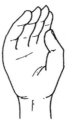

B̈ *(same as left but hand bent)*

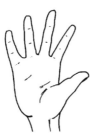

5 *(same as* B *but fingers spread)*

˙5˙ *(bent 5, 'clawed hand')*

C *(fingers and thumb bent to form curve as in letter 'c')*

G *(index finger extended from fist)*

O *(fingers bent and all touching thumb)*

F *(index finger and thumb touching: all other fingers extended)*

H *(index and middle fingers extended from closed fist and held together)*

I *(little finger extended from closed fist)*

L *(index finger and thumb extended from closed fist)*

V *(index and middle finger extended from fist and held apart)*

V̈ *(as above, but with fingers bent)*

W *(the middle three fingers extended from fist, may or may not be spread)*

X *(index finger extended and bent)*

Y *(thumb and little finger extended from fist)*

λ *(middle finger extended from fist)*

ষ *(middle finger bent, rest of fingers open)*

This list does not include all the dez symbols used for ASL, particularly those handshapes that are used primarily for American fingerspelling, such as 'R' (index and middle fingers extended and crossed, as in 'crossing one's fingers' for good luck). This handshape is included in the list of Brennan et al. (p. 133), but they state that its use is restricted to the Catholic deaf community. A symbol which is added for BSL, λ (middle finger extended from fist), represents a handshape not found in ASL, most likely because of its obscene connotation in American culture. So we see that just as the tab inventory for BSL and ASL is different, so is the dez inventory.

The above list also does not include all of the dezes listed in Brennan et al., particularly those that are considered 'phonetic variants' of a distinctive handshape. For example, Brennan et al., following Stokoe, use the symbol 'Ḃ' to represent a B flat hand with the thumb extended. This handshape never contrasts with B with the thumb not extended (in the sense of distinguishing a minimal pair of signs) but seems to be required in certain phonetic contexts, especially when thumb contact is used (cf Brennan et al., p. 105).

As well as leaving out the non-distinctive variants that Brennan et al. include, I have also left out their 'E' dez because of its infrequent usage and because I am not convinced that it is functionally distinct from 5̈. I have also left out some other hand-shapes listed by Brennan et al., for similar reasons.

Earlier I mentioned that a hand can act as tab in a two-handed sign where the non-dominant hand is stationary, and the dominant hand acts upon it. In this case the non-dominant hand is the tab, and the dominant hand the dez. Only certain handshapes can occur as tab in BSL: the main ones are A, B, 5, C, G and O. It is interesting to note that these handshapes are considered 'unmarked' or neutral in that they appear to occur most frequently, are maximally distinct in their formation, occur in all known sign languages, and are learned first by children (cf Battison, 1974, 1978, and chapter 7). Examples of signs occurring with these tabs are as follows:

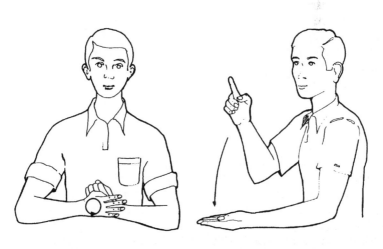

SATURDAY (A tab, B dez)   *LAW (B tab, G dez)*

THROUGH (5 tab, B dez)   *SPRING (C tab, O dez opening to 5)*

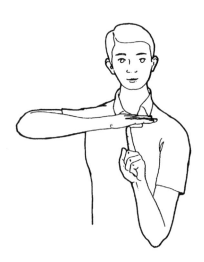

IMPORTANT (G tab, B dez)

MEDICINE (O tab, I dez)

In all the examples above, the dez handshape is different from the tab, but these tabs can also occur with identical dez handshapes. Other dezes which can occur as tabs (and which do not belong to the 'unmarked' or neutral set) seem generally to require identical dez handshapes. This appears to be true of F, H and X, as shown by the following examples:

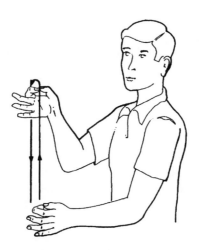

SEW (F tab and F dez)

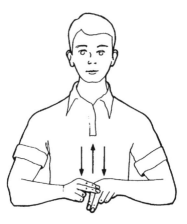

*FATHER (*H *tab and* H *dez)*

The I tab, which is occasionally used, seems to be an exception in that it can have a non-identical dez, as in the following:

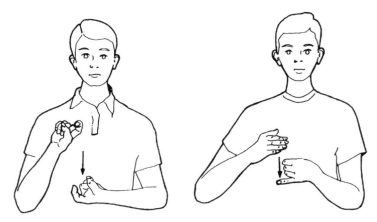

*DEPEND (*X *tab and* X *dez)*   *END/LAST (*I *tab,* B *dez)*

However, I suspect the structure of this example may be explained by its relatively iconic nature, and since I have not found many other similar examples, I would not place 'I' in the category of unmarked or neutral handshapes.

Sig

Most of the sigs identified in ASL and which have symbols in the Stokoe system seem to be important in BSL. Brennan et al. divide them into three categories: directional movement, interaction and manner. The following list of sigs and their symbols used in BSL follows Brennan et al.'s categorization roughly:

Direction

ʌ	up
v	down
ʌ/	up and down
>	right
<	left
ꝫ	side to side
т	towards signer
⊥	away from signer
ɪ	to and fro

Manner

a	supinating rotation
ᴅ	pronating rotation
ω	twisting
⊚	circular
ŋ	nodding or bending
□	opening
#	closing
⋌	wiggling
₩	crumbling action
∅	no movement

Interaction (between two hands, or between one hand and tab)

)(approach

x contact

ⲭ link or grasp

✦ cross

÷ separate

⟨⟩ interchange

~ alternation

The symbols ₩ (crumbling action) and Ø (no movement) were added for BSL. (₩ is from Gestuno, World Federation of the Deaf, 1975.) It is particularly interesting to note that a symbol denoting no movement is necessary for BSL, but apparently not for ASL. So whereas in ASL signs there is always some kind of significant movement, in BSL the absence of movement, or neutral movement, can be equally significant.

Now that the symbols for tab, dez and sig have been listed, we can demonstrate their use in the notation of some signs of which we have already seen illustrations, i.e. I, THINK, KNOW, CLEVER, GIVE, MEET, TRUE, RIGHT, NAME, BELIEVE. (See illustrations on pp. 54–8.) Note that all the following formulae will be used to notate these signs: TD^S, TD^S_S, TDD^S, and TD^{SS}_S (see p. 58).

I:	$[]G^X$	TD^S
THINK:	$\cap G^X$	TD^S
KNOW:	$\cap \dot{A}^X$	TD^S
CLEVER:	$\cap \dot{A}^X_{<}$	TD^S_S
GIVE:	$\emptyset BB^{\perp}$	TDD^S
MEET:	$\emptyset GG^X$	TDD^S
TRUE:	BB^X	TD^S
RIGHT:	BA^X	TD^S
NAME:	$\cap H^X_{\omega}$	TD^{SS}_S
BELIEVE:	$\cap G^X \text{ :: } BB^X$	$TD^S \text{ :: } TD^S$

The last sign, BELIEVE, is treated as a compound because it has two tabs: it will be seen that its notation is actually a combination of the notation for THINK and TRUE. Later we shall discuss the classification of signs like BELIEVE as compounds rather than as 'double tab' signs.

Non-signers who try to use the notation system outlined to form signs without looking at the drawings will probably not be quite accurate. This is because notation of tab, dez and sig does not give all the 'phonetic' detail that is necessary to form a sign. In the case of the sign TRUE, for example, it does not specify that the hands are at right angles and perpendicular to one another. The notation only gives information about the components of signs that appear to function 'phonemically' to distinguish signs from one another in the language. However, it is not clear that the notation system as outlined even gives sufficient information to distinguish all signs from one another (let alone to actually make them), and some researchers believe that other components must be specified, in particular, orientation of the hands.

The notation system outlined above did not include information about the orientation of the hands. However, the original Stokoe system does allow for the incorporation of such information by the use of sig symbols as subscriptions to tab or dez symbols. Thus, for example, the symbols α and D can be used as subscripts to the dez symbols, to show whether the palm is facing upwards or downwards. So adding subscripts to the notation for the sign GIVE (see above), thus: $\emptyset B_\alpha B_\alpha^\perp$, specifies that the hands are held with the palms facing upwards.

Stokoe's system allowed for the specification of orientation as extra 'phonetic' detail, but some of those following on from his work (cf Battison, 1974, Friedman, 1977) have argued that orientation should have the same phonological status as tab, dez and sig, so that a sign should be considered to have four important parameters or aspects. The notation of BSL described in Brennan et al. gives equal weight to orientation in that, just like tab, dez and sig, both palm and finger orientation are specified for every sign. Brennan et al. also state explicitly that they 'regard orientation as a separate parameter' for two reasons: 'the fact that orientation *alone* distinguishes pairs of otherwise identical signs and the fact that transcriptions excluding orientation have proved descriptively inadequate' (Brennan et al., 1980, p. 159). Their first reason could be described as 'phonemic', and relevant for the phonological description of the language, while the second is 'phonetic', and less relevant in this regard. Orientation seems to function contrastively to some extent in BSL, in that it is the only factor which distinguishes some signs from one another. Brennan et al. (p. 162) say that finger orientation 'accounts for very few minimal pairs' and in any case there are certainly fewer minimal pairs accounted for by orientation than by tab, dez and sig. So it is not clear whether we can accord orientation the same phonological status as the other three components. The fact that it is useful in adequately describing signs for researchers or learners (the second of Brennan et al.'s reasons for its recognition as a major para-meter) is not really an argument for its phonological status, as researchers and learners often need extra 'phonetic' information which may later turn out to be predictable from phonological information.

Two other aspects of manual signs whose phonological status has been questioned are hand arrangement and point of contact. As stated earlier, signs can be made with either one or two hands. Brennan et al. (pp. 214–15) give three minimal pairs which are apparently distinguished by having one vs two hands, but there do not seem to be many. This may be because one hand may be deleted in a two handed sign in a phonological process (see below), or one may be added in a grammatical process to indicate a plural subject as in 'they look', where LOOK is made with two hands instead of one (cf Brennan et al., p. 215). The other aspect of hand arrangement in signs is the relationship between the hands in two handed signs. Additional details of the Stokoe notation system allow for the representation of one hand above the other, both hands close together or behind one another, and both hands linked or crossed (cf Stokoe et al., 1976, p. xiii). However, these details, although important in the phonetic or concrete representa-tion of signs, do not seem to play a major role in distinguishing signs from one another (though see Brennan et al., 1980, pp. 217–19, for a few minimal pairs).

Point of contact is not specified in the Stokoe system, but is considered by some ASL researchers to have phonological import-ance (cf Friedman, 1977, Klima and Bellugi, 1979). Brennan et al. argue that point of contact information is essentially phonetic detail that can be predicted from orientation and hand arrange-ment, but suggest that for descriptive purposes it may be useful to incorporate it in the notation. The Bristol Sign Language Group propose incorporating point of contact in the notation by using symbols placed immediately in front of dez symbols which represent either dez or tab hand configurations. Thus the notation of the sign RIGHT, for example (represented above as BA^X), would have a symbol placed before both B and A to show that contact is made on the palms of the hands (see Appendix of Woll et al., 1981). Point of contact specification is referred to by the Bristol group as 'secondary tab', although this may be a little confusing since both tab and dez hands may have 'secondary tab' specified. Also, point of contact seems only to be specified for two handed signs involving contact between the hands, and yet the term 'secondary tab' might lead one to expect point of contact to be specified also in signs where there is contact between a dez and non-manual tab. The term also implies phonological status for point of contact, which does not seem to be justified. Nevertheless, we can agree with Brennan et al. that it may be useful to specify point of contact for phonetic or descriptive, if not phonological, purposes.

One possible solution to the problem of the phonological status of orientation, hand arrangement, and point of contact is to adopt Klima and Bellugi's (1979) suggestion (made for ASL) that signs can be analysed as made up of both major parameters (equivalent to tab, dez and sig) and minor parameters, such as orientation, hand arrangement and point of contact. Minor parameters are seen as sub-classifications of hand configuration or dez, and differ from major parameters in that they function to distinguish fewer minimal pairs. Klima and Bellugi also present some psycholinguistic evidence for the status of these parameters, which is worth considering in the absence of comparable evidence for BSL. Their evidence is of two kinds: (1) memory and (2) production of signs. Results from a memory experiment show that when signers make mistakes in recalling signs, the errors often differ from the target in only one major parameter (tab, dez, or sig). So for example, HOME was remembered as YESTERDAY: in ASL these two signs differ only in hand configuration or tab. As well as errors of tab, dez and sig, errors of orientation were also made. From this one might conclude that in ASL orientation has some phonological importance, and possibly more so than hand arrangement or point of contact, neither of which seems to figure in memory errors. However, errors in the production of signs (or 'slips of the hand') involved hand arrangement to a greater extent than orientation. So there is some psychological evidence for the existence of the major and minor parameters proposed for ASL by Klima and Bellugi, but it is not conclusive as far as the major/minor distinction is concerned. Linguists differ in the importance which they attach to psycholinguistic evidence for their analyses, but whatever our view, we cannot draw any firm conclusions for BSL. As we have seen, what is phonologically significant in one language may not be in another, so that it is conceivable that orientation, for example, functions differently in BSL from in ASL.

So far, however, we do not know enough about the phonological structure of BSL to distinguish clearly between major and minor parameters, or between phonological and phonetic elements of sign language. It is partly because of this lack of knowledge that researchers are likely to arrive at different inventories of phonological elements. At this stage, some decisions about the boundaries between elements are likely to be fairly arbitrary. Also, focus on establishing a notation rather than on phonological analysis per se has meant that people have been primarily concerned with working out how to specify sufficient phonetic detail to arrive at a phonological analysis.

However, in the specification of phonetic detail, or the pure description of physical activity without regard to the status of that activity in the linguistic system, we may have been too limited in our scope. As was pointed out earlier, the Stokoe system and its modifications deal only with the activity of the hands. However, researchers are becoming increasingly aware of the important role of non-manual activity such as hand, face and body movement in sign language. We do not yet know at what level of the language this activity is important (e.g. phonological or syntactic), but it seems likely that it functions at more than one level. At the level of the individual sign, it seems that we may find signs that are either entirely non-manual, or signs which have an important non-manual component. (Entirely non-manual signs are attested for ASL, Providence Island Sign Language and Swedish Sign Language: see Baker, 1980, p. 44.) Brennan et al. suggest (p. 2) that the signs ENOUGH and FED-UP are distinguished only by facial expression: FED-UP is shown with the mouth turned down at the corners (see illustrations).

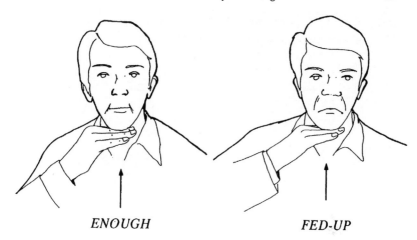

ENOUGH   FED-UP

Similarly, Brennan et al. (p. 236) state that IMAGINE and
DREAM differ only in that the eyes are closed in the case of
DREAM.

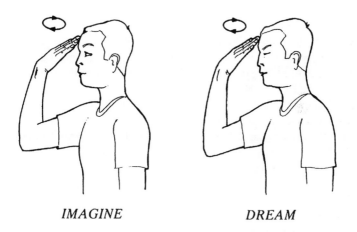

IMAGINE   DREAM

If non-manual activity can distinguish minimal pairs of signs, then
it must have phonological significance if we use the same criteria
as were used to establish tab, dez, and sig. If the phonological
significance of non-manual activity is accepted, then this will have
implications for the status of the manual components. What
seemed to be minimal pairs differentiated by tab, dez and sig may
turn out to have non-manual distinctions. For example, Brennan
et al. (p. 61) give STEEL and HARD as a minimal pair, differing

in that one is made on the teeth in the mouth, and the other on the chin (see illustrations).

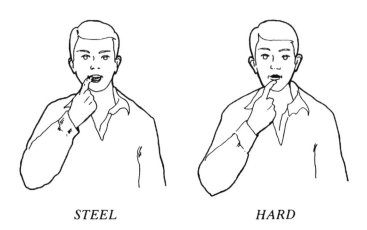

STEEL   *HARD*

This pair is actually used as evidence for the status of the mouth as a tab separate from the chin. But in the photographs provided by Brennan et al. the cheeks are puffed out in the case of HARD, but not STEEL. Could the cheek activity then be the significant difference rather than the place the sign is made? Before we can answer this specific question, we need to know about the answers to the following general questions concerning non-manual activity: (1) Is it obligatory or optional? (2) Does it function as an inherent part of individual signs, or can it be superimposed like intonation on spoken language? (3) How much variation is there between signers?

The first step will doubtless be the development of a notation system to represent non-manual activity. Not only will it have to represent movements of the face and eyes, but also of the mouth. Mouth movements in sign language research have been all but ignored (though see the work of Vogt-Svendsen (1981) on Norwegian Sign Language), doubtless through a reaction against oralism in deaf education (see chapters 2 and 7). However, it now seems that many signs may have conventional mouth shapes which sometimes represent the corresponding English word, but often do not. For example, I have observed the sign SUCCEED

(ØȦȦˣ⁺꜀) made with simultaneous mouthing of the lip pattern [blid]. Very little is yet known about such lip patterns.

More research is needed on non-manual activity in sign language, but we can already start questioning our assumptions about the phonological status of both manual and non-manual activity. Should we expect non-manual activity to be describable in terms of the same elements as manual activity? Perhaps we should if it operates at the level of individual signs. Stokoe (1979) argues that one effect of including orientation as a major parameter of sign analysis is that it cannot be applied to non-manual activity. Klima and Bellugi (1979) in fact explicitly identified their 'minor parameters' (orientation, hand arrangement and point of contact) as subclassifications of handshape or dez. So perhaps only the 'major parameters' can be used to describe non-manual activity, especially as Stokoe (1978, p. 39) redefined tab as 'where sign activity occurs', dez as 'what acts' and sig as 'the action'. However, as Stokoe himself recognizes (Stokoe, 1978, p. 86, 1979, p. 184), tab will be redundant if 'what acts' is not the hands. The greater mobility of the hands allows them to range over head and trunk for example, whereas the lips, for example, can move in only one place.

A new approach to the phonology of sign language might start by taking 'what acts' and 'the action' (or articulator and articulation) as the broad categories of description of both manual and non-manual activity. Manual activity could then be further described by subcategories or features of 'what acts' and 'the action'. Orientation of the hands and hand arrangement might subclassify 'what acts', while place of action and point of contact might subclassify 'the action'. These subclassifications might ultimately be developed into phonological features to be incorporated in some way into the grammar of the language. Features or subcategories could also be developed to specify 'what acts' and 'the action' for non-manual activity: the action of the eyes and mouth, for example, could both be described by features such as opening and closing. All this is speculative, but my own view is that all we can do at the moment is to specify a phonetic notation that is detailed enough to incorporate phonologically relevant information, but selective enough to be useful (the success of this task may depend on trial and error), while pursuing research on other levels of the language, such as the syntactic, so that a phonological description can be ultimately integrated with this.

Until now we have only dealt in any great detail with the phonological inventory of BSL, and not with constraints on the structure of signs, or phonological processes. As has been explained, emphasis on the inventory of BSL is the result of work done on a notation system. There are still many questions to be answered in connection with the inventory, but we may already glimpse some of the constraints on structure and some of the processes, at least within the limited scope of manual activity.

Discovering constraints on the structure of BSL signs means discovering how the phonological elements combine together to make possible signs and what combinations are not possible. Some constraints will result from the physical medium in which signs are produced; others may be language-specific. One obvious constraint on the structure of manual signs is that they all have a tab, dez, and sig. These elements occur simultaneously, and it is not physically possible for one to be missing. However, it is possible for a sign to have more than one tab, dez or sig. The possibility of more than one dez or sig is allowed for in the Stokoe notation: two identical handshapes may form a double dez, as in GIVE, and both sequential and simultaneous sigs may be represented (see p. 70). The fact that the two handshapes in a double dez sign are identical is captured by what we may call a Symmetry Condition (cf Battison, 1974). This condition is adhered to by both ASL and BSL, but it remains to be seen if it is a universal constraint. In the case of sigs, there are obvious physical constraints on their combination: for example, you cannot have movement towards the signer and away simultaneously, but it is possible sequentially. Signs with more than one tab such as BELIEVE (see p. 70) are generally considered to be compounds. This may be because the change of tab often involves a change of dez also: in BELIEVE the change of tab from forehead to passive hand is accompanied by a change in dez from G (index finger) to B (flat hand). Where the tab in a sign (or part of a compound sign) is a passive hand, the handshape of the passive hand must be one of a set of unmarked handshapes, listed on p. 65. The restriction of the tab handshape to this set is referred to as the Dominance Condition, and like the Symmetry Condition, was originally formulated by Battison (1974) for ASL. Brennan et al. (p. 19) point out that the unmarked handshapes have other interesting characteristics in that they occur in signs which have a change of handshapes, either where there is an opening or closing movement, or where there are two tabs in 'compound signs'.

These are just a few of the phonological constraints which seem to operate on BSL signs; we now turn to phonological processes. Until now we have been dealing with the 'citation form' (or 'normal form') of signs: that is the form which would be listed in a dictionary, or the form which might be given by a native signer in response to a question, 'What is the sign for x?' However, signs do not generally occur in isolation, but in combination, in the context of conversation and other kinds of communication. In sign sequences, signs are likely to deviate from their citation form, just as words when uttered in sequence will deviate from their pronunciation as listed in the dictionary. The modifications of citation forms can be called phonological processes, and those we shall consider here are: assimilation of dez, change of tab or sig, and hand deletion.

In some sign sequences, the dez of one sign can be assimilated (i.e. made identical) to the sign adjacent to it. So, for example, the sign I in the sequence KNOW(NEG) I ('I don't know') was observed made with the B dez used in KNOW(NEG) rather than the A dez of the citation form.

The citation form of the sign KNOW(NEG) involves contact with the upper face and then movement away. However, in rapid, informal signing I have seen this sign made lower down, approaching the chest, but often without contact. Thus both the tab and sig have been changed. This change is paralleled by a historical tendency noted by Woll (1981b) for some signs to change from head (with contact) to neutral space (without contact).

The third kind of phonological process we shall consider is one hand deletion in two-handed signs. One hand deletion seems particularly common in signs where both hands move, particularly if there is no contact. GIVE, for example (see p. 56) often occurs with only one hand. Where one hand is tab and the other dez, the tab may be deleted, especially if the tab is one of the unmarked handshapes (see p. 65). So RIGHT (see p. 56) for example, is often made without the B tab. (It is interesting to note that, according to Battison (1978, p. 63), this type of deletion does not seem to occur in ASL, so this may be an example of a language-specific phonological process.) The tab may also be deleted if it is the same shape as the dez, as in FATHER (see p. 67). Deletion of the dez alone never seems to happen: presumably because it carries more information than the tab, and also, tab deletion is equivalent to substitution of neutral space tab. Deletion of one hand, like the other phonological processes, is a variable phenomenon, but variation is found in all languages; variation in BSL will be further discussed in chapter 6. The factors affecting hand deletion seem not only to be phonological (e.g. depending on hand arrangement, type of tab, dez or sig), but also social, since hand deletion is much more common in informal, casual conversation than in formal settings (cf Deuchar, 1981, and chapter 6).

Summary

In this chapter I have tried to show how analysis at the phonological level can be applied to individual signs. Phonological analysis of BSL has been influenced by the classical phonemic rather than more modern approaches, and since it has been done in conjunction with the development of a notation system, the emphasis has been on the phonological inventory rather than on constraints and processes. However, it is clear that the phonological elements of BSL, though as yet not fully determined, are subject to certain structural constraints, and do undergo certain changes. In the next chapter we shall deal with the analysis of signs above the level of individual signs and their components.

4

The grammar of BSL

In the last chapter we looked at BSL at the level of the individual sign, and noted that signs could be analysed as made up of certain simultaneously occurring components. We also noted that parts of signs are susceptible to modification under certain conditions. However, just as spoken languages are more than just lists of spoken words, sign languages are more than lists of signs, and we must now extend our analysis beyond the limits of the individual signs to see what happens when signs are put together to produce meaningful utterances. Just as spoken languages have rules or regularities governing the way in which words are put together, we may also expect to find regularities in the construction of sign utterances, and such regularities in BSL will be part of its grammar.

How does one go about 'discovering' the grammar of a language that has not been codified, or 'written down' in a grammar book, and on which linguists have so far done little research? One possibility would be to start from a familiar spoken language such as English, and look for equivalence of its categories or processes in the grammar of BSL. This was the approach taken in the early research on American Sign Language, when it was important to establish the language as worthy of the attention of linguists, but it has not proved to be very fruitful. If the study of English grammar has been somewhat hampered by a traditional approach based on a Latin model, we might expect the model of a spoken language like English to be at least as limiting in the analysis of sign language. Even finding parallels to the units of spoken languages, let alone rules for their combination, is very difficult in sign language research. Although we saw in the last chapter that a sign is roughly comparable to a word, it is a very different kind of 'phonological' unit. Beyond the level of the individual sign, problems also arise if it is assumed that signs will follow one another in sequence like words, and that the sequence will have the same function as in a spoken language like English. In English, sequence indicates relations between words such as 'John' and 'Bill' in a sentence like 'John saw Bill'. In sign language there is a spatial as well as a temporal dimension, and information can be presented simultaneously as well as sequentially, so that not everything has to be done by sequence. A great deal of effort has been expended in research on American Sign Language in trying to establish whether its basic order is subject-verb-object or not (cf Fischer, 1974, Friedman, 1976a) while not enough attention has been paid until recently to the difficulty of defining 'subject' and 'object' in a way independent of any particular language, and to the fact that relations between such notions may be expressed in sign language using some means other than linear order.

Another example of a blind alley in BSL which the structure of English might lead us to pursue would be the search for parallels to the way in which English marks tense on verbs. The apparent absence of tense in BSL verbs has led some people who are not familiar with languages other than English to conclude that BSL cannot be a real language if it does not mark tense: there are, however, many spoken languages which do not have the grammatical category of tense, such as Chinese and Malay (cf Lyons, 1977, pp. 678–9). Languages which do not have tense have alternative ways of referring to time, and later in this chapter we shall see how time reference is accomplished in BSL. Looking for categories found in English may have a further drawback, namely, that we ignore categories which are less commonly mentioned in relation to English. An example of such a category is aspect, or 'situation-internal time' (cf Comrie, 1976, p. 5) to which less attention has been given in English grammar than to tense, but which appears to be an important category in BSL grammar, as we shall see later.

In the last paragraph I used the term 'BSL verbs', but that in itself is an example of the way in which categories from English may unduly influence our analysis. In English we are accustomed to making a clear distinction between the 'parts of speech' such as nouns, verbs and adjectives, although there is not always a distinction of form involved (cf 'measure' or 'drink' as a noun or verb). While it is doubtless worthwhile investigating (as have Supalla and Newport, 1978) whether there is a distinction of form between nouns and verbs in sign languages, we should consider the possibility that such categories may not be relevant to the analysis of BSL, or that they may not be formally marked. Although BSL 'verbs' can be identified to the extent that they appear to translate English verbs, it looks as though BSL 'adjectives' may operate in similar constructions to 'verbs', occurring with nouns to attribute qualities to them. An example from actual sign conversation is PINT CHEAP, meaning 'The pint is cheap', but without having an overt 'verb' sign. BSL does not have a copula like the verb 'to be' in English, so that what seem to be adjectives may, like verbs in English, function as predicators in that they make assertions about the properties of certain entities. This also happens in some spoken languages, such as Japanese, and it is important to beware of viewing English as the 'prototype' spoken language, attributing all differences between English and BSL to their difference of medium. Until we know more about the relation between the structure of languages and the medium in which they are manifest, we cannot be sure of the extent to which the medium of English makes it an inappropriate basis for the analysis of BSL. It is clear, however, that both English and BSL have some language-specific characteristics which they may or may not share with other languages, whether spoken or signed.

A final example of the way in which notions from the grammar of English may be misleading in research on BSL is in the search for a unit comparable to an English sentence. Later in this chapter we shall consider what the appropriate unit of analysis is for BSL, above the level of the sign, but it is worth saying at the outset that anyone looking at a sequence of signing, as in a conversation, finds it very difficult to identify sentence boundaries on a formal basis. However, I would suggest that this is not due to the unusual structure of BSL, but rather to the unusual structure of written English, on which our notion of an English sentence relies. Recent research on spoken English, however, shows that while a unit such as a clause can arguably be identified, identification of sentences is extremely difficult (see e.g. Crystal, 1980b). Since much of the data used for sign language analysis is spontaneously generated, we might expect its structure to parallel spoken rather than written English. Thus the danger of the influence of English in our approach to BSL lies not only on its difference of primary medium (vocal-auditory rather than gestural-visual), but also in that our view of English may be based on its structure in its secondary, written medium.

If we accept that BSL is most fruitfully investigated by direct analysis rather than via English, then there remain two alternative approaches to its analysis. Assuming that the main aim of a grammatical analysis is to link form and function, we can either work from linguistic structure to grammatical function, or from grammatical function to linguistic structure. Most analyses will make use of both strategies, which may be seen as complementary rather than in opposition. In what follows I shall illustrate each strategy in turn, in order to show how one might go about doing the grammatical analysis of BSL. Since research into BSL is still in its early stages, I shall not be providing a complete grammatical description of BSL, but trying to show how one might achieve the basis for such a description.

Taking the approach of proceeding from structure to function first, we shall look at some BSL data and try to identify some grammatical regularities. Two areas of structure which might be worth investigating for their possible function in the grammar are first, manual activity which involves the modification of the 'citation form' of signs as defined in the last chapter (p. 79), and second, non-manual activity, to which we have so far given little attention.

Near the end of the last chapter we saw that the citation form of signs can undergo what we called phonological processes, or physical modifications in certain contexts, but the examples we looked at did not involve a clear change or addition of meaning. If we were to find examples of modifications of signs that do affect meaning in a regular way, these might be considered to be 'morphological processes', or processes which either relate signs or have grammatical function. In the linguistics of spoken language, the term 'morphology' is used to refer to both derivation, by which words such as 'act', 'action' and 'active' are related, and inflection, a grammatical process relating forms of the same verb or noun, e.g. 'act, acts, acted', or 'house, houses'. While derivation belongs in the lexicon or vocabulary of the language, inflection is part of the grammar since it is able to represent grammatical categories such as number and tense. In spoken language, derivation and inflection are often carried out by the addition of affixes to a base form, the plural 's' or the past tense 'ed' being examples of such affixes in English. In BSL it is clear that sequentially placed affixes of this kind are not found, and those devising sign systems to represent English for educational purposes have found it necessary to invent separate signs for English affixes such as 's'. However, as we saw in analysing the phonology of BSL, sign languages have available to them simultaneity as well as sequentiality, and so we might well look for morphological processes affecting one or more of the simultaneous parameters of signs, as we saw happens in phonological processes.

I shall deal almost entirely with processes marking inflection rather than derivation, since inflection is most interesting from the point of view of the grammar, and so far has seemed a more fruitful area of analysis. Little research on derivation has yet been done, and although Supalla and Newport (1978) found a regular distinction between certain types of nouns, and verbs in BSL according to the type of movement involved, no similar derivational relationship has yet been found in BSL. This does seem to be an area worth investigating, though, since what would be English translations of nouns, verbs and adjectives in BSL are found in formationally similar pairs or groups: for example, a sign usually glossed MARRY seems to function as either a noun meaning 'wedding', a verb meaning 'marry', or an adjective meaning 'married'. The same appears to be true of a sign usually glossed as INTEREST. Dorothy Miles (1979) points out that some noun-verb pairs differ in movement; for example, translations for 'key' and 'to lock' produce similar signs except that the movement is repeated in the case of the noun, but this does not seem to be a regular process since in the pair 'enemy' and 'to battle', it is the verb which involves repeated movement. The sign which translated 'meeting' is related in form to that for 'to meet', in that both involve the same handshape with the index fingers of both hands extended, but whereas there is independent circular movement of the hands in the sign for 'meeting', in 'to meet' the hands move directly towards and touch one another. A great deal remains to be done on derivational processes in BSL.

Until researchers realized that signs could be modified in non-sequential ways, the possibility that sign languages could exploit inflectional processes was not seriously considered. However, this situation has been changed by Klima and Bellugi's (1979) work on ASL where they give detailed consideration to many kinds of inflection, thus giving support to their contention that ASL is more of an inflecting language like Latin than an 'isolating' language like

Chinese. In what follows, proceeding from structure to function in BSL, we shall look at changes in the sig or parameter of movement and in the dez or handshape which seem to function as grammatical inflections. Some changes will also involve changes in other parameters of the sign.

One way in which the parameter of movement of a sign can change is in its direction. This possibility is realized in a small set of signs in BSL including GIVE, EXPLAIN, ASK, SAY, SEE, BEAT and MOCK. These signs appear to have in common specific formational and semantic criteria: the citation form of the signs involves movement away from the signer, and semantically there is a notion of either concrete or abstract transference. They can be considered verbs because of their meaning and function. In these signs, the direction of movement is a marker of case in an egocentric system where, if there is a first person argument (that is, if the signer needs to refer to himself or herself), direction of movement will show the case of the first person, whether 'agent' or 'patient'. If the first person is agent (or source) then there is movement away from the signer, while movement towards the signer indicates a first person patient (or goal). So 'I give to you' is differentiated from 'You give to me' (or 'He/she gives to me') in that in the first the hands, open in B shape and palm upwards, move away from the signer whereas in the second they move towards the signer. Like GIVE, the sign EXPLAIN is made with two hands in neutral space, and the outwards movement of the citation form is similarly modified to an inwards movement towards the signer when there is a first person goal as in 'You explain to me', for example. The signs ASK, SAY and SEE differ from GIVE and EXPLAIN formationally in that each involves initial contact with some part of the face of the signer, and then movement outwards. So when signs of this kind undergo modification to indicate first person patient or goal, initial contact with the face remains, but is followed by movement downwards to the chest of the signer (which is the location of the first person pronoun 'I' or 'me'). A third formational category is represented by the signs BEAT and MOCK, where the dominant hand acts, as dez, upon the subordinate hand as tab. Whereas in the citation form the fingers of both hands are pointing outwards, and the dominant hand moves on top of and across the subordinate hand, modification to mark first person involves change not only in the direction of movement of the dominant hand, but also change in the orientation of both hands, so that the fingers point towards the body. Thus BEAT and MOCK have the property of what Fischer and Gough (1978), referring to ASL, call both direction-ality and reversibility, while those verbs which allow modification in their movement only, just have the property of reversibility. In all these verbs, the case of the second (or third) person is indicated by default, being complementary to that of the first person.

Having illustrated the grammatical significance of modification of the movement parameter with regard to its direction in some verbs, we can now look at another kind of movement modifica-tion: repetition (sometimes called 'reduplication'), which seems to function as a marker of aspect in verb signs, and as a marker of plurality in certain noun signs. Repetition of movement can be either fast or slow, and it seems that while fast repetition may indicate durative aspect, slow repetition may indicate iterative aspect. To give an example of the latter, the sign QUARREL in its citation form involves two hands in the 'I' shape (little finger extended from fist) contacting one another with palms facing inwards. When this contacting movement is repeated several times, slowly, the modified sign can be interpreted as meaning 'quarrel repeatedly'. If the movement were repeated quickly however, the meaning would be 'quarrel for a long time'. The category of aspect as found in BSL will be discussed later in the chapter as an illustration of how one might proceed from grammatical function to linguistic structure.

Repetition of movement to indicate plurality in nouns appears to be neutral as between fast and slow, and in addition to repeti-tion of movement, usually to involve a shift of place along a line in front of the signer. So the sign for CHILD, for example, is made plural by repetition of movement of a flat palm face down on one side of the signer, while shifting the location slightly further from the sign with each repetition. A similar process can occur with the sign BUILDING, for example, which is made by 'buil-ding' movements of both hands in neutral space in front of the signer, and which can be pluralized by repeating these movements, each time in a different location. It appears to be possible to mark plurality in this way only in signs occurring in neutral space, presumably because it would be much more difficult to shift loca-tion in signs made on the body.

We now turn to look at the modification of signs whereby the parameter of handshape, rather than movement, is altered for grammatical purposes. Alteration of handshape to incorporate number is derivational in some signs, inflectional in others. It is derivational in signs based on those referring to future time, such as TOMORROW, NEXT-WEEK, NEXT-YEAR. The handshape used in all these signs is the index finger, but more than one finger can be used to represent a corresponding number of time units. So whereas the sign TOMORROW is made with the index finger contacting the underside of the chin and then moving outwards, three fingers making the same movement in the same place would mean 'in three days' time'. The incorporation of number can be seen as an inflectional process, or perhaps a kind of external sandhi (see Matthews, 1974) in noun signs where number, acting as a modifier, can be incorporated into the sign itself by an appropriate modification of the original handshape, which may well have to be an index finger or a two-finger handshape. I have seen the two-finger handshape of the sign for a deaf person replaced by three fingers to indicate 'three deaf people'; and Carter (1980) reports on the substitution of three fingers for the index finger for the citation form of GIRL, in order to sign 'three girls'. The process, however, appears to be optional, and it is not clear what status it has in the grammar.

Another category of handshape modification affects verb or predicate signs, and involves the incorporation of what appear to be 'classifiers': these are forms which have the function of pronouns in BSL, but encode information about the type and shape of the referent (see Brennan et al., 1980, and Brennan, 1981). These classifiers are similar to the predicate classifiers discussed by Allan (1977) in that they can be substituted for the handshapes of certain predicate signs, particularly verbs of motion, to encode properties of the 'subject' or 'object' of the action. This can be particularly clearly illustrated with the example of the incorporation of the classifier for people, an open hand with the fingers spread, which is held horizontally to indicate people covering large areas of horizontal space, as in crowds, and vertically to indicate one behind the other, in single file.

PEOPLE (in single file)   *PEOPLE (in crowds)*

This classifier in either of its orientations can be incorporated into the sign GO, of which the citation form is an index finger moving away from the signer. Incorporation of the classifier is achieved by substituting the open handshape for the index finger and retaining the movement of the verb. The incorporated classifier indicates that 'people' are the subject of the verb, and that these people are spatially arranged as indicated. Other classifiers include those for round, flat and curved things (see Brennan et al., 1980). When incorporated into verbs these are likely to be objects rather than subjects for semantic reasons (they refer to passive things). As Woll (1983) has shown, some handshapes seem to have semantic content at the level of the individual sign in its citation form, so that, for example, a large number of signs with a meaning of 'goodness' have an A ('thumbs up') handshape, while many signs involving 'badness' have an I (little finger extended) handshape.

Having looked at modifications in signs involving either the parameter of movement or handshape, we shall now turn to a group of signs where change in both the handshape and movement during the course of the sign has the function of negation. This process, usually referred to as 'negative incorporation', affects a small set of signs which include WILL, LIKE, WANT, BELIEVE, AGREE, GOOD and possibly KNOW. It is difficult to see what these signs have in common, since they are formationally quite different from one another and functionally similar only in that they occur in predicates. It is interesting to note, however, that a very similar process appears to affect a lexically similar set of signs in ASL and French Sign Language (see Woodward and DeSantis, 1977). In BSL this process involves the addition of an upward (or optionally, downward) movement of the hand(s) immediately after the normal movement of the sign. This additional movement is accompanied by an opening movement of the hand (if the hand is closed) towards an open, 5 handshape. Thus WILL, for example, made by a forward movement of a closed fist by the cheek, is negated by adding an opening and upward movement of the hand. LIKE, made with a flat open hand on the chest, only needs the addition of an upward movement to negate it, since the handshape is already open. KNOW is a slightly different case, since the negated form already has the open hand-shape throughout the sign, whereas the affirmative form has an À ('thumbs up') handshape. It seems likely that through time, the final handshape of the negated KNOW has been assimilated backwards, thus replacing the initial handshape, so that we now have what looks like a distinct lexical negative form, though still with the final upward movement. The only reason I can suggest that such a change should have been undergone by only one of the signs allowing negative incorporation is that, of the set, negated KNOW seems to be the most frequent. In any case, the process undergone by the other signs in the set illustrates the fact that more than one parameter of a sign (in this case, movement as well as handshape) can be affected by a modification of form which has grammatical function. It should just be pointed out, before leaving the topic of negative incorporation, that the signs in the set it applies to can also be negated in alternative ways which are not limited to any specific set, for example by the addition of a sign glossed as NOT or another sign, NOTHING, the latter being more common in informal signing. There is also a common non-manual means of negation, which we shall discuss below in connection with non-manual activity that has grammatical function.

As we saw in the discussion of the phonology of BSL in the last chapter, researchers have paid much more attention to manual than to non-manual activity in sign language. The assumption has been that the core of the language is in what the hands do, while activities of the head and face, for example, are 'paralinguistic' in that they are not an integral part of the sign language, though they may function to express the signer's personality or feelings, rather in the way that it is thought that such activity functions in spoken language. However, the fact that hearing signers can often be picked out just by their inability to use non-manual expression 'correctly', and the fact that hearing people often comment on the apparently 'bizarre' facial expressions and body movements of deaf signers suggest that the role played by non-manual activity in spoken language is in fact very different from its role in sign language. Recently researchers have begun to pay more attention to the role of non-manual activity, both at the level of individual signs (see last chapter) and at the level of sign language grammar. In what follows we shall look at those aspects of non-manual activity that appear to have grammatical function, proceeding from those activities whose function is clearer to those where it is less clear.

As I said above, there is a common non-manual kind of negation. This involves the shaking of the head while simultaneously signing what would otherwise be an affirmative utterance. So, for example, shaking the head while signing GO (index finger moving away from the signer), could be translated as 'I'm not going'. This kind of negation is extremely common.

Another kind of non-manual activity which seems to have clear grammatical function is the movement of the eyebrows to mark questions. The eyebrows may be either raised or lowered and 'knitted' as in a frown. In BSL, as in other languages, questions can be divided into two categories, 'Yes–No' or 'Wh-'. Yes–No questions require a choice between a 'Yes' or 'No' answer, as in the English question 'Are you coming tomorrow?' while Wh-questions, introduced in English mostly by 'Wh-' words like 'Why', 'What', and 'When', require a specific kind of information as an answer. It is clearly inappropriate to answer 'Yes' or 'No' to the question 'What is your name?' In English there is a characteristic intonation associated with questions, but questions can also be identified by a change of word order. In BSL, where it is not clear whether there is a basic temporal order anyway, non-manual activity seems to be the only way of distinguishing Yes–No questions from statements. Non-manual activity also accompanies Wh- questions, although these also include a question sign such as WHY, WHAT, etc. which may be placed at the beginning or end of the question, or both. In Woll's (1981a) discussion of questions in BSL, she suggests that the non-manual features associated with Yes–No questions are different from those associated with Wh- questions. In Yes–No questions, she says, 'Eyebrows are raised, and chin, head and shoulders are brought forward for the duration of the question', while in Wh- questions, 'the eyebrows are knitted, and the shoulders are hunched as well as forward' (p. 146). The main contrast suggested here seems to be in the position of the eyebrows: raised versus lowered or knitted. Checking Woll's suggestion against the few examples in my film data, however, the position is not so clear: three Yes–No questions have raised eyebrows, while one has them lowered, and two Wh-questions occur with raised, while two occur with lowered eyebrows. Worswick (1982), analysing data from the Edinburgh Sign Language Project, broadly agrees with Woll about the ways in which Yes–No questions can be differentiated from Wh- questions, and yet finds one Yes–No question with lowered eyebrows, and one Wh- question with raised eyebrows. She tries to explain these exceptions by saying that whereas the lowered eyebrows with Yes–No questions indicated particular puzzlement, the raised eyebrows with Wh- question may have marked a clarification question. One could develop this explanation to suggest that raised eyebrows may indicate a smaller requirement for information on the part of the signer (or a lesser degree of puzzlement) than lowered eyebrows, which would indicate a greater requirement for information. Since Yes–No questions logically only require a choice between two options in their answer, whereas the number of possible answers to Wh- questions could be infinite, it seems reasonable to suggest that the information required when a Yes–No question is asked is generally less than that required by a Wh- question. However, there would be exceptions to this generalization where a Yes–No question is asked by someone who thought that they knew the answer, but now think they may have been wrong. Worswick's example of a Yes–No question with eyebrows lowered is HEARING BORN YOU ('Were you born hearing?') where the person asking had always before assumed that his addressee was born deaf but now thinks he may have been wrong. Thus we could argue that the likely answer to this question ('Yes') would bear a heavier load of information than is normal in answers to Yes–No questions, because it would be contradicting a strong previous assumption. Conversely, raised eyebrows with a Wh- question could indicate (perhaps unusually) that the signer thinks he/she may know the answer, but wants clarification or confirmation. In my data one signer asks another

when his holiday is (WHEN HOLIDAY WHEN) with raised
eyebrows, asks whether it is in July by means of a Yes–No question with raised eyebrows (J-u-l-y YOUR), and then asks what
the exact dates are with lowered eyebrows (WHEN BETWEEN).
Following the argument outlined above, we could attempt to
explain the difference of marking in the two Wh- questions in the
sequence by suggesting that the signer already had an idea that
his addressee's holiday was in July (hence raised eyebrows for low
degree of information needed) but did not know the exact dates
(hence lowered eyebrows for high degree of information needed).
If further research confirms this suggestion, then we may wish to
conclude that questions in BSL are grammatically marked by
movement of the eyebrows from their neutral position, and
semantically marked as to degree of information required by their
actual position, whether raised or lowered.

Earlier we looked at the grammatical function of headshaking as
a means of negation, but what about headnodding? Like English
speakers, signers use headnods in isolation as answers to questions
meaning 'Yes' and also to indicate agreement, or that they follow
what is being said to them. In addition, Lawson (1983) suggests
that a headnod may function as an 'existence/assertion marker' in
a similar way to that suggested by Liddell (1980) for ASL. Lawson
gives an example of a manual sign co-occurring with the headnod
and having the existential meaning 'there is'. I also found a
headnod in my data, co-occurring with a sign that was the first in
a comment made upon a topic consisting of a long string of signs
(Deuchar, 1983). Since the topic usually contains relatively given
information (see Chafe, 1976), and the comment asserts something new about that, this analysis seems to be in line with the
proposed function of headnod as an assertion marker (cf Liddell,
1980). It is not clear to what extent the headnod with this function
is obligatory, however, in the way that moved eyebrows, for
example, mark questions.

The function of the headnod in BSL is just one of the many
kinds of non-manual activity discussed by Lawson (1983) in her
paper 'Multi-Channel Signs' where she suggests that activities such
as cheek movements and mouth patterns may have grammatical
(as well as lexical or idiomatic) function. Lawson suggests that
the cheeks may be puffed out or sucked in with the function of
intensification: thus a sign for 'brilliant' is made 'very brilliant' by
the co-occurrence of puffed out cheeks. Among the mouth

patterns analysed by Lawson is one which she calls 'um', which involves opening and closing of the mouth. She suggests that this has associated with it a meaning of 'contrary to expectation' and gives two examples of sign sequences with which it co-occurs, one being translated as 'shorter than expected' and the other as 'would have been'. It is thus possible that 'um' realizes a modal category of some kind, but further research is needed on the generalizability of this phenomenon.

So far I have illustrated one approach to BSL grammar, according to which one moves from linguistic structure to the analysis of its grammatical function. I should now like to illustrate the alternative approach whereby one moves from grammatical function to the identification of linguistic structure. Up till now I have used the term 'grammatical function' without really defining it, so it is worth making clear here that I am using it to refer to the realization of a particular grammatical category defined in a language-independent way. To give an example, I suggested earlier (p. 87) that repetition of movement in verb signs could have the grammatical function of marking aspect, which is another way of saying that the grammatical category of aspect is found, or realized, in BSL. On the other hand, the grammatical category of tense does not seem to be found in BSL because there does not seem to be a modification of verb signs in BSL which marks time. Instead, time appears to be marked lexically, as we shall see below. If a grammatical category is not found in BSL or any other language, then the function or meaning of that category will usually be expressed lexically rather than grammatically, by an individual lexical item (sign or word) rather than a regular modification of form, or a particular grammatical construction (combination of lexical items). The distinction between grammaticalization and lexicalization should become clearer in the discussion which follows, but it cannot be made sharply in an absolute way (cf Lyons, 1977, p. 234 and p. 678).

The 'structure to function' approach relies on the assumption that there are certain regularities that can be discerned in a language, and then related to the function they fulfil. The alternative 'function to structure' approach relies on the assumption that there are certain grammatical categories that might be realized in a given language, because of the communicative ends they serve. In what follows I shall focus on some basic categories which are realized in BSL, specifically the deictic categories of person and time, and the category of aspect, which was partially discussed earlier (p. 87).

Deixis is defined by Lyons (1977, p. 636) as the function of 'grammatical and lexical features which relate utterances to the spatio-temporal co-ordinates of the act of utterance'. Since all utterances occur in a spatio-temporal context, most languages will presumably have ways of referring to that context: deictic categories are therefore possible candidates for grammaticalization in BSL as in any language. Person deixis is a subcategory of deixis in that the context of an utterance must include the participants in it, minimally a speaker (or a signer) and an addressee. Lyons (1977) emphasizes the importance of person deixis in pointing out that 'There is much in the structure of languages that can only be explained on the assumption that they have developed for communication in face-to-face interaction' (p. 638). This statement refers to languages in general, but seems particularly apposite for sign language in that it is almost impossible to use it without face-to-face interaction, unless in television broadcasting or by means of experimental writing systems. A further statement by Lyons on person deixis could also have been written with BSL in mind, although, again, it is intended to be more general: 'The canonical situation-of-utterance is egocentric in the sense that the speaker, by virtue of being the speaker, casts himself in the role of ego and relates everything to his viewpoint. He is at the zero-point of the spatio-temporal co-ordinates of . . . the deictic context' (Lyons, 1977, p. 638). In the earlier discussion of case-marking on certain BSL verbs by the modification of direction of movement, we saw that the system was egocentric in that direction of movement indicated the case of the first person. This would be an example of the grammaticalization of person deixis in BSL, in which the egocentric position of the signer has direct spatial representation. I would argue that this has grammatical function in that it only applies to a small set of verbs, and that in these verbs, it is obligatory: it would be ungrammatical to sign 'You say to me', for example, with the direction of movement being outwards from the signer rather than inwards towards her or him.

Another way in which the grammaticalization of person deixis is reflected in BSL is in the existence of a category of personal pronouns (as well as in the classifiers discussed earlier) and in the constraints governing the deletion of pronouns. BSL has the following pronoun signs: I (index finger touching chest); YOU (singular) (index pointing away from signer), HE/SHE/IT (index pointing away from signer, to left or right), WE (dual) (index and middle finger moving away from and then towards signer), WE (plural, inclusive) (left and right index fingers moving in symmetrical semi-circles from centre to periphery), WE (plural, exclusive) (as inclusive WE, but smaller semi-circles), YOU (plural), (index finger moving across signing space), THEY (index or flat hand moving across signing space). (The terms 'inclusive' and 'exclusive' refer to the inclusion or exclusion of the addressee.) There are also possessive pronouns, with clenched fist handshape in similar locations. The first and second person pronouns (i.e. I, WE, YOU) will always have deictic function (i.e. they will always refer to people involved in the act of utterance) whereas the third person pronouns may either have deictic function (in which case they will point to the individuals involved) or anaphoric function, which means that they will have the same reference as a previous nominal.

Pronouns may be deleted under certain conditions, which are different for deictic and anaphoric pronouns. For deictic pronouns, the egocentric nature of the deictic system is again reflected in that the first person subject pronoun appears to be the only one that can normally be deleted with first person reference still understood. This is illustrated by the following example:

INJECTION WANT
'I want an injection'

Here no subject pronoun appears overtly, so first person reference is assumed. In verbs which allow modification of their direction of movement, however, as described on p. 86, neither subject (agent or source) or object (patient or goal) pronouns of any person need be overtly indicated if their location is marked by the initial or final point of the movement. Thus in 'You give to me', the pronouns YOU and ME do not have to be overtly indicated since their location is already marked in the direction of movement of GIVE, from the location of YOU (away from the signer) to the location of ME (close to signer).

Third person subject anaphoric pronouns, however, can be deleted if the referent remains the same as that of the last nominal. This is illustrated in the following example:

TWO THREE FOUR HELP HE MARSHALL KNOW IT
USED-TO IT
'He helps to marshal numbers two, three, four. He knows it,
he's used to it.'

In this example about a speedway rider, the anaphoric pronoun
HE refers to Michenik, a speedway rider who has been named a
little earlier in the discourse. The same person is also subject of
the verbs which follow, KNOW and USED-TO, but the pronoun
does not need to be repeated since the reference of HE has not
changed. In both deixis and anaphora, only subject pronouns are
deleted. This is not really surprising, since subjects are often topics
(cf Li (ed.), 1976), or that which is being talked about, and topics
often include known or given information, which therefore does
not need to be made explicit. (There are parallels to this pattern
of subject pronoun deletion in spoken languages such as Spanish
and Japanese.) Thus in the last example about the speedway rider,
a pronoun referring to Michenik is deleted since Michenik is the
topic of the discourse, what it is about. The third person pronouns
IT in KNOW IT USED-TO IT, however, are not deleted since
they are not part of the topic. (IT probably refers to the speedway
track.)

We have now seen that the category of person in BSL seems
to be at least partly grammaticalized in that there is a category of
personal pronouns, and regular constraints governing their deletion. However, deixis of time, in contrast to person deixis, does
not appear to be grammaticalized. Verbs do not inflect for tense
in the way in which they do in many European languages. Nevertheless, deictic time can be indicated lexically in the use of adverbials. These adverbials reflect the egocentric nature of the system
in that neutral or 'unmarked' time is the present time, the time
of the signer's utterance. Present time need not be marked overtly,
though if it is a present time adverbial such as NOW is used.
The egocentric nature of lexical time reference in BSL is further
reflected in that the location in space of the time adverbials relative to the signer is directly related to the time represented, relative to the present. The sign for NOW is made in neutral space
immediately in front of the signer; signs representing past time,
such as BEFORE, LAST-WEEK are made or move behind this,
and signs representing the future, such as FUTURE, NEXT-
WEEK, are made or move in front of this. Thus BSL can be said

to have a 'time line' similar to that found in other sign languages such as ASL (cf Frishberg and Gough, 1973).

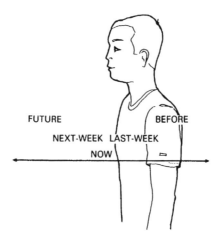

FUTURE   BEFORE
NEXT-WEEK LAST-WEEK
NOW

The Time Line in BSL

When the time referred to by the signer is not the present, it will normally be marked as non-present at the beginning of discourse, or at the point where the time reference changes. To give an example, the following utterance, from data, is marked as referring to the past by the adverbial BEFORE:

WE BEFORE t-h NIGHT DART DART MATCH
'We went to a darts match last Thursday night'.

Future time can be marked either by a future adverbial such as NEXT-WEEK or by the sign glossed as WILL, which was mentioned on p. 89 as allowing negative incorporation. This sign seems to function as an auxiliary verb, since it co-occurs with verb signs, either being placed before or afterwards, as in the following examples:

WILL ASK
'I will ask'
AGREE WILL YOUNG
'The young will agree'
COME COME COME YOU WILL(NEG)
'Come, come, come: you won't!'

The fact that WILL appears to function as an auxiliary verb, with another verb, rather than a lexical adverbial, and the fact that it allows negative incorporation like other signs functioning as verbs, but unlike the time adverbials, suggest that, exceptionally, one kind of time reference may be grammaticalized in BSL. However, I would suggest that not only tense, but also modality, may be represented by WILL. According to Crystal (1980a, p. 230) modality involves a wide range of meanings, 'especially attitudes on the part of the speaker towards the factual content of his utterance, e.g. uncertainty, definiteness, vagueness, possibility'. As Lyons says, 'Futurity is never a purely temporal concept; it necessarily includes an element of prediction or some related modal notion' (Lyons, 1977, p. 677). An element of prediction is particularly clear in the second and third signed examples with WILL: prediction that the young will agree, and realization that the addressee is not going to come. Further evidence for the idea that modality may be grammaticalized in BSL is found in the existence of two other BSL auxiliary verbs, MUST and CAN. MUST occurs in examples such as MUST GO ('I must go') and CAN in examples such as DRIVE CAN ('I can drive') and CANNOT SAY ('I cannot say'). (As the second example suggests, there is a separate lexical sign, CANNOT.) In addition, Lawson (1983) describes a mouth movement 'um' which has the meaning 'contrary to expectation', which also appears to be an expression of modality.

Returning to past time marking in BSL, Brennan (1983), in a discussion of time marking in BSL, reports on the discovery in Scotland of some 'past tense' forms of a small number of verbs, including SEE, WIN and LEAVE. These would seem to be examples of the lexicalization rather than grammaticalization of past time marking, but Brennan does suggest that the past form of SEE, for example, might result from a 'blend' between SEE (index finger moves out from eye) and what she calls the 'completion sign' FINISH, which in Scotland involves an open palm ('B' shape) closing to a tapered ('O' shape) hand. In England there is a variant of this sign which is formed differently ('thumbs-up' À handshape circling in neutral space). FINISH will be further discussed below under the category of aspect.

So far we have considered the deictic categories of person and time, but the next category to be considered, aspect, is non-deictic in that, while its meaning is related to the concept of time, it does not refer to the time of the utterance, but to the 'internal temporal constituency of a situation' (Comrie, 1976, p. 3). Comrie differentiates tense and aspect by saying that while tense is concerned with 'situation-external time', aspect is concerned with 'situation-internal time' (Comrie, 1976, p. 5). Lyons suggests that the term 'aspect' primarily refers to the perfective/imperfective distinction as grammaticalized in the Slavonic languages, but that 'it is extended to cover a variety of other oppositions, in so far as they are grammaticalized in the structure of particular languages – oppositions based upon the notions of duration, instantaneity, frequency, initiation, completion etc.' (Lyons, 1977, p. 705). Notions of duration and so on can of course be expressed in all languages, but they are generally considered aspectual only in so far as they are grammaticalized rather than lexicalized.

According to Comrie, perfective aspect is distinguished from imperfective aspect in that, while 'perfectivity indicates the view of a situation as a single whole, without distinction of the various separate phases that make up that situation . . . the imperfective pays essential attention to the internal structure of the situation' (Comrie, 1976, p. 16). This particular distinction seems to be grammaticalized in languages, if at all, rather than lexicalized. The other aspectual notions, based on duration, etc., are semantic distinctions which can be either lexicalized or grammaticalized, but which would be subcategories of imperfective aspect, in that it is only this which pays attention to the internal structure of the situation. The perfective aspect, on the other hand, treats the situation as a complete, 'unanalysed whole' (cf Brennan, 1983, p. 12), and so we would not expect it to be combined with grammatical marking of aspects referring to the internal structure of the situation.

In BSL there does not seem to be a perfective/imperfective distinction marked by verb inflections, but there is an auxiliary verb, FINISH (ØÅÅ), which seems to be used optionally to indicate perfective aspect. The following are examples from my data in which it occurs:

I KILL ALL FINISH
'I've killed all (the weeds)'
I FINISH WIN
'I('ve) won' (said immediately after a game of darts)
SUGAR PUT-IN FINISH
'I've put in the sugar'

HE SAY YOU ALL READ FINISH
'He says, "Have you finished reading all (of the newspaper)?"'

All of these examples seem to suggest the notion of completeness, so that FINISH may well be an optional perfective marker. Since all the examples given use the past tense in their English translations, one might wonder if FINISH has in fact been misleadingly glossed and is really a past tense marker, despite the earlier suggestion (p. 94) that BSL does not have the grammatical category of tense. I do not have any examples of FINISH co-occurring with present or future time reference, whereas the perfective in Russian, for example, can occur with future time reference (cf Comrie, 1976, p. 18). However, the relative infre-quency of FINISH and its apparent current association with the notion of completeness indicate that it is at the moment a perfec-tive aspect rather than a past tense marker.

The imperfective aspect in BSL appears to be marked occasion-ally by an auxiliary verb glossed as BEEN (Ø5ᴰ), but more often by a particular inflection, reduplication of the movement parameter, which indicates durative, iterative or habitual aspect (these being subcategories of the imperfective: cf Comrie, 1976, p. 25). The category of aspect as marked by inflection in BSL was mentioned on p. 87, but we shall look at it here in more detail. The kinds of aspectual categories which are marked on verbs in BSL, and the way in which that marking is achieved, will depend on their inherent meaning or 'aspectual character' (cf Lyons, 1977, p. 706). In describing the situations to which verbs characteristically refer, we can distinguish, following Lyons (1977, p. 707), between events, states and processes. Each of these categories can be distinguished from the others by the presence or absence of the semantic features 'stative' (non-dynamic) and 'punctual' (non-durative), as shown in Table 1.

Table 1

Situation	± Stative	± Punctual	BSL example
state	+	−	SIT ('be sitting')
event	−	+	COME
process	−	−	TALK

As I said on p. 87, 'Repetition of movement can be either fast or slow, and it seems that while fast repetition may indicate durative aspect, slow repetition may indicate iterative aspect'. However, this is only true of processes, as Table 2 shows.

Table 2

| Situation | Meaning of repetition of movement | |
	Slow repetition	Fast repetition
state	–	durative
event	iterative	habitual
process	iterative	durative

Table 2 should be interpreted as meaning that slow repetition of movement in verbs referring to states does not occur, but that fast repetition in such verbs indicates durative aspect, and so on. The generalizations contained in the table are based on my own findings and the published reports of the Edinburgh project (see Brennan et al., 1980, Brennan, 1981, Brennan, 1983). However, they should be seen as tentative as findings are sparse and more research is needed. If we compare Table 2 with Table 1, we see a striking parallelism between aspectual character and marking. Durative aspectual marking, for example, parallels −punctual aspectual character in that it only applies to verbs which are inherently −punctual, or durative. This is because durative marking indicates that the state or process was particularly lengthy: so BSL SIT or TALK with fast repetition would be translated as sitting or talking 'for a long time'. Durative aspect cannot apply to an event, which is inherently +punctual, or non-durative, and so fast repetition is 'free' to take on the meaning of habitual for events. Table 2 shows habitual aspect as applying only to verbs denoting events (+punctual) but further research is needed on whether and how habitual aspect is marked for processes and states. Iterative aspect is shown in Table 2 to be marked by slow repetition for events and processes (both being −stative), as shown in Table 1: it does not appear to apply to states.

According to Brennan (1983), the distinction between slow repetition for iterative aspect and fast repetition for habitual aspect is not only found in 'event' verbs like COME, but also in time adverbials such as WEEK-AFTER-WEEK (slow repetition, iterative aspect) and WEEK-AFTER-WEEK (fast repetition, habitual aspect). Adverbials can clearly refer to states, events and processes as well as verbs, but it is questionable whether we would want to say that aspect is grammaticalized in adverbials in the same way as it appears to be in verbs.

Having looked at some grammatical categories as realized in BSL, we shall now turn briefly to categories of other kinds, those that might be termed 'parts of speech', and the category of 'subject'. As I said earlier (p. 83), it is not yet clear whether there is a distinction of form between nouns and verbs in BSL of the kind we find in English. However, as Lyons (1968, 1977) points out, the definition of noun and verb in various languages, and the assumption that the two categories are universal, is related to their typical function as important elements in the 'subject' and 'predicate' of a sentence. As Lyons (1968, p. 399) says:

> Every language may be assumed to have, as its most typical sentence-type of minimal syntactic structure, a class of sentences whose nuclei are composed of a nominal and a verb (the term 'nominal' is intended to include nouns, pronouns and noun-phrases; and the term 'verb' is to be understood in the wider sense which also embraces adjectives . . .). The notions of 'subject' and 'predicate' are first defined . . . with reference to such sentences.

In BSL it is certainly possible to identify nouns and verbs on the basis of functional criteria, and these criteria also help to explain why what appear to be verbs and adjectives in BSL and ASL not only 'operate in similar constructions' (see p. 83), but also seem to be affected by similar formal processes. Not enough research on aspect in BSL has been done to see whether 'adjectives' undergo aspectual marking in a similar way to 'verbs', as they do in ASL (see Klima and Bellugi, 1979), but it is worth noting that one of the signs to undergo negative incorporation in BSL (see p. 89) is an 'adjective', while the rest are 'verbs'.

Lyons (1977, p. 435) suggests that languages will have three kinds of nuclear structure: intransitive, transitive, and ascriptive. These three are illustrated in BSL by the following examples:

intransitive: FATHER FALL ('Father fell')
transitive:.   TEN p PUT-IN ('I put in 10p')
ascriptive: FARE THERE BACK TEN p
                 ('The fare there and back is 10p')

These structures seem much more comparable to English sentences if we analyse them in terms of 'topic' and 'comment', which are notions used in modern linguistics to refer to what the sentence is about and what is said about that. (See Deuchar, 1983, for discussion of the application of these notions to BSL.) They are equivalent to the traditional notions of subject and predicate as developed by grammarians and logicians (see Lyons, 1968), but not quite equivalent to the notions as used in English grammar, by which we are often unduly influenced. Nevertheless, the notions 'subject' and 'predicate' in their traditional sense can be used to describe the components of the three structures above, the subjects being what we can call the 'nominals': FATHER, understood I and FARE THERE BACK, and the predicates being the 'verbal expressions' FALL, TEN p PUT-IN, and TEN p (see Lyons, 1977, p. 429, for definitions of 'nominal' and 'verbal'). The fact that the 'subject' can be left out in the second example (TEN p PUT-IN) supports the traditional idea that the predicate is the most important part of the sentence. (The notions of 'subject', 'object' and 'topic' will be further discussed in relation to BSL as well as to ASL in the next chapter, p. 126.)

The possibility of deleting the subject in BSL also explains why we do not find units exactly equivalent to English sentences in BSL. Another problem in identifying the sentence in BSL is that, since it is primarily an abstract, theoretical notion, it may not be clearly recognizable in the concrete data of spontaneous utterances generally used as data for BSL analysis. A related problem is what the basic unit of grammatical analysis should be for BSL. This is a question that is being discussed in relation to the grammar of spoken language, since it is becoming clear that a unit larger than the sentence may be necessary in order to fully understand certain kinds of grammatical phenomena. In BSL, we have seen that the way in which person and time reference work suggests that we need a fairly large unit of grammatical analysis, and certainly not one confined to a single subject and predicate alone. We can conclude that the approach of 'discourse analysis' (see e.g. Coulthard, 1977) should be taken seriously in BSL analysis.

Summary

In this chapter I have not achieved anything near a complete grammatical analysis of BSL, partly for reasons of space, but mostly because no complete analysis is yet available. Instead, I have tried to give an idea of the framework for a possible analysis, which would look both at structures in BSL and how they are modified to fulfil grammatical functions, and at possible grammatical functions or categories and how they are represented in structures. Future research on BSL will doubtless prove some of the details in this chapter incorrect, but I hope that the general approach will prove fruitful for future researchers.

5

BSL and ASL

As I pointed out in the first chapter of this book, BSL is different from other sign languages used in other countries, such as American Sign Language or French Sign Language. On p. 11 I said that BSL and ASL are considered to be mutually unintelligible (users of ASL cannot understand BSL and vice versa) despite the fact that they are both used in English speaking countries (cf Stokoe, 1973, p. 365, Wilbur, 1979, p. 1). Stokoe (1973) considers a large number of sign languages, including American, Irish, Spanish and Russian, to be descended from French Sign Language, whereas he considers British Sign Language to be unrelated to this family, but possibly related to Australian Sign Language. It is difficult to determine genetic relationships of this kind, partly because of the lack of historical evidence, and also because languages can be related in other ways, such as through contact between users of different systems. In chapter 1 (p. 3) I referred to Woodward's suggestion that ASL was influenced by, or creolized with, French Sign Language (FSL) rather than directly descended from it, and Boyes-Braem (1981, p. 223) in observing similarities in the handshapes of BSL and FSL, implicitly raises the question of whether this is due to a historical relationship or contact.

In this chapter I aim to compare the structure of BSL and ASL without drawing conclusions about whether or not they are historically related. The reasons for making such a comparison are as follows: it is often stated that BSL and ASL are different, but it is not shown how; sign languages are often compared with spoken languages, but not often with one another (though see Klima and Bellugi's (1979) comparison of Chinese and American signs); BSL and ASL are a good pair for comparison because they are both used in English speaking communities, and finally, given that more research has been done on ASL than on any other sign language, this chapter may serve both as an introduction to that literature for readers not familiar with it, and as an introduction to BSL for those already familiar with the ASL literature.

For the convenience of the reader who has already read chapters 3 and 4, I shall compare BSL and ASL first at the level of phonology, and then of grammar. At the level of phonology I shall compare the inventory of elements (tab, dez and sig), constraints on structure, and phonological processes, and at the level of grammar I shall compare inflectional processes, non-manual activity, deixis of person and time, aspect, the 'parts of speech' and 'functional' categories such as subject, topic, etc.

As I said in chapter 3, the system developed by Stokoe et al. (1976) for the notation of ASL was adapted for BSL, and the changes that had to be made may give us some idea of differences in the phonological structure of ASL and BSL. However, we should beware of assuming that the Stokoe notation perfectly reflects the phonological structure of ASL, since, as we shall see, other researchers have shown some of the ways in which it does not.

The general area within which signs may be made seems to be similar for ASL and BSL, and to include the head, trunk, arms, hands, and space in front of the upper part of the signer's body (cf Battison, 1978, p. 49). Within this general area, the possible locations for ASL signs seem to be similar to those for BSL signs, though it was necessary to add six tabs to the Stokoe notation for BSL: top of head, eyes, mouth/lips, ear, upper trunk and lower trunk (see p. 60). Of these, Friedman (1977) indicates that 'eyes' would also be needed for ASL, since she says that the eyes and nose contrast in ASL. Friedman suggests that ASL signs made in the other locations needed for BSL are iconic, and that these locations are not contrastive. For example, she says that 'All signs made at the ear are iconic and refer to the ear in some way, as in EAR, HEAR, EARRING' (Friedman, 1977, p. 39). However, she says that the sign for DEAF, which originally entailed contact of the index finger with the mouth and then the ear, now makes its second contact at the cheek, so that the ear can be considered a variant of the cheek in location. In BSL, however, the ear and cheek appear to contrast with one another, as in the signs CHEEKY and LUCKY (cf Brennan et al., 1980, p. 65). In these signs the thumb and index finger hold the cheek, or ear (respectively), shaking it to and fro. One tab in the Stokoe notation which does not appear necessary for BSL is that for wrist face up (see p. 60). This does not seem to be contrastive for BSL, and even in ASL there does not seem to be a minimal pair distinguished only by the side of the wrist. Friedman (1977, p. 42) considers both sides of the wrist to be distinct locations in ASL but marginal ones.

The dezes or handshapes which appear to be contrastive for BSL were listed on pp. 61-4, and can be compared with those listed in the Stokoe notation in Stokoe et al. (1976). Dezes needed for BSL but not included in the Stokoe notation for ASL are A, B̈, 5̇, V̈ and ⋏ . In ASL Ȧ is found as a phonetic variant of A, as are S, made with the thumb on the middle fingers, rather than touching the index finger, and T, with the thumb between the index and middle finger (see Stokoe, 1978, p. 45 and Friedman, 1977, p. 19). S and T are used mainly for fingerspelling the corresponding letters in the one-handed manual alphabet, which is not used in BSL. In BSL, Ȧ (with thumb extended from fist) is clearly distinct from A, being used for the sign GOOD (ØA⁰), and also in other signs incorporating notions of 'goodness', such as BETTER, (AAˣ), PRAISE (ØȦÁ⁀) (cf Woll, 1983). The fact that Ȧ tends to have a distinct meaning ('goodness') whereas A does not, is probably the reason why analysts have treated them as contrastive, although they may not contrast formationally to distinguish two signs in a minimal pair. (Brennan et al. (1980), p. 100, give a possible minimal pair, YOUR, with A, and RIGHT, with Ȧ, but RIGHT as they give it has tab deleted (cf chapter 3, so could be considered not to be a citation form (the 'normal form': see p. 79).)

The next extra dez symbol needed for BSL, 'bent B' (B̈), is listed as a separate symbol in Stokoe (1978, p. 68) but it seems to be a phonetic variant of B and therefore not contrastive. In BSL, however, Brennan et al. argue that B and B̈ contrast, and they give a minimal pair, UNDER (with B) and VISIT (with B̈) (Brennan et al., 1980, p. 106). The next handshape, 5̇ ('bent 5') is not listed in the Stokoe notation as distinct from 5, but Friedman suggests that they can be considered distinct in ASL. However, Friedman's analysis is not in line with the classical phonemic approach taken here (see p. 51), since she wishes to consider 5̇ as a variant of 5 in other signs. According to the classical approach, 5̇ would have to be considered either as distinct from 5 in the system or non-distinct and a phonetic variant, but not both (see Wilbur, 1979, p. 53 for further discussion of this problem). In BSL, 5 and 5̈ do appear to contrast, as in the minimal pair given in Brennan et al. (1980, p. 112), DIRTY and THIEVE. V and V̈ are not represented as contrastive with one another in the Stokoe notation, but Friedman (1977) argues, as she does for 5 and 5̈, that V̈ can be both in contrast with V and a variant of V. As we have seen, this would pose problems for a classical phonemic approach, and again, she does not give a convincing example of a minimal pair involving V and V̈. In BSL, however, there is such a pair: OFFICER and CAPTAIN (Brennan et al., 1980, p. 142). In OFFICER a V hand touches the top of the left shoulder twice, while in CAPTAIN a V̈ (bent V) performs the same action. The final extra handshape needed for BSL (λ), is not included in ASL because of its obscene connotation in American culture, as I pointed out on p. 64.

Dezes included in the notation for ASL but not needed in BSL are: E, K, 3 and R. E, K and R represent letters in the American manual alphabet, which might account for their lack of occurrence in BSL. Although something similar to E occurs in the BSL sign NAILBRUSH, this can be considered a variant of 5̈. Stokoe (1978, p. 46) suggests that E might be considered a variant of C, and Friedman (1977) does not include it in her 'phonemic inventory' of handshapes, but considers it to be a 'loan phone', a term she uses for 'those hand shapes which occur only in loan words from English – using the hand shape corresponding to the first letter of the English word' (Friedman, 1977, p. 15). Her list of loan phones also includes K and R. K (index and middle finger extended, thumb touching junction between them) is not found in BSL at all as far as I know, and R (middle finger crossed over index) only appears in Catholic signing in Britain (cf Lawson, 1981). 3 (thumb, index and middle finger extended) is the shape used for the number 'three' in ASL, and in other signs including the classifier for vehicles (see later in this chapter, p. 117): in BSL the number 'three' is normally signed with three fingers (excluding the thumb) extended, and the ASL 3 handshape is not used in any other signs.

One handshape which is neither included in the Stokoe notation for ASL nor needed for BSL is the 'horns' handshape ┡ (index and little finger extended from fist). Friedman argues that this is needed for ASL, but although she says that it is used in the signs CIGARETTE and KID, whereas Y (thumb and little finger extended from fist) is used in other signs, she does not give an example of a minimal pair where ⅄ and Y contrast. In any case it seems that signs made with ⅄ can sometimes have the thumb extended as well, and she suggests that a merger with Y will eventually take place, involving the loss of ⅄ as a significant element of the language. However, I do not find the evidence for the significance of ⅄ convincing, and assume that it can in fact be considered a variant of Y.

As in BSL, signs in ASL can be made with one or two hands, and two handed signs are of the same two types given on p. 55. On p. 65 we saw that in two handed BSL signs of the second type, where the non-dominant hand remains stationary as tab, and the dominant hand acts as dez, the tab hand can only be one of a limited set of handshapes, principally A, B, 5, C, G and O, which, as we noted, can be considered the 'unmarked' hand-shapes. It is interesting to note that the same set of handshapes (plus S, which is considered a variant of A in ASL) seem to be possible tabs in ASL (see Friedman, 1977, Battison, 1978). Battison states that these handshapes 'are maximally distinct, basic geometric shapes' (Battison, 1978, p. 36) and Boyes-Braem (1981) show that they are anatomically among the easiest to produce. Battison suggests that they are also phonologically the most natural because they are acquired first by children (cf chapter 7), because they are highly frequent in occurrence, and 'they are found in all other sign languages for which information is presently available to us' (Battison, 1978, p. 37). It is interesting, in the light of the last statement, that these handshapes are not only present in BSL, but that they occur under similar conditions to those found in ASL.

While the discussion of the comparative phonological structure of BSL and ASL has so far been in terms of the classical phonemic approach of isolating phonological elements which contrast with one another, a more modern approach has been attempted by some people working on ASL, who have tried to isolate smaller units, or 'distinctive features' (cf p. 51). Of all the parameters of a sign, the handshape or tab is the one that has been the most analysed in terms of distinctive features. So just as phonologists working on spoken languages might suggest that instead of viewing [p] and [b] as minimal units, they might be considered clusters of features such as +labial (formed by closure at the lips), +stop (formed by complete closure and then release), and ±voiced ([p] is −voiced or voiceless while [b] is +voiced). Lane, Boyes-Braem and Bellugi (1976), for example, have suggested that the hand-shapes 5 and B share the features −compact (not closed), +broad (three or more fingers extended), +full (at least four fingers extended), and that they are distinguished by the feature ±radial (5 is +radial because it has the thumb extended, whereas B is −radial because it does not). Wilbur (1979, chapter 2) discusses various feature analyses for the handshape in ASL and uses distinctive features and phonological rules to argue that S may be considered an 'underlying' handshape from which A and Å are derived. Boyes-Braem (1981) also reviews feature analyses of the handshape in ASL and proposes a combination of primary, 'morpho-phonemic' and secondary, 'perceptual' features. An example of a morpho-phonemic feature is 'grasp', which is related to the semantic notion of 'grasp' as in the signs FIND, PROFIT, WIN, CLIMB. The secondary features are more similar to those proposed by Lane, Boyes-Braem and Bellugi (1976) and include ± full, for example. Phonological analysis of BSL has unfortunately not progressed far enough to use feature analysis to compare it with ASL, though it is worth noting that Woll (1983) has sugge-sted, without breaking handshapes down into features, that certain handshapes may have semantic function.

Returning to a classical phonemic framework, as represented by the Stokoe notation, almost the same set of distinct movements, or sigs, seem to be found in ASL as in BSL. The most important difference would seem to be that absence of movement does not seem to be a possible sig in ASL, whereas it is quite common in BSL, where the only movement in a sign such as GOOD ($\emptyset A^\emptyset$), for example, is that necessary to bring the hand into its position in neutral space. Signs in ASL, on the other hand, tend to trace a path in their motion, to involve internal hand or finger movement, or to interact with the hand or body tab (cf Stokoe, 1978, p. vi). Otherwise, the only other sig found necessary for BSL that is missing in the Stokoe system was a sig for a 'crumbling action' of the fingers (ѡ) (cf World Federation of the Deaf, 1975). The one sig which is in the Stokoe system but which does not seem to be found in BSL is the one for 'enter' (ѻ), where one hand is placed inside the other. Although I have no particular explanation for these differences of sig inventory, they serve, like the differences of tab and dez inventory, to illustrate that sign languages can differ in their phonological inventory just like spoken languages (cf p. 47). In research on ASL there has been some attempt to do a feature analysis of movement analogous to that of handshape. Friedman (1977) suggests that there are four main aspects of movement: interaction of the hands, contact with the body, direction of movement, and manner of movement. Within these categories she suggests various features of movement, such as 'alternate' and 'approach' for interaction. However, she gives little idea of how these features could be used to advantage in a phonological analysis. Wilbur (1979) also includes discussion of possible features of movement in ASL. In adapting Stokoe's notation for BSL, Brennan et al. (1980) divide sigs into the categories of direction, manner, and interaction (see pp. 69–70) which is similar to Friedman's approach except that they do not replace the sigs with features. Klima and Bellugi (1979) raise the question of the extent to which the movements involved in distinguishing signs from one another can be described in the same terms as those which are involved in inflections (to be discussed later in this chapter): they conclude (p. 315) that further research is needed to answer this question decisively.

If we now leave the comparison of the phonological inventory in ASL and BSL, and turn to comparing constraints on the structure of signs in the two languages we shall find that they are very similar. In chapter 3, p. 78, I said that a constraint called the 'Symmetry Condition' accounted for the fact that the two handshapes in a double dez sign are identical, and that this constraint was adhered to by signs in both ASL and BSL. The Symmetry Condition, which was first formulated for ASL by Battison (1974) and which applies to two-handed signs of category (1) (see chapter 3, p. 55), actually requires that the two hands must be identical not only in handshape, but also in location and movement, or, more informally, 'If a two-handed sign is going to bear the added complexity of having both hands move, then both hands must perform roughly the same motor acts' (Battison, 1978, p. 34). Stated this way, it looks as though the constraint is a motor or physical one, and therefore not specific to one sign language. It certainly applies to BSL as well as ASL, but it remains to be seen if it applies to all sign languages. Battison's related Dominance Condition applies to two-handed signs of the other category, category (2) (chapter 3, p. 55) (which are not governed by the Symmetry Condition), and rules that where the handshapes of the two hands are not identical, a passive hand must remain stationary, and must have one of the unmarked handshapes (see p. 110). Battison suggests that this Condition, like the other, reduces complexity in signs, and thus it may not only apply to both ASL and BSL (as was pointed out on p. 100), but may be universal. The final aspect of phonology in which we may compare BSL and ASL is that of phonological processes (cf chapter 3, p. 48). There are many kinds of phonological process possible, but here we shall consider just those dealt with for BSL in chapter 3, that is: assimilation of dez, change of tab or sig, and hand deletion (see p. 79).

In BSL we saw that the handshape of a sign can be assimilated to that of the sign before it, so that 'I' in the sequence KNOW(NEG) I took on the handshape of KNOW(NEG). This is known as 'progressive' assimilation in that the first sign influences the formation of the second. 'Regressive' assimilation, where the second sign influences the formation of the first, is also possible in BSL, as in the following sequence from my data: L WILL CLOSE-DOWN. In this, WILL, which normally has an A (closed fist) handshape, takes on the B handshape of the following sign, CLOSE-DOWN. In ASL examples of assimilation I have found are regressive, as in the example given by Wilbur (1979, p. 73) where the handshape of WE (normally G or H) takes on the A handshape of REFUSE in the sequence WE REFUSE. Another example of regressive assimilation is given by Friedman (1976b, p. 116), where the handshape of TEMPT (normally X) took on the V handshape of STEAL in the sequence TEMPT STEAL. Friedman suggests that handshape assimilation will always be regressive or 'anticipatory', because she argues that handshape is the first parameter of a sign to be formed, so that 'in connected discourse, the hand shape of the articulator anticipates the following sign, while the shape of the place of articulation hand lags or perseverates the shape of the previous sign' (Friedman, 1976b, p. 117). This does not seem to hold for BSL, however, since there is an example of progressive assimilation of handshape, where the handshape of KNOW(NEG) 'lags or perseverates' into I. There may be grammatical constraints which affect the type of assimilation which occurs: since it is not obligatory in BSL to sign the first person pronoun (see chapter 4, p. 96), this might explain why the sign I was assimilated to KNOW(NEG) in its formation rather than the reverse.

Change of tab occurs in ASL as well as in BSL. Battison (1978), referring to the findings of Frishberg (1975 and 1976), suggests that one-handed signs made without contact on the face tend to centralize, moving 'towards the central area of signing space, the upper chest and lower face' (Battison, 1978, p. 75), and often acquiring a second hand. This tendency is historical, and accounts for some of the changes in ASL signs over time. The change of tab in the BSL sign KNOW(NEG) from upper face to chest in informal situations (see chapter 3, p. 79) could be said to represent the tendency towards centralization once contact with the face had been lost. Although this sign may be made with two hands, particularly in formal situations (cf chapter 6), I do not have data to determine whether two hands are also more likely to occur when the tab is centralized. This would be an interesting area for investigation, which would help to determine the extent to which tendencies observed in ASL are universal for sign languages, and to what extent language-specific. (Change of sig is also observed in ASL: see Battison, 1978.)

The third and final phonological process to be compared here in BSL and ASL is that of hand deletion in two-handed signs. As I said in chapter 3, p. 80 (and see chapter 6), deletion of one hand in two-handed BSL signs is more likely to take place in some types of sign than in others, more in some social situations than in others (and it may also operate over time as a historical process to change the form of a sign). Battison (1978) suggests that in ASL also, hand deletion is more likely in 'casual' or informal situations, or when only one hand is physically available for signing. He also reports (Battison, 1974) that the phonological structure of signs may have an effect on whether or not a hand is deleted, since in a study of the acceptability of hand deletion in informal situations, his informants judged that deletion of one hand was more acceptable for some types of signs than others. Deletion was most acceptable in two-handed symmetrical signs where both hands move (our type (1), p. 55), less acceptable in signs of our type (2), where one hand is active and the other passive, but within this category it was more acceptable if both hands had the same handshape, and 'almost completely unacceptable' if the passive hand had a different handshape from the active hand. I do not have comparative data from BSL on the acceptability of deletion in various kinds of sign, but deletion of one hand in signs of type (1) certainly seems to occur more

frequently than in signs of type (2). Within type (2) deletion of
the passive, though not active hand, is possible both for signs
where both handshapes are the same, as in the case of FATHER
(see p. 67), and where they are not, as in the case of RIGHT (see
p. 56). Battison (1974) found deletion in signs of this last type
unacceptable in ASL, whereas in BSL deletion seems to be just
as frequent, if not more so, in signs of this type as in signs of the
FATHER type. So it appears that the constraints on hand deletion
may be slightly different for ASL and BSL, but further research
is needed on this.

Thus far I hope to have shown that ASL and BSL have some
similarities and some differences in their phonological inventory,
similarities in the constraints on the structure of signs, and some
similarities and differences in the phonological processes that can
be undergone. We now turn to the comparison of BSL and ASL
at the grammatical level.

Comparing inflectional processes in BSL and ASL we shall
look, as we did in chapter 4, at changes in the sig or parameter
of movement and in dez or handshape changes which function as
inflections. The changes in movement we looked at in BSL
involved both changes of direction and repetition, and both these
are found in ASL also. According to Fischer and Gough (1978),
ASL has a set of verbs comparable to those in BSL (see p. 86)
which have the properties of directionality, and sometimes also
reversibility. In ASL the verb GIVE, as in BSL, is directional in
that its movement is from source to goal in a similar egocentric
system where the signer's body represents first person. Among
their list of reversible verbs (where hand orientation represents
case relations), it is interesting to note that Fischer and Gough
include the ASL verbs BEAT and TEASE (presumably equivalent
in meaning to BSL MOCK), as we saw that BSL BEAT and
MOCK are also reversible. Edge and Herrmann (1977) present
an analysis of ASL verbs which divides them into three classes:
multidirectional, multiorientational, and bodily anchored. Multidirectional verbs are the same as Fischer and Gough's directional
verbs in that they move from the location of the source to the
location of the goal, and involve the semantic notion of transference (cf BSL, p. 86). Edge and Herrmann point out that these
verbs are 'three-place predicates' incorporating three arguments,
patient as well as source and goal. So the verb GIVE, for example,
has as its arguments the source of the gift, the gift itself (patient),

and the goal to which the gift is directed. Multiorientational verbs, on the other hand, are not only formationally different in that the orientation of the hands represents case relations, but they are also semantically different in that they are 'two-place predicates', where 'the argument represented by the location behind the hands is always that of the agent of the verb' (Edge and Herrmann, 1977, p. 147), and the other argument is the patient, the one being acted upon. (Fischer, personal communication, has pointed out that there are examples of multiorientational verbs which are three-place predicates). These verbs appear equivalent to Fischer and Gough's reversible verbs, and to those verbs in BSL which I described as both directional and reversible (see p. 87). Edge and Herrmann's third category of verbs, bodily anchored, are those which are 'articulated on or at the body and the body functions as a marker for the experiencer' (Edge and Herrmann, 1977, p. 146). These verbs cannot indicate case relations by their direction or orientation because of their physical characteristics, and it is interesting that a consequence of this appears to be that they are 'one-place predicates', and only have one argument, the experiencer, which need not be overtly marked if it is the first person (cf chapter 4, p. 96 and below, p. 122). ASL verbs in this category include ANGER, EMBARRASS, FEEL, FRIGHTEN. A similar category of verbs with no inflection for movement is certainly also found in BSL.

As we saw in chapter 4, another inflection involving the movement parameter is repetition (or reduplication), which in BSL 'seems to function as a marker of aspect in verb signs, and as a marker of plurality in certain noun signs' (p. 87). Fischer (1973a) distinguishes between two kinds of reduplication in ASL, fast and slow, and suggests that while fast reduplication can indicate plural or habitual in verbs, slow reduplication represents iterative or continuative. She says that slow reduplication in verbs will be interpreted as representing iterative aspect (repeated action) in verbs which are 'point action' (like English 'kill'), and as representing continuative aspect in verbs which have inherently durative meaning (like English 'wait'). She does not describe what happens with verbs that are neither inherently durative nor inherently 'point action', like the BSL verb QUARREL mentioned on p. 87, but this will be further discussed later in this chapter under the category of aspect. Meanwhile it is worth comparing Fischer's findings concerning reduplication with those of Klima and Bellugi (1979) who suggest that 'iterative' and 'continuative' aspect are marked by reduplication both in verbs and adjectives and that they can be distinguished as follows: for iterative aspect 'the reduplicated movement is tense and end-marked (hold manner), with a slow elliptical return'; and continuative aspect is marked by 'slow, elongated, continuous reduplications that are elliptical in shape' (Klima and Bellugi, 1979, p. 294). Klima and Bellugi (1979, p. 239) find reduplication to be used for plurals also, but suggest that the repetition occurs in different places in the signing space, as I suggested for BSL. Wilbur (1979) cites an unpublished study by Jones and Mohr (1975) as indicating that other modifications as well as reduplication are used in forming the plural in nouns, depending on the formation of the noun sign, and that 'In general, any noun that involves repetition of movement in its singular does not undergo the above modification of movement for plural, but takes a plural quantifier such as MANY instead' (Wilbur, 1979, p. 95).

In BSL we saw that not only movement, but also handshape, could be modified for grammatical purposes. In ASL this is also possible. Number can be incorporated into noun signs in a similar way according to Wilbur (1979) who calls this process 'blending': it seems especially common in time indicators such as HOUR, DAY, WEEK (this is common in BSL also), and Wilbur suggests that the numbers 1, 2, and 3 have a greater degree of freedom to incorporate into other signs. It seems that this is true of BSL also, and certainly the examples I gave on p. 88 of number incorporation involved only the numbers 2 and 3.

Wilbur (1979) also discusses another kind of handshape modification we found in BSL, the incorporation of 'classifiers' into the verb. In ASL, as in BSL, the index finger can be used as a classifier for person, and Wilbur shows that this can be incorporated into verb signs by changing the handshape of the verb. She gives the example of the verb FOLLOW, which in its citation form has one Å hand following another Å hand, and where a G hand (with index finger extended) can be substituted for one or both of the Å hands to represent a person following a thing or another person. Similarly, in indicating movement underneath something, Wilbur says that the Å handshape in UNDER can be replaced by an upside down V classifier (representing legs) for a person walking, or a 3 hand for a vehicle.

Like BSL, ASL also has an inflectional process called 'negative incorporation', involving the modification of both movement and handshape. As I pointed out in chapter 4 (p. 89) negative incorporation only applies to a small set of signs, but this set seems very similar in BSL, ASL and French Sign Language (FSL), as Table 3 shows.

Table 3 Signs allowing negative incorporation

BSL	GOOD	HAVE*	KNOW	LIKE	WANT	AGREE	WILL	BELIEVE
ASL	GOOD	HAVE	KNOW	LIKE	WANT			
FSL		HAVE	KNOW	LIKE	WANT			

*not in my data, but Jones (1968, p. 120) describes it

BSL appears to allow negative incorporation in all the five verbs which were researched by Woodward and DeSantis (1977), as well as a few others. Negative incorporation as described in ASL seems to involve a similar modification of movement and handshape to that which occurs in BSL: 'Negative incorporation involves a bound outward twisting movement of the moving hand(s) from the place where the sign is made' (Woodward and DeSantis, 1977, p. 381). According to Wilbur (1979), the final handshape is always a 5 (as in BSL). Woodward and DeSantis's explanation for the similarity of the process in ASL and FSL is based on the assumption that FSL creolized with ASL in the nineteenth century when Thomas Gallaudet returned to the US from France, having learned how sign language was used in deaf education in France (see chapter 2, p. 32 and Woodward, 1978). Woodward and DeSantis (1977) say that negative incorporation is a phonological process of assimilation in FSL, because the movement in the FSL sign NOT is similar to that incorporated in certain verb signs. They say (p. 385) that:

> FSL NOT assimilates location and handshape to that of the preceding verb sign and loses its movement. This results in an outward twisting movement (to obtain the outward orientation of FSL NOT) from the place where the verb sign is made.

However, they say that negative incorporation in ASL cannot be derived from phonological assimilation, since the ASL sign NOT is a distinct lexical item. Instead, they suggest that negative incorporation in ASL arose through contact with FSL and became a grammatical rule, which in addition to the verbs affected in FSL, was also applied to the ASL sign GOOD. Although this seems a

convincing explanation, Woodward does not mention an alternative sign for NOT in ASL (ØBB⁺, cf Hoemann, 1976, pp. 32–3)
which is somewhat similar in movement and handshape to that
involved in negative incorporation: thus it is conceivable that
similar processes might have evolved independently in FSL and
ASL. Also, Woodward's explanation for the similarity of the
process of negative incorporation in ASL and FSL does not
explain why there is such a similar process in BSL also, unless we
assume that FSL and BSL had similar contact to that between
FSL and ASL. (Boyes-Braem's (1981) observation that FSL and
BSL have similar handshapes could be taken as evidence for such
contact.) So far there is not enough evidence to decide whether
negative incorporation in BSL, ASL and FSL developed independently or through language contact. So far the second seems more
plausible to me than the first, as I cannot find strong linguistic
reasons why such a similar set of verbs should be affected in the
three languages (though Fischer, personal communication, points
out that all the verbs are stative). More research is needed on
the existence or lack of negative incorporation in additional sign
languages, and on the history of their contact with FSL or other
sign languages. It is worth noting in passing that Danish Sign
Language appears to have a similar process of negative incorporation affecting similar verbs (Hansen, personal communication)
and that Danish Sign Language may have been influenced by
FSL through the spread of Epée's method of deaf education (see
chapter 2, p. 31) to Scandinavia (cf Hodgson, 1953).

We now turn to comparing the function of non-manual activity
in BSL and ASL. The non-manual means of negation by headshaking used in BSL, which I mentioned on p. 91, also seems to
be used in ASL, sometimes in combination with certain facial
expressions or movements. Wilbur (1979, p. 137) describes non-
manual negation as involving 'a side-to-side headshake, and a
special facial expression in which a primary feature is the turning
down of the corners of the mouth'. Baker and Padden (1978, p.
50) list 'frown, lowering brows, wrinkling nose, sticking out
tongue' as possible facial movements indicating negation. We saw
in chapter 4 (p. 91) that questions in BSL are marked by the
movement of the eyebrows from their neutral position. I suggested
that the amount of information required by the person asking
the question may determine whether the eyebrows are raised or
lowered in a question, rather than that Yes–No questions involve

eyebrow raising, while Wh- questions involve eyebrow lowering, as some researchers have suggested. In Baker and Padden's (1978) list of the possible functions of facial movements in ASL, they list 'raised brows, retracted eyelids, head and posture forward' for question signalling, apparently not differentiating between possible types of question. Wilbur (1979), however, differentiates between 'a leaning forward of the body, the head forward, and the eyebrows raised', which she says marks Yes–No questions, (Wilbur, 1979, p. 137) and the marking of Wh- questions, where she says, 'the eyes are narrowed and the eyebrows are squished' (Wilbur, 1979, p. 146).

Research on non-manual activity in ASL has progressed considerably further than in BSL, and it has been suggested that non-manual activity may serve additional functions to those of marking negation and questions. As we saw on p. 93, Liddell (1980) has suggested that a headnod may function as an assertion marker in ASL, and we saw that this may also be the case in BSL. Liddell (1978) has also investigated the possible non-manual marking of restrictive relative clauses in ASL. (An example of a restrictive relative clause in the English translation of one of Liddell's examples is the part in italics in the following: 'The dog *that recently chased the cat* came home'.) Liddell argues that a tilted head together with raised eyebrows marks the extent of a restrictive relative clause. However, we should bear in mind that his data are based on asking signers to translate English sentences, and so may not be representative of normal sign syntax (see chapter 8 for discussion of this kind of problem). The problem of defining the sentence in ASL is as difficult as that in BSL (cf chapter 4, p. 83), and Thompson (1977) suggests that the non-manual activity which Liddell identifies may not be marking subordination or relativization within a sentence, but may instead be 'a discourse level marker of material either mentioned earlier in the discourse or present in the common speaker-hearer context, which material the speaker wishes to return to prominence' (Thompson, 1977, p. 188). In chapter 4 I warned against investigating sign language via English, and Liddell's study could be said to be an example of this, since he started out with English sentences containing restrictive relative clauses (which are a kind of grammatical structure specific to English) rather than with a particular grammatical category (cf p. 94) whose realization one could compare in ASL, English, and many other languages. However, one can take the non-manual activity that he has identified and proceed from structure to function (cf p. 84), trying to determine what function this activity fulfils, rather than assume that it is parallel to a particular structure (the restrictive relative clause) found in English.

Baker and Padden (1978) show how it is possible to proceed in the alternative direction, from function to structure, by investigating how conditionals may be marked non-manually. They find that various kinds of non-manual activity occur at the juncture between the 'if' and the 'then' clause, such as eye blinks, brow lowering, headnodding, although there is considerable variation between signers and they conclude that 'it is the *configuration* or pattern of co-occurring behaviour that serves a given function rather than any *specific* behaviour' (Baker and Padden, 1978, p. 33).

Although research on non-manual activity in ASL is relatively well advanced in general, little work seems to have been done on the analysis of mouth movements, possibly because of a reaction against the oralism prevailing in the education of the deaf. However, as I said in chapter 4, Lawson (1983) has some preliminary findings on mouth movements in BSL, and Vogt-Svendsen (1981) has done some pioneering work on the notation and functions of mouth movements in Norwegian Sign Language.

We now take a function to structure approach in the comparison of BSL and ASL, and look at deixis of person and time. In chapter 4, p. 95, I argued that the category of person deixis is grammaticalized in BSL in the existence of a category of personal pronouns, and in the constraints governing their deletion. Friedman (1975, p. 947) discusses a similar set of what she calls 'indexing gestures' in ASL, since she rejects the idea that they are pronouns. She says (Friedman, 1975, p. 946):

> The ASL lexicon contains no signs classifiable as 'pronouns'. The equivalent of pronominal reference is achieved by the signer's first establishing a frame of reference, in front of his body, within which he establishes points of reference identified with the objects, persons and locations to which he will refer.

One could nevertheless argue that Friedman's 'indexing gestures' might be considered pronouns, for although they mark person by the direction in which they point, they mark number in their hand configuration: whereas a G (index finger) represents singular. V (two fingers) represents dual, 3 (three fingers), trial, and 5 (fingers extended and spread: Friedman labels this 'B spread'), plural. Wilbur (1979) interprets Friedman as suggesting that the points in space are the actual pronouns; she herself, following Kegl (1976) proposes that pronouns may be 'realized' at certain points in various ways: by the position of the signer's body, which is shifted from neutral position (with first person reference) for third person reference (see Wilbur, 1979, p. 106); by a classifier handshape as part of the verb (and we have seen that there are classifiers in ASL as in BSL); by an index to a point, or in various other ways (see Wilbur, 1979, p. 130). All these seem possible for BSL, although we dealt in chapter 4 mainly with pronouns formed by indexing points. The constraints on the deletion of pronouns in ASL appear similar to those in BSL, in that first person subject pronouns can always be deleted, and third person subject pronouns can be deleted if the referent remains the same as that of the last nominal. These constraints are stated by Friedman (1976a) as a way of assigning subject to verbs without overt arguments.

Deixis of time in ASL is very similar to that in BSL as outlined in chapter 4. Verbs do not inflect for tense, but time is indicated by adverbials, and the present time is unmarked (cf Friedman, 1975, p. 951). The time adverbials are located, as in BSL, on a 'time line' relative to the signer (cf Frishberg and Gough, 1973). ASL has a sign glossed as WILL, but whereas in BSL there are two separate signs, an adverbial, FUTURE (ØB$^{\perp}$), and a tense modal auxiliary WILL (see p. 98) ($\cup$A$^{\perp}$), Wilbur states that in ASL, 'many authors treat WILL and FUTURE as a single sign' (Wilbur, 1979, p. 96). Friedman (1975, p. 952) describes ASL WILL as a 'lexicalized modal', but it is not clear what is meant by this, apart from the fact that it translates English 'will'. It seems that ASL WILL may be more like a time adverbial than a modal auxiliary. One piece of evidence that BSL WILL is more 'verblike' than ASL WILL, is that BSL allows negative incorporation (see p. 89), whereas ASL WILL does not. So WILL as a modal may be lacking in ASL, but it is worth noting that ASL does, like BSL, have separate lexical signs for CAN and CANNOT, and a sign glossed as MUST (which BSL also has).

BSL and ASL are similar not only in that they do not have the grammatical category of tense, marking time lexically, but also in that they do have the grammatical category of aspect. We noted on p. 100 that BSL has an auxiliary verb, FINISH, which appears to have the function of marking perfective aspect. ASL also has an auxiliary glossed as FINISH which is described as perfective (see Fischer, 1974), and apparently also a negative equivalent, glossed as NOT-YET. (There is a sign in BSL glossed as NOT-YET ($\emptyset$AA^Z) with simultaneous headshaking, and it is possible that it may function in a similar way to NOT-YET in ASL.)

We saw earlier in this chapter (p. 116) that aspect can also be marked by reduplication of the movement parameter in verbs. We saw that a distinction has been made between fast and slow reduplication in ASL, comparable to the distinction we found in BSL. As Table 2 in chapter 4 shows (p. 102), fast repetition in BSL seems to indicate durative aspect in verbs referring to states and processes, though it indicates habitual aspect in verbs referring to events. Slow repetition, on the other hand, indicates iterative aspect in verbs referring to events and processes. We saw earlier (p. 116) that Fischer (1973a) finds that fast repetition can indicate habitual aspect in ASL, and that slow repetition indicates iterative aspect in 'point action' verbs (those referring to events in the terms of Table 2, chapter 4) but 'continuative' (probably equivalent to durative in our terms) in verbs which in our terms refer to a process. So Fischer's findings could be represented in Table 4 below, in order to compare them with my findings in Table 2, chapter 4.

Table 4 Fischer's (1973a) findings on repetition of movement in ASL verbs

Situation	Meaning of repetition of movement	
	Slow repetition	Fast repetition
state	–	–
event	iterative	habitual
process	durative	–

If we compare this table with Table 2 in chapter 4 (p. 102), we see that there is apparently no marking in ASL for durative aspect in verbs that refer to states, and no marking for iterative aspect in verbs that refer to processes, whereas both these kinds of marking are found in BSL. All the examples given by Fischer of verbs referring to processes are interpreted as having durative aspect with slow repetition: DRINK ('drink for a long time'), FLY-BY-AIRPLANE ('to fly for a long time'), IRON ('to keep on ironing' for a long time), and BE-STANDING ('to keep on standing for a long time'). Klima and Bellugi (1979) also do not deal with iterative aspect in verbs referring to processes, but they deal with a wide range of aspectual inflection in ASL (including some inflection which would not come under our definition of aspect in chapter 4, p. 100), as applied to both verbs and adjectives, and distinguish various kinds of movement change in addition to slow and .fast repetition. In general, their category of adjectival predicates is equivalent to our category of verbs referring to states, while their verbs refer to states and processes. Their findings can be presented in a simplified form, but using a similar format to Tables 2 and 4, in Table 5 below.

Table 5 Klima and Bellugi's (1979) findings on modification of movement in predicates

Situation	Meaning of modification of movement		Other
	Slow repetition	Fast repetition	
state	durative(1)	–	
event	iterative(2)	habitual(3)	incessant(4)
process	durative(1)	–	protractive(5) durational(6)

Notes
(1) 'continuative' in Klima and Bellugi's (1979, p. 294) terms
(2) 'tense and end-marked . . . with a slow elliptical return' (ibid., p. 294)
(3) 'rapid, nontense repetitions' (ibid., p. 294)
(4) 'short tense' repeated movement (ibid., p. 292)
(5) 'a long tense hold and without motion' (ibid., p. 292)
(6) 'smooth, circular reduplicated movement' (ibid., p. 294) (this seems similar in meaning to durative)

If we compare this table with Table 2 on p. 102, we can conclude that BSL and ASL both mark aspect by modification of the parameter of movement in predicates, but that they do not mark exactly the same categories in exactly the same way. BSL and ASL both mark durative aspect in states and processes, but by slow repetition in BSL, fast repetition in ASL. Also, ASL marks incessant aspect, which has not been found in BSL so far, and BSL marks iterative aspect for processes, which does not seem to be reported for ASL. Because of the paucity of the findings on aspect in BSL (see chapter 4, p. 102) and the absence of further studies in ASL to compare with the rich findings of Klima and Bellugi (1979), no definitive comparison of aspect in ASL and BSL can yet be made.

In chapter 4, (p. 103), in a brief consideration of the 'parts of speech' in BSL, I said that verbs and adjectives seemed to undergo similar grammatical processes both in ASL and BSL, and we have just seen that the 'adjectival predicates' studied for their aspect marking by Klima and Bellugi (1979) refer to situations that one can describe as states, while their 'verbs' refer to situations that can be described as events and processes. So one might argue for a single primary category 'predicate' in both ASL and BSL.

In chapter 4 also, we saw that no systematic difference had been found in the formation of nouns and verbs in BSL, although there is some evidence for such a difference in ASL. Supalla and Newport (1978) studied 100 pairs of nouns and verbs in ASL that were related in form and meaning, and that referred to a concrete object and activity. Within this carefully defined set, they found that nouns and verbs were systematically related in their formation, differing in their manner and frequency of movement: 'while verbs are either continuous or hold in manner, nouns are restrained in manner; while verbs are either repeated or single, nouns are always repeated' (Supalla and Newport, 1978, p. 119). They suggest that the relation between these nouns and verbs is best captured if one postulates an abstract, underlying form from which both nouns and verbs are derived. This underlying form is specified for all features except manner of movement, which is added when deriving a noun (+restrained) or a verb (+hold or +continuous, depending, roughly, on whether the verb refers to an event with a spatial end-point, or a process without one). The frequency of movement in the underlying form is given as −repeated: this remains unchanged for a punctual verb (referring to an event), but is changed to +repeated for a non-punctual verb (referring to a process), and also for all nouns. Inflections on nouns and verbs can then be specified by a change in the frequency of the noun or verb thus far derived. They say that slow reduplication can be applied to both nouns (for 'serial pluralization') and verbs (for iterative or durative aspect, or what they call 'iteration' and 'elongation'), but that this is applied to the single movement of the underlying form common to nouns and verbs, rather than to the repeated movement of all nouns and some verbs. So there is no repetition of cycles of repetition, but only repetition of single movements. What they call 'dual inflection' for plurals in nouns and verbs also involves repetition of only a single movement at two locations in space. Nouns and verbs inflected in one of these two ways remain distinguishable, however, in that their manner of movement is unchanged.

We now turn to a brief comparison of the 'functional' categories, particularly the notions of 'subject', 'predicate', 'object', 'topic' and 'comment'. I suggested in chapter 4 (p. 103) that BSL structures are easily analysed in terms of 'topic' and 'comment', and the same appears to be true of ASL. Woodward (1972) and Ingram (1978) have argued for a topic-comment analysis for ASL, Friedman (1976a) has shown its usefulness in analysing ASL discourse, and Binnick (1978) quotes an unpublished paper by Anderson (1977) which argues for a topic-comment analysis on the grounds that old information tends to be presented before new information. Anderson argues that the 'old before new' principle also determines the relative order of the object and verb:

> by showing that the object will follow the verb if it is an effective object and precede it if it is affective: this follows from the distinction of new and old information, as effective objects only exist (or are only identified) after the action of the verb is performed. Anderson contrasts . . . MAKE CAR . . . with . . . FOOD PUT-IN (Binnick, 1978, p. 33).

Although, as I said on p. 104 the notions of 'topic' and 'comment' are similar to 'subject' and 'predicate' in their traditional sense, the term 'subject' in particular has taken on a slightly different meaning in modern linguistics, partly because of the way in which 'subject' functions in English. 'Subject' is now seen as more of a grammatical notion than the semantic 'topic', and there is considerable controversy about whether 'subject' is the same notion in all languages (cf Li, 1976, Comrie, 1981). Li and Thompson (1976), in a discussion of the difference between the notions subject and topic in modern linguistics, say that the topic occurs sentence-initially, and has the function of announcing the theme of the discourse. The subject, on the other hand, 'has a minimal discourse function in contrast with the topic' (p. 466), but is closely related to the verb: it is determined by the verb and 'agrees' with it. To illustrate this, we have already seen how certain verbs in both BSL and ASL have inflections which agree with what semantically can be called the agent or source of the verb, or syntactically the subject.

Li and Thompson (1976) suggest that whereas all languages will have both subjects and topics, subjects will be basic in some languages, which they call 'subject-prominent', and topics will be more basic in others, which they call 'topic-prominent'. English seems to be a subject-prominent language, and topic is not particularly salient since subject and topic often coincide. Chinese, however, can be considered a topic-prominent language because the topic is more salient than the subject. Li and Thompson list several criteria for a topic-prominent language, many of which are satisfied by BSL and seem to be satisfied by ASL also. These criteria include the absence of passive constructions (needed in a subject prominent language like English in order to make the subject coincide with the topic, cf Givón, 1979b), the absence of 'dummy subjects' like 'there' and 'there is' (this is translated by a single sign glossed as HAVE in both BSL and ASL) and the existence of 'double subject' constructions (topic followed by subject) as in an example from my BSL data: ARAB THEY DON'T-LIKE RUSSIA ('The Arabs don't like the Russians').

However, some of the work on ASL grammar assumed that it was a subject-prominent language without question, reflecting what Li and Thompson call the bias of modern linguistics in favour of a subject-predicate analysis. They say, 'The assumption remains that the basic sentence structure should be universally described in terms of subject, object, and verb' (Li and Thompson, 1976, p. 461). This assumption explains the controversy among researchers in ASL grammar about whether it had a basic order (of subject, verb and object relative to one another) or whether its order was free. This controversy was partly about how grammatical relations were indicated in ASL, and some of those involved in it were committed to showing that ASL did indeed have a 'proper' grammatical structure, using English structure as their reference point for what a proper grammatical structure should be like. Because of the bias of modern linguistics and the influence of what is known about English structure, the discussions about the relative order of subject, verb and object in ASL took place with very little discussion of whether these were significant notions in ASL. Fischer (1974, 1975) argued that ASL was basically an SVO (subject-verb-object) language, although this order could be altered under certain conditions, such as when inflections on the verb indicated subject and object. (She is supported in this view by Liddell, 1980.) Friedman (1976a) disagreed with this, criticizing the sentence-oriented approach whereby signers were asked to translate written sentences. She stressed the importance of using 'continuous textual material' or discourse for analysis, and claims, on the basis of her own data, that 'Word order is relatively free, with the exception of the tendency for the verb to be last' (Friedman, 1976a, p. 142). She points out that many structures do not have an object overtly appearing, and although this in itself might have been a good reason for analysis in terms of topic-comment rather than subject-verb-object, Friedman still assumes the viability of subject, verb and object as basic notions. She does recognize topic and comment in addition to these, however.

The discussion about 'word order' in ASL not only fails to question the viability of the notions 'subject', 'verb', and 'object' for that language, but it also fails to question the assumption that linear, or temporal order will be the only significant dimension in the language. Sign languages have the spatial as well as the temporal dimension available to them, and as we have seen, some aspects of grammar, such as negation by headshaking, and verb inflections, are coded simultaneously rather than sequentially. It is possible that topic-comment might be coded sequentially in ASL and BSL, with topic occurring initially, and possibly marked non-manually (cf Deuchar, 1983), while subject-predicate might be coded spatially in verb inflections. Noun signs may have a tendency to act as topics, while pronouns, referring to them and yet syntactically connected to the verb, may act as subjects and objects. This seems to fit in with Kegl's (1976, 1977) conception of the noun phrase (cited in Wilbur, 1979), where a noun is initially (i.e. in the temporal dimension) introduced into the conversation and then indexed pronominally by a 'deictic marker' pointing to an 'agreement point' (spatial dimension). If the topic noun can be marked in the temporal dimension while the subject pronoun is marked in the spatial dimension, BSL or ASL will clearly appear to be topic-prominent if we look at the temporal dimension only.

So we should not be too hasty in classifying BSL and ASL as topic prominent. In any case, even if we were to decide that this classification is correct, we should be aware of the variable and changing nature of language (cf chapter 6) and the way in which its structure can be influenced by the situation in which the language is produced. BSL and ASL may appear to be topic-prominent because they are used mostly in informal conversation, and not for written, literary purposes like English. I have been suggesting that English is classifiable as subject-prominent, and yet we should note that topic-comment structure becomes more salient in English when it is used, like sign languages, in informal, spontaneous discourse (cf Givón, 1979b, Ochs, 1979). So although frameworks such as topic-prominence can be useful for analysis of data, we should beware of classifying an entire language irrevocably as of one particular type, since languages vary from situation to situation, and change over time. Variation in BSL will be discussed in the next chapter.

Summary

We have seen that BSL and ASL exhibit considerable similarity, but also some differences, at the levels of both phonology and grammar. While the similarities may be due to the constraints of the visual medium combined with possible historical relations and or language contact, they do not appear to be due in the least to the English of their hearing communities. The differences between the two languages show that when two sign languages develop in two separate communities, their structures will differ just like the structure of spoken languages which have different developmental histories.

6

Variation in BSL

In the last two chapters we discussed BSL as if it were a homogeneous system without variation. However, if it is as fundamentally similar to other languages as I suggested it is, then we would expect to find variation within it, since all languages may be considered inherently variable (cf Labov, 1969). Linguists often ignore this variation for the purpose of achieving a reasonably coherent (if idealized) description of the language, and leave the study of it to those who are interested in sociolinguistics, or the study of language in relation to society (Labov, 1972b, Trudgill, 1978).

Languages are known to vary in their lexicon or vocabulary, in their phonology, and in their grammar. In English, for example, the word 'bairn' is used by some speakers, such as in Scotland, whereas 'child' is used elsewhere. At the level of phonology, as is well known, speakers in the north of England pronounce the words 'put' and 'putt' (as in golf) similarly, whereas in the south the vowel in 'put' is different from that in words such as 'bus', 'under', 'cup' and 'putt': speakers in the north use the vowel in 'put' for all these words. Variation in language may be related to factors other than geographical background, such as social class, age, sex, and degree of formality of the situation. In English grammar, for example, multiple negation as in 'I ain't seen no one' (as well as 'ain't' rather than 'haven't') is used in many parts of the country by working class speakers in informal situations (cf Hughes and Trudgill, 1979).

Just as we find variation in English, we also find it in BSL, at the same kinds of levels of the language, and linked to the same kind of social factors. When comparing some items of vocabulary as used in Reading and York deaf clubs, the following items were signed differently in the two places (notation system, as used in

chapter 3, first represents the Reading, then the York sign):
LEARN ($\emptyset$GG$_\frac{x}{1}$;$\frown$55$_\top^{\#}$), SUNDAY ($\emptyset$BB^x; $\emptyset$VV^x), WHO ($\emptyset$G$^\circledR$; $\cup$ L^{Xʂ}). Geographical distance between deaf people may not be the only factor affecting difference or similarities in vocabulary, but also frequency of contact between the clubs. Differences of vocabulary between individuals may also be accounted for by the location of the school for the deaf which they attended. As suggested in chapter 2 (p. 35), schools seem to have their own sign language varieties, though little is known about them, but it seems reasonable that they might influence adult BSL. In a small investigation of variation in number systems that I did among deaf adults in Lancaster, I found that a certain variant of the number SIX (right index on left fist) was only used by people over the age of forty who had attended a school for the deaf in NW England (see Deuchar, 1981 for further details). So in this case both the social factors of age and schools seem to be significant.

At the level of phonology in BSL, we also find variation. So far not enough research has been done to establish whether the inventory of elements can vary (cf chapter 3, p. 48), but there does seem to be variation in a particular phonological process, hand deletion in two-handed signs, which we discussed on p. 79. As we saw there, the deletion of one hand from an otherwise two-handed sign is most likely to occur if both hands move without contacting one another, or if one hand is a tab with an 'unmarked' or neutral handshape such as A or B. As I suggested earlier (p. 80), the likelihood of hand deletion is affected not only by phonological factors like those mentioned, but also by the social factor of formality, since hand deletion is more common in informal than in formal settings. So a signer who makes the sign RIGHT with two hands as in the illustration on p. 56 in a relatively formal setting might make it with one hand, without the passive B hand, in an informal setting. I do not have figures to suggest how often RIGHT might be made with one hand in an informal setting, but in an investigation of the frequency of deletion of one hand from the type of sign where both hands move, without contact, I found that 50 per cent were made with only one hand in an informal setting, compared with 6 per cent in a formal setting (see Deuchar, 1981). So this is a small piece of evidence for the idea that phonological variation in BSL is related to social factors, as in most languages. Language variation is often related to language change (cf Romaine, 1982), and we may note in this connection that hand deletion may also be a historical process. Woll (1981b) has found that certain signs (such as AGAIN (ØVᵛ) which are now one-handed, were formerly two-handed (cf Woodward and DeSantis (1977) for a similar change in French Sign Language and American Sign Language).

In the area of BSL grammar, it is not yet known whether there is a difference between individual signers on the basis of factors such as their age or social class or the region where they live, but formality of setting does seem to be a significant factor again. In chapter 4 I said that two alternative ways that negation can be marked are by using a sign usually glossed as NOT (ØBB⁺), or a sign glossed as NOTHING (ØFF↕), the latter being more common in informal signing. Some evidence for this generalization is found in that in a half hour film of BSL made in both formal and informal settings (religious service vs bar setting), there were 7 instances of NOT in the formal setting, versus 3 instances in the informal setting. NOTHING occurred 5 times in the informal setting, and not at all in the formal setting (Deuchar, 1978a, 1978b).

This brief overview of variation in BSL at the levels of the vocabulary, phonology and grammar has shown that as yet we know little about the influence of social factors such as age, religion, social class and sex, but that the factor of formality vs informality of setting does seem to be a significant factor. It seemed such a significant factor in an early investigation of BSL (Deuchar, 1978a, 1978b) that I suggested that BSL exhibited the phenomenon of diglossia as discussed by Ferguson (1959). Ferguson introduced this notion to refer to speech communities where two or more separate varieties of the same language were used for formal and informal functions respectively. The four speech communities on which he based his discussion, Arabic, Swiss German, Haitian creole and Greek were all shown to have what he calls a 'High' or 'H' variety for formal functions and a 'Low' or 'L' variety for informal functions. The formal functions covered by H would include its use in church, education, and written communication, while L would be used for conversation with family and friends. The H and L varieties could be distinguished from one another, Ferguson suggested, on the basis of their vocabulary, phonology and grammar. In addition to differing according to the function for which they were used, H and L would also differ in their prestige, their literary heritage, their acquisition, and their standardization. H would be more prestigious than L, would be used almost exclusively in written literature, would be acquired later than L, at school rather than home, and would be more standardized than L. This separation of linguistic and social characteristics would be fairly stable over time. The notion of diglossia has been criticized, particularly with reference to its application to Arabic, for being an oversimplification of the real situation (see e.g. Kaye, 1970, El-Hassan, 1977), and it has been suggested that the linguistic separation between H and L is not as clear as had been imagined, so that there might be a continuum of varieties rather than two distinct varieties, and also that the separation of function described by Ferguson is not always rigidly maintained. Nevertheless, it seems that there may be something special about the communities which Ferguson describes, not least that the communities themselves seem to recognize that there are two separate varieties, and to use separate terms to refer to them. In English, for example, which was not proposed as one of the defining communities of diglossia, we do not have terms equivalent to 'Classical' and 'Colloquial' Arabic, or 'Hochdeutsch' and 'Schweizerdeutsch'.

Stokoe (1969) was the first to suggest that the notion of diglossia might be applicable to sign language communities when he argued that it was exhibited in ASL. He argued that two separate varieties of ASL, which he termed H and L, exhibited the same separation of function described by Ferguson for diglossic communities. Another term for H was Manual English, whereas L was generally referred to as just 'signing' or 'chat'. H was quite similar to English in structure, whereas L was quite different. Later Woodward (1973a, 1973b) suggested that it would be more accurate to speak of a 'deaf diglossic continuum' between ASL and Standard English, thus getting rid of the notion of separate varieties of ASL, but at the same time distinguishing ASL more clearly from English in his terminology. Woodward (1973b) suggests that ASL and English are linked by a continuum of sign varieties, and he terms these intermediate varieties 'Pidgin Sign English' and says that they 'will show reduction and mixture of grammatical structures of both languages as well as some new structures that are common to neither of the languages' (p. 40), as is the case with pidgins. Later in the chapter we shall discuss the problems arising from Woodward's use of the term 'pidgin' in this connection.

With the benefit of research on diglossia in ASL, and also the suggestion that there was also diglossia in Danish Sign Language (see Hansen, 1975), it seemed a good idea to investigate whether there was diglossia in BSL. Although BSL is different from ASL, its sociolinguistic situation is similar in that it is used in a country where the dominant language is English, so one might expect to find a similar relation between English and sign language in Britain and the US.

In investigating BSL, I soon discovered that hearing adults who worked with deaf people distinguished between two kinds of signing: what they called 'grammatical' signing and 'deaf and dumb signing'. We saw in chapter 2 that social workers with the deaf tend to agree with the opinion of many teachers that BSL is not a language of the same status as English (see p. 40), and that there was an attempt by a Committee to bring BSL closer to English in structure. The sign language class I attended was given by a social worker who taught us to use what he would have seen as 'grammatical' signing or what is now often termed 'Signed English', that is, signs following the order of English words. If asked about grammatical constructions among the deaf themselves, he would say that they were incorrect, although he himself was a native signer, and would use the same constructions himself when talking to the deaf. Of course this is similar to the belief held by English speakers that the way they use their native language is not 'correct', so that when asked about their language, they may try to produce what they think is correct rather than what they would normally say (Trudgill, 1974). While in the case of English, people's prescriptive attitudes tend to come from a particular variety of English that has social sanction (that is, standard or 'BBC' English) in the case of BSL they come from another language (albeit the same variety, standard English) which, in mainstream (hearing) society, has superior status.

In the deaf community itself, two distinct varieties of sign language also seem to be recognized, and although I was not able to establish whether there were conventional labels used to distinguish the two varieties, I was told that the sign CLEVER might be used to describe what might seem to be an H signer, and that L sign could be designated by a modification of the sign SIGN ($\emptyset 5,5,^{\circledcirc}$) where the hands would move up and down rather than in circles, as follows: $\emptyset 5,5,^{N}$. This modified sign could also be translated as 'conversation'.

Another indication that two separate sign language varieties might exist or be thought to exist was found in a book dealing with deaf people and deafness, where the author (Firth, 1966, p. 126) says:

> We have *two languages*, one the pure deaf sign language, based on the spontaneous mode of expression of deaf people, but using as vocabulary a body of gestures which have become known over the years to generations of the deaf.
> Secondly we have another language of gesture, also based on this accepted vocabulary of conventional deaf signs, but which uses them in relation to grammatical English . . .

An article by a chaplain to the deaf makes the same kind of distinction and also refers to the different functions of the two varieties. Corfmat (1970, p. 1) refers to the 'indigenous sign language' which deaf people use when 'communicating in an uninhibited manner', but he says that 'when they speak to the hearing person, or someone in authority such as the chaplain and welfare officer they endeavour to express their thoughts in something nearer to *our* expression of the Sign Language'.

It thus seemed that two varieties of sign language were recognized in Britain, both by deaf people and by those working with them. I also observed these two different kinds of sign language in use, not only comparing what we were taught in sign language classes with what deaf people used in actual conversation, but also by observing the sign language used in the two main social activities at the deaf club in Reading where I did nine months' field work: church services in the chapel at the deaf centre, and informal social evenings at the bar. Given that Ferguson (1959) listed sermons in church as one of the functions of H, and conversation with friends as one of the functions of L, a difference between these two might suggest diglossia.

I did find a clear difference between church signing and signing in the club, and found that the church signing was similar both to that variety taught in sign language classes and to that I observed at occasional formal meetings or talks by deaf people (Deuchar, 1978a). The formal, church variety, which I called 'H' in line with Ferguson's usage, was similar to what Stokoe (1969) called 'Manual English' in that it followed English structure fairly closely, with the signs in English word order, and a large amount of fingerspelling of English words. This is shown in the following example from a sermon in my film (fingerspelling is represented by lower case letters joined by hyphens, while signs are represented by upper case letters):

SOMEt-i-m-e-s WE ALL GO t-o PLACES a-n-d t-o-w-n-s a-n-d c-i-t-i-e-s WHERE WE HAVE NEVER b-e-e-n BEFORE

'Sometimes we all go to places and towns and cities where we have never been before'

This variety of sign language was very different from that used informally in the club, where people mostly only fingerspelled names, as in the following from the film data:

K-i-l-b-y BEFORE GOOD NOW GOOD?

'Is Kilby, who was good before, now good?'

In this utterance, the fact that it is a question was signalled by raised eyebrows over NOW GOOD. As we saw in chapter 4, the grammar of this 'L' variety, to which I have previously referred simply as 'BSL', is quite different from English, and includes the use of simultaneous devices such as eyebrow raising while signing as the sole means of asking a Yes–No question.

Having established that the sociolinguistic situation with regard to BSL seemed to be akin to that characteristic of diglossia, with two separate varieties fulfilling separate functions, roughly formal and informal, in the deaf community, I then went on to explore the differences in grammar between 'H' and 'L', assuming that whereas the former would be constrained by English grammar, the latter would be freer to exploit the visual medium. The areas of grammar which I focussed on to test this hypothesis were negatives, questions and case relations. These have all been discussed with reference to BSL (equivalent to 'L' in the diglossia study) in chapter 4, on pages 89–91, 91–3, and 86–7 respectively.

Considering negation, the types of negation covered which appeared to have different frequencies in H and L included the following: fingerspelled, NOT (see p. 90), NOTHING (see p. 90), negative incorporation (see p. 89) and simultaneous negation (see p. 91). While fingerspelled negation and NOT were more common in H (see also p. 141 this chapter), the other kinds were more common in L. I then divided the types of negation into only two categories, medium-specific and medium-non-specific, in order to test the hypothesis that L would use devices that exploited the visual medium to a greater extent than H. I considered negative incorporation and simultaneous negation to be medium-specific, because they depended on the simultaneity possible in a visual-spatial language. The other kinds of negation were considered to be non-medium-specific because they utilized a sequential dimension equally available to the oral and visual medium. The result showed that 54 per cent of the occurrences of negation in L were medium-specific, whereas in H none were medium-specific (Deuchar, 1978a, 1978b). Thus at least in negation, L seemed to exploit the visual medium to a greater extent than H.

In analysing the signalling of Yes-No questions in H and L, it was found that although eyebrow raising might occur with questions in H, these questions were also indicated by changes of order or 'do-support' as in English. The following example from film data shows the use of 'do-support' with fingerspelled 'do':

D-o YOU KNOW WHERE THIS p-l-a-c-e i-s
'Do you know where this place is?'

In L, however, 'do' was not introduced, nor any comparable sign, but Yes-No questions were marked by simultaneous eyebrow-raising as in the example on p. 93, or the following:

eyebrows
raised
WILL GO
'Will you go?'

In these examples, simultaneous eyebrow raising, which is something only possible in the visual medium, was the sole means of indicating that a question was being asked. There was just one example in the L data of a question with non-medium-specific, English structure, as follows:

A-r-e y-o-u a-w-a-y HOLIDAY
'Are you going away on holiday?'

The English structure here comes from the extensive use of finger-spelling, which may be explained by the fact that the woman was elderly, as the old seem to fingerspell more. She may also have been more conscious of the camera than the others. This kind of example was in any case the only one out of eleven.

In the third area of grammar investigated, H and L data were compared to find out to what extent either used medium-specific ways of indicating the relation between source and goal in the verbs GIVE, ASK, SAY and SEE. As we saw in chapter 4 (p. 86), case relations in these verbs can be indicated by direction of movement from source to goal or agent to patient. In all the occurrences of the verbs in both the H and L data, direction of movement was found to indicate case relations, but in the H data order, as in English, was another indicator. The following is an example from the H data:

SOME ONE SAY US THIS RIGHT WAY
'Someone tells us this is the right way'

In this the movement in the verb SAY is downwards, close to the signer, indicating that there is a third person source (SOMEONE) and a first person goal (US). However, since the order of the signs is similar to the order of words in English, one might argue that case relations are indicated by sign order. This cannot be said of L, where source and goal are not always overtly indicated, as in the following example:

HOSPITAL LETTER GIVE
'We gave the letter to the hospital'

As we saw in chapter 4 (p. 96), it is quite common to leave out subject and object (or source and goal) pronouns if their location is marked by the initial and final point of the movement, as in this example, where the movement in GIVE is towards the signer, as from third person source towards first person goal. Thus relative order of overtly indicated source and goal in relation to the verb does not seem to be a way of indicating case relations in L, which, unlike H, relies entirely on medium-specific devices.

Thus it is possible to view the British deaf community as diglossic in that it makes use of at least two sign varieties which are both functionally and formally distinct. Both varieties are produced in the visual medium, but H is heavily constrained in its structure by English, as is shown by the absence of medium-specific grammatical devices compared with their exploitation in L, which is clearly not constrained by English.

Criticisms of this analysis of the British deaf community may be made on various counts, and fall into two main categories: (1) those which accept the linguistic analysis of the two varieties 'H' and 'L' (which are now more commonly called 'Signed English' and 'BSL' respectively, as in the usage I have followed in other chapters), but which do not accept the analysis of functions as manifesting diglossia; and (2) those which would modify the linguistic analysis. Llewellyn-Jones et al. (1979) accept the existence of two varieties of sign language, BSL and Signed English, but suggest that Signed English is not used normally within the deaf community, but mainly to communicate with hearing people. Hearing people are seen as outside the deaf community, even if they know BSL as well as Signed English. Llewellyn-Jones et al.'s main argument here is thus that Signed English is not central to the deaf community in the way BSL is, but that it really belongs to the hearing community. One could question their assumption that the deaf and hearing communities are mutually exclusive, and that BSL and Signed English are completely distinct (we shall question this later), but as far as the applicability of the notion of diglossia to the deaf signing community is concerned, it is worth pointing out that the 'H' variety (in this case Signed English) in Ferguson's defining communities is never central to the majority of the community, most of whom are not native speakers of it. The 'H' variety may also be associated primarily with another speech community. So in Haiti, for example, the H variety, French, is spoken natively by only a minority of Haitians, and is primarily associated with France, the former colonial power. Whereas Llewellyn-Jones et al. suggest that the British deaf community cannot be considered diglossic because those who use 'H' are marginal to the community or part of its elite, this situation is in fact typical of diglossia in Ferguson's sense. Diglossia does not mean bilingualism, but often unequal access to the two varieties, where the elite may have privileged access to the formal, public variety which they, the minority, use in controlling or governing the majority (for further discussion see Deuchar, 1978c).

Having questioned whether Signed English can be considered part of the repertoire of a deaf diglossic community, Llewellyn-Jones et al. temporarily suspend their disbelief in order to examine another aspect of diglossia proposed by Ferguson, the idea that the 'H' variety has more prestige that the 'L' variety. They used an adaptation of the matched guise test developed by Lambert et al. (1960) which involved showing video-tapes of the same person signing in 'H' and 'L' to two separate, but equivalent groups of deaf people. The deaf people in each group were asked to rate

140 140 *Variation in BSL*

the signer on scales which included friendliness, helpfulness, good looks, intelligence and professionalism. The results showed that, overall, the 'L' version was rated more positively, and they state specifically (Llewellyn-Jones et al., p. 9) that:

> The 'L' version was rated more friendly, more pleasant, more helpful, more likeable, better looking and good, than the 'H' version. There were no significant differences in competence groupings of the scales, i.e. intelligence, professionalism, adequacy of signing, understanding of signing.

From this they conclude that the 'covert' prestige of 'L' is greater than that of 'H'. They point out that this is in line with other language attitude research which has shown that indirect means of testing attitudes, like the matched guise test, may produce more positive attitudes than direct tests for languages or varieties which do not have a high degree of official approval. Thus they suggest that 'Deaf people may produce judgements "for public consumption" that they do not hold for actual Sign Language use in practice' (Llewellyn-Jones et al., p. 10), implying that deaf people might acknowledge the prestige of 'H' overtly while denying it covertly. Rather than contradicting the diglossic situation, this actually seems to be consonant with it. Prestige as described by Ferguson (1959) appears to be overt rather than covert (see Trudgill, 1972, for a discussion of covert prestige) since he refers to speakers' overt statements about the supposed superiority of H and does not mention indirect attitude testing. However, in the defining diglossic communities one can certainly discern signs of the covert prestige of 'L', as in the appearance of literature in Swiss German, and the feeling which Arabs appear to have that their own dialect ('L') is better than any other (cf Ferguson, 1968).

So far the arguments I have discussed against viewing the British deaf signing community as diglossic have been made on the basis of the functions of the two varieties of sign language which are assumed to exist. However, the suggestions and findings put forward do not seem to conflict with the diglossia model on functional grounds. Nevertheless, applying the model does depend on assuming the existence of two separate varieties, and it is this assumption which must now be questioned.

As I pointed out earlier in my discussion of diglossia in ASL, Woodward (1973a, 1973b) modified Stokoe's (1969) suggestion of two polar 'H' and 'L' varieties by proposing instead that there was a 'deaf diglossic continuum' between ASL and English. Lawson (1981) follows Woodward in adopting the notion of a diglossic continuum between BSL and English, and she also follows him in suggesting that the intermediate varieties between the two poles can be termed 'pidgins'. To exemplify the relationship between BSL, Signed English, and 'pidgins', she gives the English glosses for signs translating the English 'I have not seen you for a long time' (Lawson, 1981, p. 173). She says that in Signed English there would be signs for each of these English words, in the same order; in BSL the translation would be glossed as I YOU SEE NO, and in pidgin sign the gloss would be I YOU SEE LONG. She suggests that not only does use of one variety depend on the formality of the situation, as in diglossia, with varieties approaching the BSL end of the continuum in informal situations, and the English end in formal situations, but also that 'Signers will possess varying ranges of competence on the BSL-Signed English continuum' (Lawson, 1981, p. 172). She expands this as follows:

> Native signers will be competent in the varieties near the BSL end and, depending on their command of English, will have greater or lesser competence in varieties approaching the English end. Non-native signers will have more competence in varieties approaching English than in those approaching BSL. However, all signers will get as close to the BSL end of the continuum as their competence allows in informal situations, and will approximate the English end as far as possible in formal situations.

Thus Lawson is suggesting that signers will indeed use a form of sign approximating to English in formal situations, although its proximity to Signed English will depend on their competence. Similarly, the proximity to BSL of signing in informal situations will again depend on the signer's competence. Lawson's view of the situation might be reflected in Figure 1.

This figure shows that, while the general notion of diglossia seems to hold in a social sense for the community of signers, in that a distinction is made between formal and informal sign varieties corresponding to formal and informal situations, individuals will vary in the range of sign varieties they have available. So while a hearing native signer might be considered bilingual (an individual

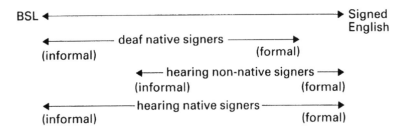

Figure 1

notion, whereas diglossia is social) in BSL and English, other signers will have other kinds or ranges of 'bilingualism'.

Thus Lawson shows that formality of situation is not the only factor which determines the variety of sign language used, but that individual factors may also be important. Woodward's work on ASL supports this idea. He found that people who were deaf or who had deaf parents were more likely to use varieties of sign language with specifically ASL (non-English) constructions, like negative incorporation, than those who were not deaf or who did not have deaf parents (Woodward, 1973a, 1974, 1975). He also found that factors, such as age, race and region (Woodward, 1976) could be related to sign language variation. At the beginning of this chapter (p. 131) I suggested that age and region of school might be significant social factors in BSL, in addition to formality of setting. Further research is clearly needed on the relative effect of the various social factors, and also on the nature of linguistic variation. We are particularly ignorant about the nature of syntactic variation, for although we have assumed that it can be defined in terms of approximation to English or BSL, the reality may actually be more complex. (Peter Jones (personal communication) has suggested for example that formal signing may involve a reduction in facial expression.) The linguistic situation may instead be one of overlapping sign varieties which are related to social factors (see p. 149).

Before considering other views of the nature of variation in BSL, we should consider some problems that may arise from the use of the term 'pidgin' to refer to sign varieties on a diglossic continuum between 'pure' BSL and English. A fairly conventional definition of the term 'pidgin' follows (DeCamp, 1971, p. 15):

A pidgin is a contact vernacular, normally not the native language of any of its speakers. It is used in trading or in any situation requiring communication between persons who do not speak each other's native languages. It is characterized by a limited vocabulary, an elimination of many grammatical devices such as number and gender, and a drastic reduction of redundant features.

Research in America on intermediate varieties between ASL and English suggests that there is a variety (or varieties) which serves as a contact vernacular between the deaf and hearing communities ('Pidgin Sign English'), and that it lacks redundancy. Reilly and McIntire (1980), for example, found that Pidgin Sign English (PSE) contained features found in both ASL and English, such as the use of directional verbs as in ASL and constituent order as in English, but that PSE lacked redundancy in that the facial behaviour associated with ASL tended to be eliminated, although mouth movements characteristic of English words tended to be added. So it is not clear whether PSE actually contained fewer grammatical devices or less redundancy overall. However, Woodward and Markowicz (1975, p. 13) claim that PSE does show reduction and admixture, and that 'The loss of ASL features sometimes decreases redundancy in the system without complete compensation by the introduction of redundancy via spoken language features'. They also suggest that a hearing person's PSE is more reduced in structure than a deaf person's PSE, because since PSE is produced in the same medium as ASL, more features from ASL (especially phonological) can be transferred than from English.

As regards the function of PSE, both Reilly and McIntire and Woodward and Markowicz agree that it acts as a contact vernacular between the deaf and hearing communities, but Woodward and Markowicz suggest that it actually helps to maintain the cultural boundary between the deaf and hearing communities since 'it does not allow extensive integrative and expressive communication between hearing and deaf communities' (Woodward and Markowicz, 1975, p. 31).

As we saw earlier, Lawson (1981) adopts the practice of using the term 'pidgin' to refer to varieties of sign on a diglossic continuum between BSL and English. However, there is a potential problem, both for the American and British situations, in using

144 Variation in BSL

the term 'pidgin' to refer both to a contact vernacular between communities who do not share a native language, and to a variety on a continuum which comes within a signer's repertoire of formal and informal signing. A pidgin is not normally a native language, and yet if we follow Lawson's model as depicted in Figure 1, we might have to accept the conclusion that a native deaf signer signing appropriately in a formal situation is producing a pidgin which he or she does not know natively. It therefore seems preferable to restrict the term 'pidgin' to a sign contact vernacular which is used primarily for deaf/hearing communication in whatever situation, which is native to none of its users, and which combines features of both sign language and English. The variety of sign language used by a native signer in a formal situation would then not be considered a pidgin, in that the signer would have command of this variety, and would not be using it as a contact vernacular, but because of the formality of the situation. The fact that this variety manifested English influence in its structure would not make it a pidgin any more than the influences from French in the English language make English a pidgin: they would simply be the result of language contact in the predominantly public sphere where the institutions of one group are dominated by another group (the deaf and hearing; or the Britons and the Normans). On the other hand, hearing non-native signers' attempts to sign informally might be considered pidgins because they are an inaccurate attempt at BSL, which they do not know natively and they are also an attempt at hearing-deaf communication. Thus I would accept the term 'pidgin' for sign varieties used in contact between the hearing and deaf communities, but would not use it for varieties used within the deaf community itself (unless those varieties were developed by deaf children in the absence of linguistic input, see chapter 7). It is worth pointing out, finally, that some linguists would not even use the term 'pidgin' to refer to a contact vernacular between two communities trying to approximate each other's language, but suggest that pidgins must develop either by 'tertiary hybridization', where a third target language is being aimed at, or by 'relexification', where the grammar of a previously existing pidgin is taken over, but new lexical items are introduced (cf Whinnom, 1971, Trudgill, 1974).

Another approach to variation in BSL which deserves serious consideration, is that proposed by Ladd and Edwards (1982), who suggest that BSL is a creole (a language which has developed from a pidgin to become the native language of a speech community). Ladd and Edwards take West Indian Creole as their basis for comparison, and suggest that BSL and West Indian Creole are not only linguistically parallel, but that there are also social, attitudinal and educational parallels. A similar point of view is taken by Fischer (1978) with reference to ASL. Just as Ladd and Edwards find similarities between BSL and West Indian Creole, Fischer finds similarities between ASL and Hawaiian Creole English. She finds, for example, that they both have an existential word/sign translatable as 'have', that they both mark aspect rather than tense, and they both lack a passive construction. She also says that ASL has all of the nine characteristics listed by Craig (1971) as found in English-based creole syntax. Fischer also points to similarities in the social conditions under which ASL and creoles developed. She suggests that Woodward (1978) may be right in suggesting that ASL resulted from a creolization process between the indigenous sign language in America and the French system taken to America by Gallaudet in the early nineteenth century (see chapter 2, p. 32). In addition, she suggests that one reason why ASL may still look like a creole 150 years later is because of the way in which 90 per cent of deaf children learn it, from their peers at school, or from hearing parents who know signed English at best. (This acquisition situation is discussed in relation to BSL in chapter 7.) As Fischer (1978, p. 329) says, 'Most children are forced to *re*creolize ASL in every generation'.

Having established the similarity between ASL and Hawaiian Creole English, Fischer goes on to suggest that there is a post-creole continuum from ASL to English. She says that a post-creole continuum may develop 'If, through continued contact, speakers of a creole continue to be exposed to a "standard" language, that is, the language that provided the lexical base for the creole' (Fischer, 1978, p. 316), and suggests that this has happened in the case of ASL and English. She follows creolist terminology in distinguishing three levels of such a continuum, the 'acrolect', 'mesolect' and 'basilect', where the acrolect would be the closest to standard English, the basilect further away, and the mesolect somewhere in between. Like those who described variation in ASL as a diglossic continuum (cf Woodward, 1973a, 1973b), she defines the continuum in terms of its closeness to or distance from English, and what she calls the 'mesolect' looks rather similar to Woodward's Signed English. However, the way in which ASL developed does not seem to satisfy the conditions for a post-creole continuum to arise, since English has not provided the lexical base for ASL, and ASL appears to have developed quite independently from English, and certainly not through English relexification of a pre-existing pidgin. In other creole situations where the standard, 'official' language is not related to the creole, a post-creole continuum does not develop: this is true in Surinam, for example, where the creole is related to English, but the official language is Dutch (cf DeCamp, 1971, p. 29). In my view the only way of seeing the apparent continuum between ASL and English as a post-creole continuum would be to consider Signed English to be the basilect, formed by the relexification of English with ASL signs, while maintaining English syntax, and ASL the acrolect. However, the sociological conditions which make the acrolect dominant in a society do not prevail in the case of ASL. It seems therefore more convincing to argue simply that ASL is a creole, but to account for the continuum to English in another way, as a continuum of contact vernaculars between the deaf and hearing communities.

Returning to BSL, I would not consider it to be at the end of a post-creole continuum any more than I would ASL, but I would agree with Ladd and Edwards (1982) that it does appear to be a creole, both on the basis of its structural characteristics and because of the way it is acquired (see chapter 7). Bickerton (1981) surveys the key areas of grammar found to be similar in many creoles, and we shall pick out the following as applying also to BSL: tense-modality-aspect (TMA) systems (Bickerton, 1981, p. 58), existential and possessive (ibid., p. 66), copula (ibid., p. 67), adjectives as verbs (ibid., p. 68), question words (ibid., p. 70), and passive equivalents (ibid., p. 71).

Bickerton suggests that many creoles express tense, modality and aspect by particles placed before the verb, usually in that order. While BSL makes use of the spatial (simultaneous) dimension as well as the temporal, because of its medium, we can say that BSL appears similar to creoles in its TMA system in that tense is furthest from the verb, followed by modality, followed by aspect, which is the closest. In chapter 4 we saw that time is generally marked by adverbials such as BEFORE, and NOW, rather than in tense inflections on the verb. I suggested that although there is an auxiliary/verb glossed as WILL, which might seem to act as a tense auxiliary, this auxiliary also represents modality, which following Bickerton's generalization, would account for its being closer to the main verb. There is also an auxiliary CAN, placed, like WILL, adjacent to the main verb. As we also saw in chapter 4, aspect is marked either by an auxiliary (FINISH), or by verb inflections indicating durative, iterative and habitual aspect. Thus we see a progression from distance from the verb, to proximity to it: time adverbials (T), often not adjacent to the verb, are distant, modal (M), and aspect auxiliaries, adjacent to the verb, are closer, and aspectual verb inflections (A) are incorporated within the verb itself.

With regard to the existential and possessive, Bickerton (1981, p. 66) states that 'over a wide range of creoles, the same lexical item is used to express existentials ("there is") and possessives ("have")'. This is true of BSL, in that the sign usually glossed as HAVE (Ø5ᵛ) can be used in the sense of e.g. 'I have' as well as 'there is'. Fischer (1978) reports the same for ASL.

Creoles tend not to have a copula (like 'to be' in English), which is linked to the characteristic of adjectives behaving like verbs, which is also common in creoles, and which was mentioned on p. 103 (chapter 4) in connection with ASL and BSL. In my film data there is an occurrence of HE GOOD(NEG), which in English would be translated as 'He is no good', using the copula. In BSL, however, the adjective acts more like a verb, and in this particular case, undergoes negative incorporation like some verbs (see p. 89).

Bickerton says that in Wh- questions in creoles, the question word is placed in front of the declarative form of the sentence, and that such words are generally composed of two elements, a question word and the thing to which it relates. So English 'where', for example, may be translated as 'what place', and 'what thing'. In BSL, there are Wh- signs for questions, which are generally placed at the beginning of a sentence, but may also be placed at the end, or both the beginning and end (cf Woll, 1981a, p. 142). These questions are not made up of two linearly separate elements, as Bickerton suggests is the case for creoles, but Woll (1981a) points out that three particular question signs, WHEN, HOW-MANY and HOW-OLD, have handshape and movement in common, but differ in location in a way related to their meaning. All three signs are made with five fingers extended, separated and wiggling, which could be considered as indicating that they are question signs; then the location of WHEN (on the cheek) seems to indicate time in that it is similar to that of the time signs YESTERDAY and TOMORROW; the location of HOW-OLD indicates age in that it is the same as that of AGE and OLD, and the location of HOW-MANY indicates quantity in that it is the same as that of MANY (this actually has wiggling fingers as well as the question HOW-MANY). Thus two meaning elements seem to be incorporated into these question signs in a comparable way to that which apparently happens in the case of creoles.

Finally, BSL appears to be similar to creoles in its lack of a passive construction. Lack of a passive is also characteristic of what Li and Thompson (1976) call 'topic-prominent' languages or languages that are best analysed in terms of topic and comment. We suggested on p. 127 that BSL might best be analysed in these terms, and this may well be both because of its creole-like nature and because of the informal communicative situation in which it is generally used. Bickerton (1981, p. 272) suggests that 'the first word-order in early language was topic-comment', so since creoles are languages in a relatively early stage of development, we should not be surprised if they have this structure. In addition, both Givón (1979b) and Ochs (1979) suggest that a topic-comment structure is most common in informal, unplanned discourse, even in English. (For further discussion of possible explanations for BSL topic-comment structure, see Deuchar, 1983.)

How do we now view BSL in relation to the sign varieties mentioned earlier? We rejected the idea of a continuum of pidgin varieties from BSL to English, and would also reject the notion of a BSL-English continuum, since BSL is not based on English. Instead, I would suggest that we may view BSL as part of a complex of overlapping varieties, relating both to social characteristics of individuals (age, class, etc.) and to characteristics of the setting of a given interaction (formal vs informal). Some of these varieties may show influence from English in their structure, as one would expect in a language contact situation (cf Haugen, 1977), and may overlap with 'pidgin' sign varieties used primarily for contact between the English-speaking and deaf communities, and manifesting a compromise between English and BSL. These 'pidgin' varieties would then overlap with English in the form of Signed English (English represented as accurately as possible on the hands). In addition there might be a complex of pidgin BSL varieties, developed primarily by children in the absence of sufficient input from BSL, or with English-influenced input from hearing parents. The linguistic relationships as I see them are as presented in Figure 2. However, more research is needed to relate them to their social context and to determine the relative importance of social factors such as formality/informality of setting (which looms so large in the diglossia model) and other factors.

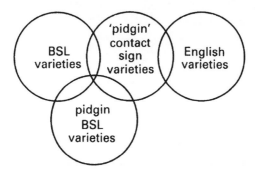

Figure 2   Variation in BSL

Summary

At the beginning of this chapter we saw how variation could be found at various levels, and that it could be related to social factors. One factor which appeared to be particularly important was formality/informality of setting, and this led to consideration of whether there was diglossia in the British deaf community, with an 'H' variety used in formal settings, and an 'L' variety used in informal settings. Different varieties in different settings were found, with English structure clearly influencing the formal variety, and the visual medium more obviously exploited in the informal variety. It was then suggested that the idea of two separate varieties should be modified by postulating a linguistic continuum, where people's range of competence as well as the setting would influence their sign language usage. It was also suggested that the idea of a linear continuum from BSL to English was probably an over-simplification, and that linguistic factors other than just approximation to English should be considered. Problems arising from the use of the term 'pidgin' were then discussed, and a further idea was then considered: that BSL might be a creole. Support was found for this, both on linguistic and social grounds, but the idea that there might be a post-creole continuum was rejected. Instead, a model involving variation within intersecting circles was proposed, as in Figure 2 (p. 149).

7

The acquisition of sign language

This chapter is called 'the acquisition of sign language' rather than 'the acquisition of BSL' because we do not know very much yet about the acquisition of BSL alone. What we do know, however, can usefully be combined with the results of research on other sign languages, especially ASL, to give a good idea of the way in which BSL is most likely acquired.

Until now we have been concerned with what BSL, as a language, is like, and how it compares with other sign languages (see last chapter). Now we shall be concerned with how it is learned, or acquired, as a first language. The reason for including a chapter on this topic is twofold: first, comparison of what we know about spoken language acquisition with what we know about sign language acquisition may give us further insights into the nature of sign language and the difference or similarity between signed and spoken languages; and second, knowledge of the way in which sign language is acquired may give us further insights into the process of language acquisition in general. This is an important issue in current linguistic theory, as well as being interesting in itself.

As Lyons (1981, p. 252) says, 'The term "language-acquisition" is normally used without qualification for the process which results in the knowledge of one's native language'. The term 'acquisition' is often used in preference to 'learning' because one's first or native language is not taught in a planned way, but acquired naturally by a process which we are just beginning to understand. A common attitude to language is that it must be 'properly taught' to be 'correct' (one teacher's criticism of BSL was that it was 'picked up on the buses'), but a linguist would take the point of view that the notion of correctness is a social or cultural one, and that young children will generally learn the language to which they are exposed relatively effortlessly, without the intervention of a teacher. Children do not seem to be predisposed to learn one language more than another: a British child brought up in a Chinese speaking environment, for example, will learn Chinese just as easily as a Chinese child.

Research on the acquisition of spoken language by hearing children (see Fletcher and Garman, 1979, for a good selection of studies) has shown that there is a remarkable similarity in the stages through which children progress, even though they may pass through these stages at different ages and at different speeds. After an initial period of crying, cooing and babbling during the first year of life, children start to produce single words which generally appear to refer to objects or people in their environment. They then go on to produce two-word utterances expressing a variety of grammatical relations such as 'nomination' (e.g. 'that book'), 'locative' (e.g. 'sweater chair') and 'action-object' (e.g. 'put book') (reported in Dale, 1976, p. 24). The length of children's utterances then gradually increases, and they also begin to produce inflections, like the plural 's' in English or the past tense of verbs. Like their syntax, their phonology also develops from a simple system with few contrasting items towards the full adult system. The way in which children use word order varies according to the language they are acquiring (see Dale, 1976): if it is a language which uses order consistently to indicate semantic relations, like English, where order distinguishes 'Susan sees Mary' from 'Mary sees Susan', children will use order in a similar way. However, where the order in the adult language is relatively free, as in Finnish, for example (see Bowerman, 1973), children may or may not produce utterances with their own fixed word order. Gradually, children acquire structures of increasing syntactic complexity, to express increasingly complex semantic relations, until by the age of about five they have acquired something fairly close to the adult linguistic system. They will acquire some new syntactic constructions after this (see Chomsky, 1969), and of course the acquisition of vocabulary will continue throughout their lives, though usually at an increasingly slow rate.

Until relatively recently, studies of early language acquisition concentrated on the second year of life, when vocalizations begin to be meaningful. However, recent studies have investigated the non-vocal beginnings of communication and language, not only by early vocalizations, but also by bodily movements such as eye gaze, and hand and arm movement (see e.g. Lock, 1978, Bullowa, 1979, Givens, 1978). The finding that non-vocal signals may be important in the early stages of communication seems a particularly significant one for those hearing parents of deaf children who are advised by oralists to avoid the use of 'natural gesture'. Oralists' concern to emphasize spoken language often leads them to ignore the fact that hearing children and their parents normally make use of visual-gestural communication as well, so that advising parents to avoid this actually makes their communication less rather than more normal.

An important point about language acquisition is that it does not proceed by mere imitation of the adult language. Children produce utterances which they have not heard adults produce, like the example 'sweater chair', which could be analysed as a reduced version of an adult utterance such as 'the sweater is on the chair'. Some child utterances show that not all the rules of the child grammar are the same as those of the adult, such as when certain rules have a broader application: this may be called 'overregularization' (see Dale, 1976, p. 34). Children learning English, for example, commonly apply the past tense 'ed' to what for adults are irregular verbs, to produce forms like 'bringed', 'comed', 'doed' etc. This happens after they have produced the adult forms 'brought', 'came', etc. which they now seem to 'forget' for a while. It is generally thought that the irregular forms are used earlier as unanalysed ways of representing the past tense, but that once a regular rule has been discerned by the child ('add "ed" to form the past') then this is applied to all verbs, the irregular exceptions to the rule being learned only later. This kind of phenomenon is taken as evidence for what Chomsky (1965, p. 6) calls the 'creative aspect' of language, or what Lock, from a slightly different perspective, calls the 'guided reinvention' of language (Lock, 1980).

As we have seen, there is by now a considerable amount of information available on how spoken language is acquired, and shortly we shall see that there is considerable similarity in the process by which sign language appears to be acquired. First, however, we shall take a brief look at the background to the other reason for studying sign language acquisition, mentioned at the beginning of this chapter, that is, to see what light it may throw on the process of language acquisition in general. As Bickerton (1981) and others have pointed out, the way in which language acquisition was viewed during the 1960s is somewhat different from the recent view of it, which became established during the 1970s. The view prevalent in the 1960s developed largely under the influence of the work of Chomsky (e.g. 1957, 1965, 1972) in generative grammar. The view which developed was one which saw the child as innately endowed with a 'Language Acquisition Device', which was similar to Chomsky's idea of a universal grammar in that it would include some constraints on the possible forms a human language might take. This would make it easier for the child to acquire any human language. The process of acquisition, according to this view, involved the child formulating hypotheses about the possible structure of the language to which he or she was exposed, and then modifying these hypotheses as more data became available. We should note that this view is not concerned with the nature of the interaction between a parent and child in the acquisition process, but simply assumes the presence of some language 'input' or evidence, which according to Chomsky (1972, p. 27) is 'restricted and degenerate', or poor in both quantity and quality.

Opposition to Chomsky's view of language acquisition came first from those who disagreed with his view of the Language Acquisition Device. The philosopher Putnam and the psychologist Piaget, for example, have suggested that language acquisition can be explained by the application of general intelligence or cognitive abilities, rather than by the existence of a device specifically designed for language. (The debate between Chomsky, Piaget and others is reported in Piattelli-Palmarini (ed.) (1980).)

As discussion of these questions continued, and as predictions, based on generative grammar, about the nature of the Language Acquisition Device, seemed not to be borne out by the results of psycholinguistic research (see Aitchison, 1976, chapter 9), researchers also began to question Chomsky's assumptions about the nature of the input to the proposed Language Acquisition Device. In particular, they questioned whether it was 'restricted' and 'degenerate' as Chomsky suggested, and thus began to study the role of parent-child interaction in the acquisition process. Some of their results suggest that parents' speech to children may be more structured in a way to aid acquisition than was previously thought (see Snow and Ferguson, eds, 1977). According to Bickerton (1981, p. 138), this has led to a new consensus view on language acquisition, which he states as follows:

The mother, it is claimed, models language for the child, adapting her outputs to his linguistic level at every stage. Far from being degenerate, the data she provides are highly preadapted, highly contextualized, and patiently repeated. 'Mothers teach their children to speak', Bruner (1979) states. When all these factors are taken fully into account, the consensus claims, the need to posit an innate component in language acquisition shrinks to near zero or even disappears altogether.

Bickerton argues against this view, pointing out that the development of creoles from pidgins involves the introduction of complexity into the relatively simple input of a pidgin. Taking the first creole generation in Hawaii as an example, Bickerton (1981, p. 139) says, 'Mother could not teach these children to speak, for the simple and inescapable reason that Mother herself did not know the language – the language didn't exist yet. But even so, without Mother, those children learned how to speak'. ('Mother' presumably spoke Hawaiian pidgin, which was no-one's native language.) Bickerton's view of language acquisition involves assuming 'the existence of an innate bioprogram for language', which puts him more in line with the Chomskyan approach (though see Mühlhäusler, forthcoming, for a comparison of Bickerton's and Chomsky's approaches). In addition, Bickerton suggests that creoles, which have developed in the absence of a language input, and which he demonstrates have somewhat similar structures, reflect particularly well the effect of the 'bioprogram'. Bickerton suggests that other, more established languages, differ from creoles in their structure because they have been subject to other influences, such as cultural and processing factors. Later in this chapter we shall review studies of sign language acquisition which suggest that Bickerton may be right in playing down the role of language input.

In chapter 6 I discussed the possibility that BSL might be considered a creole. In the light of Bickerton's comments about the development of creoles, we might now consider to what extent the social conditions under which BSL is acquired are similar to those prevailing in the acquisition of a creole, either by the first or subsequent creole generations.

In her discussions of the acquisition of ASL, Meadow (1980) uses the term 'linguistic socialization' to refer to both the acquisition of sign language, and entry into the deaf community. She suggests that there are three possible times at which linguistic socialization may occur: from birth, at school entry and in adulthood. This pattern of sign language acquisition seems to apply to BSL also, and can be contrasted with the normal process of linguistic socialization of the hearing child, who will begin to learn his or her parents' language at birth, and will not have to begin the process of linguistic socialization at school entry or in adulthood again, unless acquiring a second language or language variety and thus access to another speech community. So why is the pattern of sign language acquisition, in particular that of BSL, different from that of most spoken language acquisition?

If the process of BSL acquisition were to begin at birth, as in the case of most spoken languages, the parents of deaf children would have to be native users of BSL. However, about 90 per cent of deaf children are born to hearing parents (cf Conrad, 1981, p. 14), who are unlikely to be native signers unless they themselves were born to deaf parents. Hearing parents are unlikely to acquire BSL as a second language and use it with their deaf children, partly because of oralist attitudes discouraging the use of sign language, and also because of the lack of availability of high quality instruction in BSL. Some hearing parents may, however, learn Signed English, which (see chapter 6) is based on the vocabulary of BSL but follows English structure. It cannot be considered equivalent to a 'BSL input' to the child, but might arguably provide the basis for later acquisition of BSL. This is pure speculation, however, in the absence of relevant research.

Those relatively few deaf children who are born to deaf parents may learn BSL from birth if the parents use it to them. As Meadow (1980) points out, not all deaf children of deaf parents are exposed to sign language, since some deaf parents may avoid using it with their children in compliance with oralist suggestions. However, if BSL is the first language of deaf parents, I suggest that this kind of a ban would be difficult to maintain, and that in fact most deaf children of deaf parents would learn BSL from birth. Again, virtually no research has been done to establish whether this is so.

For the majority of deaf children who have not learned BSL from birth, entry into a school for the deaf will be the next possible point of linguistic socialization. Not all deaf children will attend special schools for the deaf since the alternatives include units attached to hearing schools (see Rodda, 1970, p. 31), but for

those who do and do not already know BSL, entry to the school
will be the beginning of linguistic socialization for them. As I said
in chapter 2, most schools for the deaf are residential, and
although very few of them have a positive attitude to the use of
sign language, the children will certainly use sign language among
themselves. Assuming that not more than 10 per cent of the
children at the school will have learned BSL from their parents,
we have an unusual situation in that the remaining 90 per cent of
deaf children will be learning sign language from their peers, only
10 per cent of whom have been exposed to the adult system of
BSL. Although we know that children may learn language partly
by talking to other (usually older) children, it is rare that they are
not exposed to the adult language at all. Not only are deaf children
of hearing parents generally not exposed to adults using BSL, but
only 10 per cent of their peers will presumably be competent in
something approximating adult BSL. Since anecdotal observations
have suggested that school sign language is somewhat different
from adult sign language, it seems reasonable to assume that
schools for the deaf are developing their own sign language to
some extent, as the input from adult BSL is fairly small and
indirect for most deaf schoolchildren. This suggests that, in answer
to the question raised on p. 155, children learning BSL in deaf
schools are similar to first generation creole speakers, in that they
are at least partially inventing their own linguistic system. This
system then presumably undergoes some modification when children leave school and enter the adult deaf community. So it may
not be surprising if BSL has some of the structural characteristics
of a creole, since it seems that, as Fischer (1978, p. 329) has
suggested happens with ASL, BSL may be 'recreolized' every
generation (cf Schlesinger and Namir, 1978, p. 1: 'Sign language
is a form of communication which is used in every community of
deaf persons and seems to be invented anew by them whenever
such a form has not been previously established'.) In order to test
this hypothesis, research is clearly needed on the process of sign
language acquisition in deaf schools, and on the extent to which
the sign language used by deaf children is comparable to adult
BSL.

As I have already suggested, some deaf children will learn BSL
neither from their parents nor from their peers at school. These
are children who may have attended a school or unit for partially
hearing children, or who, because of a relatively small hearing

loss or unusual oral ability, have attended a normal hearing school. Such children may never wish to belong to the adult deaf community and may never learn sign language. However, those who attend adult deaf clubs will generally learn sign language to communicate with other members, which justifies considering adulthood as another possible point of linguistic socialization. Because of the lack of research in this area also, it is not clear to what extent those learning BSL as adults are able to attain a 'native-like' competence in it, that is, to what extent they know it as well as those who learned it in childhood. This question is particularly interesting for language acquisition theory because of the idea that language acquisition must be completed by puberty in order to be fully successful. This is sometimes known as the 'critical period hypothesis' (cf Lenneberg, 1967) and is a controversial question (cf Krashen, 1973, and discussion in chapter 9). Any research into the question would have to determine the extent and type of any sign language competence already possessed by the deaf adult apparently learning BSL for the first time. Even in a primarily oral environment, a deaf person might have developed some kind of a sign system to use either with those few deaf people he or she knew, or with hearing friends or relatives who would accept it. It would clearly be important to establish to what extent this kind of sign language acquisition is distinct from that of children acquiring a school sign system and then adapting it to the adult system when they enter the adult deaf community. Research is needed to determine to what extent primary linguistic socialization is carried out on entry to the adult deaf community, and to what extent a kind of secondary linguistic socialization. A related question is whether BSL acquisition in adulthood is a case of first language or second language learning, since many deaf adults will have been through an oral education designed to teach them English.

Readers whose prime concern with deafness is the question of how deaf children can be integrated into the majority hearing community may wonder why I have so far talked only about the acquisition of BSL, when most deaf people might be expected to acquire some degree of competence in English. My response to such readers would be that I am primarily interested in BSL rather than deafness as a phenomenon, but I shall be discussing the acquisition of English later in this chapter (see p. 173), in the context of a discussion of the possible bilingual acquisition of BSL and English. Now, however, we shall turn to a review of the available evidence concerning the details of the process of sign language acquisition, and the extent to which this is similar to spoken language acquisition. Most of the evidence is from ASL, but there is also a small amount of information from studies of the acquisition of Swedish Sign Language as well as BSL.

All the studies of sign language acquisition which I have come across deal with acquisition at the first possible stage of linguistic socialization, that is, in the home with the parents, from birth onwards. Children falling into three separate categories are studied: deaf children of deaf parents, deaf children of hearing parents, and hearing children with deaf parents or with other exposure to sign language. The kind of language input to the children varies according to the extent to which it follows the syntax of the spoken language.

One of the first acquisition studies of ASL is reported by Schlesinger and Meadow (1972). They studied four children, all of whom were exposed to both sign language and spoken English, and two of whom had deaf, two hearing parents. Their results show similarity to the results from spoken language in that all the children used one sign at first with a variety of meanings, and then progressed to two or more signs in combination. Like the phonology of young hearing children, the phonology of the signs used by the children was different from the adult system in tab, dez or sig (see chapter 3). One of the children, Ann, had an unusually large vocabulary at the age of 19 months, when compared to hearing children. This raises the question of whether sign language acquisition might take place at a faster rate than spoken language acquisition, and Schlesinger and Meadow have some additional relevant evidence. They looked at the diaries of language acquisition kept for two hearing children who were learning both English and sign language, the latter from their deaf grandmother. It is interesting to note that for both hearing children, the first sign appeared before the first word, and in the case of one of the children, the first sign is thought possibly to have appeared at the age of five and a half months. (Dale, 1976, reports that the first word usually appears between ten and thirteen months, although there are difficulties in deciding what criteria must be satisfied for the first word to be recorded.) Schlesinger and Meadow's finding is paralleled by the observation in a BSL acquisition study (Llewellyn-Jones, 1982) that the younger brother of a deaf child with hearing parents could produce considerably more signs than words by the age of one year. We shall discuss the reasons why signs might appear earlier than words further on (see p. 162). Schlesinger and Meadow also studied the spoken language development of the deaf children, since all were receiving spoken language input as well as sign language, and they found that spoken output increased with signed output. Their general conclusions are as follows (Schlesinger and Meadow, 1972, p. 87):

> The analysis thus far indicates that the milestones in sign language acquisition generally parallel the milestones of spoken language acquisition. We have also found that knowledge of sign language at these early ages has not interfered with speech acquisition; on the contrary, the number of spoken words and lipreading facility increased with sign language acquisition.

Klima and Bellugi conducted a study of the acquisition of ASL at about the same time as Schlesinger and Meadow, and conclude, in a similar vein, that 'some of the basic processes of language acquisition are the same across modalities' (Klima and Bellugi, 1972, p. 96). In common with hearing children learning a spoken language, the child they studied, Pola, showed evidence of over-generalization (similar to overregularization as described on p. 153). She used negative incorporation (see chapter 4, p. 89) in a wider range of constructions than it is used in the adult language, and she also used directionality (see chapter 4, p. 86) inappropriately in extending it to the verb FINGERSPELL, which does not have directionality in the adult language. This feature of Pola's sign language acquisition thus showed clear similarity with the acquisition of spoken language.

A study by Prinz and Prinz (1979 and 1981) throws further light on the way in which sign language compares to spoken language acquisition, since they studied the acquisition of both ASL and spoken English in a hearing child who has a deaf mother and a hearing father. Like Schlesinger and Meadow, Prinz and Prinz found that signs were acquired earlier than words, so that at any given age between 7 and 21 months, the number of signs in the child's vocabulary was larger than the number of words. They found that her first combinations sometimes included both signs and words, although later she would choose entirely sign or entirely speech according to who her addressee was. Her sign vocabulary initially complemented her spoken vocabulary, so that she seemed to have 'one lexical system with separate entries from both languages' (Prinz and Prinz, 1981, p. 83). Later, however, she began to distinguish between the two lexical systems, as usually happens in bilingual language development. Prinz and Prinz conclude (1981, p. 85) that the child 'is successfully acquiring language in two different modalities and that her linguistic development in sign and in speech is parallel to that of hearing children simultaneously learning two or more spoken languages'.

This brief overview of ASL acquisition studies thus far indicates that sign language acquisition appears to be similar to spoken languages in the stages through which it passes, though sign language acquisition seems to begin earlier. Ahlgren (1977), in a study of the acquisition of Swedish Sign Language, also found that sign language developed earlier than spoken language, and she suggests that this is because 'Sign language is an ontogenetically more basic means of communication and it is cognitively more closely linked to the most important source of information about the world than is spoken language' (Ahlgren, 1977, pp. 170–1). Brown (1977), however, makes a different point. He proposes that the early stage of sign language learning is easier than spoken language learning because many of the first signs learned will be iconic. His argument is based on the fact that children's first items of vocabulary are at the 'Basic Object Level' (i.e. referring to basic objects in the child's environment, like 'chair', 'table', 'apple', etc.), and on the assumption that signs for such objects will have a high degree of iconicity. He argues as follows (Brown, 1977, p. 20):

> At the Basic Object Level, referents have a maximal number of distinctive attributes and movements. Distinctive attributes and movements constitute the raw material of iconic signs. Therefore, there is a maximal potential for iconicity at the Basic Object Level.

Brown reports that hearing children who did not know ASL found iconic signs easier to remember than non-iconic signs, and Mandel (1977b) found that hearing adults remembered signs better if they perceived them as iconic (Luftig and Lloyd, 1981, report a similar finding). However, neither of these results tell us of the function of iconicity for first language learners of sign language, and we should not over-estimate it, given Klima and Bellugi's (1979) finding that iconicity did not have a role in deaf signers' recall of

ASL signs, and given the problems in what is meant by iconicity (see chapter 1).

We should also question Brown's assumption that the majority of early signs are in fact iconic. Schlesinger and Meadow (1972, p. 59) argue that not more than half their subject Ann's vocabulary at the age of 18 months could be iconic (or have 'ideographic meaning') to her; Prinz and Prinz (1979) and Woll and Lawson (1981) question to what extent signs which are iconic to adults will be so to children, since perception of iconicity depends on perception of etymology, for example that the BSL sign MILK comes from the motion involved in milking a cow. Bonvillian (1983) reports that only about one third of the signs produced in his own study of early sign language acquisition were iconic, presumably to him, so perhaps fewer were iconic to the children themselves.

Bonvillian's study of the acquisition of ASL produced results similar to the others in that his deaf subjects produced their first recognizable sign, ten different signs, and then combinations of signs, all earlier than is normal in the acquisition of spoken language (Bonvillian, 1983). He suggests that the accelerated appearance of the first individual signs may be due not to their iconicity, but to the fact that children's hands can be moulded and guided by parents (whereas this is not true of the vocal organs), the fact that they receive direct visual feedback from their productions, and the fact that the motor system seems to develop more rapidly than the speech system. Similar suggestions are also made by Prinz and Prinz (1979) and Wilbur (1979). However, Bonvillian suggests that such factors are operative mainly in the early stages, since the onset of sign combinations in the children was not statistically related to their early vocabulary growth. Bonvillian suggests that studies of the further development of sign language skills might be expected to parallel the development of spoken language more closely, 'as both systems would be substantially reflecting underlying cognitive abilities' (Bonvillian, 1983, p. 124). Another finding from Bonvillian's study was that the relation between his subjects' sign language development and their cognitive development, measured on conventional scales, was not as clear as has been suggested for spoken language development. This may mean, he suggests, that although cognition is important in language acquisition, it is not the only factor, and factors such as mechanical skill (previously thought unimportant, see Lenneberg,

1967, p. 131) may play a part. This finding also leads Bonvillian to question the way in which measures of language development are usually based on production rather than comprehension. Comparisons of sign and spoken language development based on comprehension rather than production measures might reveal more similarity in the timing of the early stages of language development. Bonvillian's study is interesting not only for the light it throws on sign language acquisition in particular, but also for language acquisition in general.

We now turn to a more detailed look at the acquisition of particular parts of the sign language system. We shall look at relevant studies under three headings: phonology or 'sublexical components' (see chapter 3, p. 47), syntax or grammar, and semantics or meaning relations. So far, more is probably known about the acquisition of sign language phonology than about any other aspect of the language, and within phonology, about acquisition of the dez or handshape rather than about acquisition of the tab or sig (see chapter 3 for explanation of these terms).

Studies of the acquisition of phonology in spoken language have found that sounds tend to be acquired in a certain order (for example, stops like 'p' before fricatives like 'f': see Dale, 1976, p. 214), and that children make regular substitutions for adult sounds (for example replacing fricatives with stops, see Dale, 1976, p. 216). Similar results have been found in a few studies of the acquisition of handshape, in particular McIntire (1977) in ASL, and Carter (1981) in BSL.

McIntire (1977) refers to an unpublished paper by Boyes-Braem (1973), where a model is proposed for stages in the acquisition of handshape. This model is based on the assumption that the 'A' handshape (closed fist) is the unmarked or basic handshape, and that it will be acquired earliest. As McIntire explains, handshapes acquired after this one can be defined in terms of the addition of increasingly complex features, such as 'extension away from the central axis of the hand of one or more fingers (G, 5)', 'contact of the fingertips with the opposed thumb (F, O)' (McIntire, 1977, p. 250; see chapter 3 of this book, pp. 61–4, for explanation of the symbols for the handshapes). The general prediction is that children will acquire handshapes requiring control of thumb and index finger or the whole hand before others, and that handshapes which have already been learned will be substituted for those which have not yet been learned. McIntire's data, from the acquisition of ASL by a deaf child, generally support Boyes-Braem's model, though McIntire finds that the use of features such as +index, +compact in specifying the handshapes makes it possible to state substitutions in the form of rules (see McIntire, 1977, pp. 257–8). However, McIntire's rules cannot account for all the data, and she suggests that other factors apart from handshape must be taken into consideration, such as complexity of movement or sig, and the availability (or not) of visual feedback in the production of the sign.

In a very interesting, unpublished study of the acquisition of BSL, Carter (1981) tests the application of Boyes-Braem's and McIntire's ideas to the acquisition of dez in BSL, and she also investigates acquisition of movement. At the age of 25 months the distinctive handshapes used by her subject, Jessica, are: A, 5, C, G, F and O (see chapter 3, pp. 61–2), the first four of which belong to Boyes-Braem's first stage, and the last two of which (F and O) belong to Boyes-Braem's second stage. Jessica also showed a regular pattern of substitutions for adult handshapes she had not yet acquired: for example, she substituted 5 (with fingers spread) for B (with fingers close together). An interesting incident is reported which suggests that her perception for some hand-shapes may have been ahead of her production: she was seen to manipulate her fingers with the other hand in order to produce the H handshape (index and middle fingers extended from the first) required for the sign TWO. (H belongs to Boyes-Braem's stage 3 of acquisition.) Carter agrees with McIntire that various secondary factors affect use of handshape by the child, especially complexity of movement as proposed by McIntire (1977). In addition, Carter suggests that two further factors might be important: hand combination and, in her subject's case, simultaneous vocalization. As pointed out in chapter 3 (p. 55), signs may be made with one or two hands, and two handed signs may be of two types: (1) where both hands move, and (2) where the dominant hand acts on a stationary, non-dominant hand. Carter suggests that signs of the second type are more difficult to produce, and it seems that Jessica produced more substitutions of handshape or movement for signs of this category, that is, she found it more difficult to produce the adult form of type (2) signs than of type (1) signs.

Llewellyn-Jones (1982), in another unpublished study of BSL acquisition, found that the first handshapes to be acquired were

A, 5, C, G, B and O, the first four of which, as in Carter's (1981) study, belong to Boyes-Braem's first stage, and the last two of which belong to her second stage. Handshapes acquired later in Llewellyn-Jones' study included H, I and Y, which are in Boyes-Braem's third stage, and 5 and Å, which do not appear to be distinctive in ASL (see chapter 5, pp. 108–9). So this study gives further support to the idea that there are stages in the acquisition of handshapes, which are found in more than one sign language.

Carter also investigated the acquisition of the movement parameter or sig in BSL, and the way in which this interacts with handshape and hand combination. She suggests that in the early stages, the child may not produce the distinction between movements in the horizontal plane (like side-to-side versus to and fro), but may simply have a contrast between horizontal and vertical. In movements from the wrist, the order of complexity seems to be: up/down, side to side, and circular. This accounts for substitutions like up/down for side to side movement in PAINTBRUSH, where Jessica cannot manage to combine side to side movement with wrist movement, even though she can produce side to side movement on its own in other signs. An example of the interaction of handshape and movement found by Carter is that opening and closing movement seems to require a handshape with the thumb touching one or more fingers. Carter suggests that it is because of this that the dez 5 is substituted for G in signs involving opening and closing movement (like BIRD), even though G is used in other signs. Carter also finds that movement interacts with hand combination. This is shown in that when producing two-handed signs of the type where both hands move, which Carter suggested were simpler for the child, Jessica seems to have less difficulty in producing the correct movement than she does in signs of the other type, where a dominant hand acts on a non-dominant, stationary hand. Thus hand combination interacts with both movement and handshape (see above).

Although we are separating acquisition of phonology, syntax and semantics in sign language for convenience of exposition, they are clearly not separate in practice, and a good example of the interaction between all these aspects of the language is found in the study by Kantor (1980) of the acquisition of classifiers in ASL. Classifiers in ASL have similar syntactic function to their function in BSL (see chapter 4, p. 88), and are used to some extent by the children in Kantor's study. However, a particularly interesting finding is that handshapes which are made correctly by the children in non-classifier signs are replaced by motorically simpler handshapes in classifier signs. Thus the 3-hand (thumb and first two fingers spread) and the V-hand are replaced by a 5-hand, which according to the Boyes-Braem model mentioned earlier is acquired earlier than either 3 or V. Kantor suggests that these substitutions in classifiers can be accounted for by the syntactic and semantic complexity of classifier usage in ASL.

As for studies specifically on the acquisition of sign language syntax, Hoffmeister and Wilbur (1980) report Fischer's (1973b) study of the acquisition of verb inflection. (For a discussion of inflection in sign language, see chapter 4, pp. 84–90.) Fischer found that the children she studied progressed from a stage of using no verb inflections to a stage of overgeneralizing by using inflections with verbs that did not allow them, to, finally, near adult-like use of inflections. This description is reminiscent of the way in which spoken language syntax is acquired. Fischer's results are complemented by the finding of Ellenberger and Steyaert (1978) that action verbs allowing spatial modification (a kind of inflection) for source-goal or location were acquired later than verbs not allowing such inflection. Like Fischer, they found that when first used, inflections were not made in an adult way. Ellenberger and Steyaert's interpretation of their results is interesting with reference to the question of the role of iconicity in sign language acquisition, for they say (p. 268): 'While one might expect spatial modifications to appear earlier because of their pictorial nature, they are, in fact, relatively late acquisitions, perhaps because such representations may require a fairly advanced mastery of cognitive skills involving spatial relationships'.

Hoffmeister and Wilbur (1980) also report on Hoffmeister's (1978) finding that children learning ASL rely on a basically SVO (subject-verb-object) order to an extent which appears to be greater than in adult ASL. This is interesting in the light of the way that word order is used by children in the acquisition of spoken language (see p. 152).

The third aspect of sign language acquisition to be considered is the acquisition of semantic relations. Several studies of ASL acquisition (Schlesinger and Meadow, 1972, Klima and Bellugi, 1972, Prinz and Prinz, 1979) suggest that children in the early stages of ASL acquisition use signs to express the same range of semantic relations expressed by children learning spoken languages. Early semantic relations include nomination or naming (e.g. MILK), recurrence (e.g. MORE), non-existence (e.g. ALLGONE), attributive (e.g. MANY CANDY), locative (e.g. GO HOME), agent-action (e.g. MAN WORK) and action-object (e.g. GRAB BOY). Of these, Carter (1981) found nomination, recurrence, attributive, locative, and action, and also negation in her study of the acquisition of BSL. Prinz and Prinz (1979, p. 289) report that the sequence of acquisition of the semantic relations by their child was similar to both that of children learning English and of deaf parents acquiring ASL. Thus far it looks as though the visual medium of language does not significantly influence the acquisition of semantic relations, and this conclusion is further supported by Ashbrook (1977), cited in Hoffmeister and Wilbur (1980), who investigated whether there was any developmental difference between semantic relations expressed sequentially, and those expressed simultaneously. Despite the fact that the latter kind is possible only in sign language because of its visual medium, she found that semantic relations were developed in the same way, whether expressed simultaneously or sequentially. This provides evidence for the relative insignificance of the difference of the medium of sign language from spoken language.

One further aspect of language acquisition which is often neglected in research, but which is a prerequisite to successful communication, is the acquisition of communicative strategies. Although sign language is similar to spoken language in some respects, for example, in that people have to take turns in talking to one another, its medium means that there are different ways of attracting and holding attention, and of signalling that one wishes to talk. Carter (1981) pays some attention to the acquisition of communicative strategies in her study of BSL, and notes that her subject Jessica shows knowledge of the necessity of establishing eye contact with the addressee, and that she uses tapping or touching the person concerned as an attention-getting strategy. Carter also describes how Jessica learns to interact with adults through give-take routines (where an object is passed round with the instruction to give it to the next person) and turn-taking (while playing or looking at picture books). Maestas y Moores (1980) looks at the very early interaction of deaf parents with their infants and finds that parents use a variety of sensory channels to stimulate communication with their children, including touching the children to obtain their attention, signing on their bodies, and moulding the children's hands into signs. Earlier in this chapter (p. 153) I mentioned research on early parent-child communication where the parents are hearing, but it would be interesting to compare this with communication where either the parents or children, or both, are deaf.

At the beginning of this chapter I suggested that knowledge of the way in which sign language is acquired might throw some light on language acquisition in general, and I suggested in particular that some studies of sign language acquisition are relevant to the question of the role of language input. As we have seen, BSL is often acquired in an unusual way, in schools for the deaf where there is little adult sign language input. Some preliminary evidence for the kind of acquisition process which might be operating under such conditions is given in Tervoort's (1961) study of the sign language system developed by children in Dutch and American schools for communication with one another. Tervoort suggests that when individual signs are first invented, they are 'natural gestures' which bear some resemblance to what they represent. These signs become 'formal signs' when they are recognized because of an established convention as to what they represent, and not because of their visual similarity to the object represented. Presumably a 'natural gesture' would be used just once in a context that required it, whereas a 'formal sign' would become part of the common sign language vocabulary of the community by convention. Tervoort deals mainly with the development of individual signs, but shows that language invention is possible in a community, at least at the level of vocabulary.

Kuschel (1973) makes distinctions similar to those between Tervoort's 'natural gesture' and 'formal sign' in his description of the sign system developed by the only deaf-mute on a Polynesian island for communication with hearing people. Kuschel divides the signs of the deaf-mute, Kangobai, into three categories: those 'immediately decipherable by members of other cultures', those 'immediately decipherable only by members of Kangobai's own culture', and those 'immediately decipherable only by a few selected members of Kangobai's own culture' (Kuschel, 1973, p. 10). Kuschel does not report with whom the signs in the third category are used, but he does say that their comprehension depends on previous explanation or learning. So it may be that Kangobai uses these signs with the people with whom he commun-

icates most often, and for whom the signs have a meaning established by convention, as in a normal speech community. Again,
Kuschel's evidence suggests that sign language invention is
certainly possible, though we have few details, and do not know
to what extent Kangobai's friends and relatives were involved in
the invention of signs, particularly those of the third type.

Feldman et al. (1978) did a detailed study of sign language
acquisition in the absence of input, in American families with deaf
children and hearing parents who did not sign. Their carefully
described results contribute significantly to the debate about the
role of linguistic input in language acquisition. Their aim was 'to
ask whether communication develops similarly for the *deaf* child
without linguistic input as for the *hearing* child *with* linguistic
input' (p. 361), and their conclusions, on the basis of data from
six deaf children, were 'that these linguistically isolated individuals
display communicative skills that are language-like, despite their
deprivations', and 'that there are significant internal dispositions
in humans that guide the language acquisition process' (p. 408).
They found that the deaf children made reference in two ways,
by pointing to people, things or locations in their environment,
and by pantomiming properties of things and events. These points
and pantomimes, which they call 'characterizing signs', sometimes
appeared in sentence-like combinations. These sentences represented the following semantic relations: actor, patient, recipient
and place. The children seemed to be using gesture order as a
strategy to indicate semantic relations: patient always occurred
before recipient, patient usually occurred before act, and act
usually occurred before recipient. (Actor and place did not often
appear.) The children's reliance on order to help indicate relations
suggests that this is a natural strategy, since we have already seen
(p. 152) that children may anyway use order to a greater extent
than the input language does. Feldman et al. also studied the
gestures of the mothers, to check whether the children could in
fact be said to be learning gestures from their mothers. They
found that although the mothers did point and use characterizing
signs in similar ways to the children, they relied more on concrete
objects as 'props' and they produced few gesture combinations
conveying semantic relations in the way the children did. Those
combinations which they did produce appeared at a later stage
than the child's combinations, which suggests that the mother was
learning from the child rather than vice versa. Feldman et al.

point out that the children's invention of the gesture system can be considered analogous to the creation of a creole, the process which we discussed earlier in relation to BSL (see page 155). I said (p. 157) that the acquisition of BSL in schools might be similar to the creation of a creole, but the case in Feldman et al.'s study is clearer because there is total absence of input from the adult sign language system rather than only partial absence, as in the case of BSL in schools.

Volterra (1981) comments on the fact that all the combinations in Feldman et al.'s data seem to include a point (what she calls a 'deictic gesture'), and that there are no examples of two or more characterizing signs (what she calls 'symbolic gestures'). Volterra suggests that the use of points or deictic gestures represents an early stage of language acquisition, and that signs are only true symbols once they are decontextualized, or used independently of the physical environment in which the conversation is taking place. She argues that Feldman et al.'s study provides 'indirect evidence for the fact that to combine two symbols it is necessary to be exposed to a linguistic input' (Volterra, 1981, p. 359). Volterra's argument is one explanation for the fact that Feldman et al.'s data differ from other data on sign language acquisition (including her own and that mentioned earlier in this chapter) in the absence of combinations of 'symbolic gestures' (gestures that are not points). However, there are other possible explanations which are only indirectly related to the absence of language input. One is that Feldman et al.'s children had simply not yet reached the stage of combining symbolic gestures. Consistent with this hypothesis would be the idea that absence of linguistic input may have a retarding, though not necessarily an obstructive effect on language development, since deaf children of the age of Feldman et al.'s subjects with language input would normally have started to produce symbolic gestures. Another, related explanation for the absence of combinations of symbolic gestures in Feldman et al.'s data is that the children were isolated from one another, each communicating primarily with his or her mother, *who did not know the system*. In these circumstances, it is not surprising if the children made maximal use of the physical environment by pointing, and that their characterizing signs were pantomimic, since it is as if they were making the system maximally transparent to the learner mother. Symbolic communication has to be based on convention or agreement between the communicating partners, as Tervoort (1961) has pointed out, so that the children in Feldman et al.'s study would have had to establish agreement with their mothers in order to develop symbolic gestures. It is interesting to note that the children used characterizing signs or symbolic gestures mainly to represent actions rather than objects or people, possibly because it was easier to produce a pantomime of an action that was transparent to the mother. Since most of their sign combinations normally include one action, which, like a verb, tends to link nominals representing objects and people, this could explain why we do not see combinations of characterizing signs. However, there is some evidence that the children in the study may in fact have been trying to use actions symbolically to represent objects as well as transparently to represent actions themselves: this evidence comes from the description of cases where 'the child first points at the noun referent, followed by the iconic sign, in non-action contexts' (Feldman et al., 1978, p. 367). The authors take the example of a twisting motion made in response to a picture of a jar, and although they consider the possibility that the motion might be intended to refer to the jar itself, they decide to classify it as an action. However, it is possible that the child's twisting motion, made in the physical context of a jar, or following pointing to the jar, may have been an attempt to agree with the mother on a symbolic gesture which would henceforward represent 'jar'. As Feldman et al. admit, there are considerable problems in interpretation of this kind of data. Because their conclusions are based on data which is difficult to interpret unequivocally, we cannot assume they are definitive, and must therefore leave open the question of whether linguistic input is necessary for symbolic communication to become established. Meanwhile we may note that some possible counter-evidence to Volterra's claim comes from a study by Mohay (1982) 'of the communication systems evolved by two deaf children in the absence of a sign language model', where combinations of two or more gestures (apart from points) do seem to be produced.

It is certainly possible that a sign system created in the absence of language input might be qualitatively different from one learned with input, and as Newport (1981) points out, Woodward (1973a, 1975) has shown that the use of certain ASL inflectional rules is related to having deaf parents and acquiring ASL before the age of six. Newport herself reports on a study she is conducting which compares control of certain aspects of ASL morphology by first generation signers (those with hearing parents) and second generation signers (those with deaf parents who are first generation signers). She finds that second generation signers show control of most of the morphological contrasts available in ASL, while that of first generation signers is only partial. These findings have interesting implications for the role of linguistic input in language acquisition, for they suggest that 'complex internal morphological analysis is performed by second-generation deaf on an input which does not itself contain this morphology' (Newport, 1981, p. 120). Thus children may 'improve' on an incomplete input, again in a similar way to the way in which a creole is created from a pidgin. However, with reference to Newport's study it should be pointed out that the suggestion is based on the assumption that the second generation signers do in fact learn from an 'inadequate' or incomplete input, whereas they may have had contact with other deaf adults or children who have a more complete mastery of ASL, either before attending school or in school itself.

The final study to be mentioned on the role of input in sign language acquisition is that by Ahlgren (1981) on the acquisition of Swedish Sign Language by deaf children with hearing parents. In this study the parents use sign language as they are themselves learning it as a second language. Ahlgren finds that their children develop sign language adequately, and to a degree that is superior to their parents. She suggests that such children can develop sign language normally even if the parents do not start attending sign language classes until the child is one year old, because the first year of communication is visual-gestural anyway. She says that language development will only be poor if communication and interaction is poor, but not because of the input. Ahlgren's subjects might seem at first sight to be equivalent to Newport's first generation signers, who Newport found did not have normal sign language skills, but the fact that the Swedish hearing parents used sign language might have made enough of a difference to make the children equivalent to second generation signers. It is also the case that the children in Ahlgren's study had some exposure to the signing of deaf adults, although Ahlgren states that this was less than two hours every other week. Unfortunately we do not know how significant quantity of input is, though we may speculate that its quality may be more important.

Unfortunately I cannot report on studies on BSL acquisition which answer questions about the role of language input or the kind of sign language which deaf children with differing kinds of input are acquiring. Detailed studies are clearly needed of BSL acquisition at the three possible points of linguistic socialization: at home, whether with deaf (first or later generation) or hearing (signing or non-signing) parents, at school among deaf children, and at deaf clubs for adults. However, in the absence of such studies we may suggest on the basis of other studies that children are certainly capable of remarkable feats of acquisition or invention in the total or partial absence of input, and that the type of sign language system acquired by each deaf individual may vary according to the conditions of its acquisition.

Our final concern in this chapter will be to look at the way in which the acquisition of BSL is related to the acquisition of English, since deaf people live in a predominantly hearing society and need to communicate with hearing people as well as with one another. Since deaf children cannot learn English on the basis of hearing English spoken around them, a special effort has to be made to teach them the language. (Although we discussed earlier the possibility of a language being invented if input were inadequate, it seems unlikely that deaf children would 'invent' a spoken language on the basis of imperfect input of English, when they have an alternative visual medium for production and feedback.) The teaching of the language will take place mostly in an educational context, though parents of young deaf children can also play a part. British people are not usually very familiar with bilingual language development (although this is the norm in many parts of the world), and although most would agree with the aim of the oralist philosophy of deaf education, to develop English skills to the full, one must question its assumption of monolingualism, or the idea that one has to make a choice between sign language acquisition and English language acquisition. This is not the place for a detailed discussion of the oral-manual controversy regarding methods of deaf education, since it was described in chapter 2 and has been extensively written about elsewhere (see e.g. Brennan, 1976, Royal National Institute for the Deaf, 1976a and 1976b, Conrad, 1979, Meadow 1980, and Freeman et al. 1981). However, the following facts, established by research, may be worth mentioning briefly: the oral method is not entirely successful in developing skills in English (Conrad, 1979, 1981); early acquisition of sign language (or Signed English) does not prevent or slow down acquisition of speech but may accelerate it

(Schlesinger and Meadow, 1972, Holmes and Holmes 1980); access to language in early childhood is important in cognitive development (Conrad, 1979); and deaf children who have learned sign language when young tend to score higher than other deaf children on tests of intelligence, educational achievement, reading and writing (Vernon, 1976, Conrad, 1979, 1981). It may be because of these facts that, as described in chapter 2, some British schools for the deaf have introduced 'Total Communication', or speech in combination with signs. Although anecdotal reports of the effects of this change by teachers who are involved suggest easier communication between teacher and child, and better adjustment of the children, research on the way in which this has affected the children's competence in English has not yet been done. In Britain, the only study which might give an indication of the kind of results to be expected is that by Fenn (1975 and 1976) on the development of English in deaf children through the PGSS system, which, as explained earlier, is an artificially devised manual system designed to represent English. Fenn (1975) concludes that while PGSS is certainly an effective medium of communication, it is not clear that it leads to an adequate representation of English, since children tended to use PGSS in ways similar to BSL by introducing simultaneity in place of sequentiality. In an American study, Marmor and Petitto (1979) point out the difficulties of simultaneous production of speech and sign, and report that signed utterances of teachers using simultaneous communication in the classroom 'were predominantly ungrammatical with respect both to rules of English and to rules of ASL'.

It is important to realize that when speech is used in combination with signs, as in Total Communication (see chapter 2, p. 36), the sign system is not BSL (or ASL), but more like Signed English (see chapter 6). Because BSL has a different grammar from English, with sign order not being the same as word order, and with facial activity that does not necessarily correspond to the production of English words, it cannot be used simultaneously with English. However, there is no reason why it should not be used alternately with English, in different lessons, for example, or in different parts of a lesson. This may happen in practice in schools where the teacher is a native signer (though this is rare) and occasionally uses BSL for ease of communication, or in classes for school leavers where the emphasis is on conveying information which will help them to survive in the adult world. However, it is not official policy anywhere as far as I know. This is probably because BSL is not widely recognized as a language in its own right, nor are many teachers competent in it, and it is easier for hearing people to learn Signed English. But since BSL is the first language of most deaf children in deaf schools (whether or not they have learned it at home) it is a resource which teachers could draw on. They could use it not only to convey important information in a way that will not be misunderstood, but they could also use it as a vehicle to teach English as a second language. I imagine that if it were recognized that English is the second, not the first language of deaf children, then it could be taught much more effectively. Stokoe (1972) wrote an article called 'A classroom experiment in two languages' advocating teaching of English via ASL, and Coye et al. (1978) describe an interesting bilingual, bicultural approach to teaching English where both English and ASL are used in the classroom by a hearing and deaf teaching team: they report very positive reactions on the part of both the students and the teachers, although they did not evaluate improvement in English specifically. In Britain, it seems likely that recognition of BSL as a full language in schools would improve the confidence of deaf people as well as their desire and ability to learn English, and would ultimately aid their integration as bilingual, bicultural adults, into both the deaf and the hearing communities.

Summary

This chapter has been about the acquisition of sign language in general, with reference to BSL as far as possible. We have seen that sign language acquisition tends to parallel spoken language acquisition in the stages it passes through, although it seems to begin earlier, possibly because of its visual-motor rather than vocal production. We have noted that the conditions under which sign language is acquired may be different from those common in spoken language acquisition, in that a deaf child's parents are often not the primary source of sign language input. This has led to interesting evidence on the role of language input which suggests that input may not be necessary in the same quality and quantity as was previously imagined. Since members of the deaf community have to function in the hearing community also, we looked finally at how BSL acquisition might contribute to the acquisition of English as a second language, and concluded that bilingualism and biculturalism was a reasonable goal for deaf people.

8

Doing sign language research

So far in this book I have presented the results of research on BSL without very much consideration of how those results are obtained. I have given the results of data analysis, but little information about the prerequisite to data analysis, which is data collection. In this chapter, however, I shall focus primarily on the methodological problems of data collection in sign language research. My aim will be to create general awareness of the extent to which the choice of methods of data collection can affect the results of analysis, and to give practical guidance to those considering doing sign language research.

I shall first give a personal illustration of one approach to sign language research, comment on its strength and weaknesses, and I shall then discuss more generally various aspects of the research process, under the following headings: *type of researcher*, *type of data*, and *data collection* and *transcription*.

My first study of BSL (Deuchar, 1978a) was based on data collected in a deaf club over a nine month period during 1976–7. I had very little knowledge of BSL when I began the research, although I did know some ASL. I chose observation as my main method of data collection (see below) because I was interested in a sociolinguistic approach to sign language research which would lead to an analysis of the difference between sign language varieties as used in formal and informal situations. As a graduate student I had a low budget, so that I could not afford expensive recording equipment, or to pay for the services of a deaf person as research assistant.

Since I chose observation in a deaf club as my main method, I had to be accepted as an honorary member of such a club for a period of time. As a hearing, non-native signer with no deaf relatives or friends, I had to have a reason for my presence in a deaf club that would be acceptable to its members. So I presented myself as someone who was interested in learning about sign language and deafness, and in return for the opportunity to attend the club, I agreed to act as a volunteer driver providing transport to and from the club for elderly deaf people once a week. This turned out to be an ideal practical reason for my presence at the club, as I would arrive with a group of deaf people, and stay until they were ready to go home. Because the hearing welfare workers at the club also provided transport for deaf people, the club members tended to assume I was a trainee welfare worker, particularly since welfare workers in training also have to learn sign language. This probably led to my being identified with the hearing welfare workers rather than with the deaf themselves, but at least it meant that my presence at the club was accepted. In addition to visiting the club whenever it was open (three times a week) I also attended two different sign language classes, in order to progress in sign language competence as quickly as possible. When at the club I was able to practise using sign language in conversation with anyone willing to talk to me: on the whole the older members of the club seemed to be more willing than the younger members, possibly because the older members had more experience and confidence in communicating with hearing people than the younger members, and perhaps also because their seniority to me in age made up for the differences between us in educational background and hearing status.

As I became more competent in BSL, I began to record data, at first in note form, and at first unobtrusively so as not to arouse suspicion or hostility. However, as the members became more accustomed to me and my activities, I began to take notes more openly. After I had been attending the club for five months, I introduced a video-recorder, with the members' permission, and made an hour long recording of part of a church service, and of conversation in the club bar. The members appeared to enjoy this, particularly as they were able to view themselves on the monitor immediately after the recording. The data produced as a result proved to be technically too poor for extensive use for analysis, but the operation of recording the data made the deaf accustomed to having a camera pointed at them.

The next stage, after two more months, was to introduce two other hearing people who were to make a cine film of data. It was necessary for me to have some data on film rather than on video-tape so that this could be shown in the USA, where I was a student. (American video standards are different from those in Britain, and the difference can only be overcome using international standard equipment, to which I did not have access, or a costly conversion process once the tapes have been made.) The two people who were to make the film visited the club several times before filming, so that the club members could become accustomed to them. They appeared to be easily accepted, perhaps because they were known to one of the deaf members, who had in fact introduced them to me. Their equipment was somewhat more obtrusive than the video recorder, since they had two cameras and bright lights (these had not been necessary with the video), but the members nevertheless seemed to produce natural, spontaneous signing (with the occasional exception: see chapter 6, p. 137) and made little reference to the camera except for one or two comments about the heat generated by the lights. As a result a half hour film was made, consisting of about ten minutes of signing as in a church service and twenty minutes of spontaneous, conversational signing. The limitations of the cameras, which needed rewinding at frequent intervals, meant that continuity was hard to achieve, and while the church service was 'staged', with breaks, to allow continuity in the film, the conversational signing recorded is in short fragments. While this was not ideal, it seemed the best solution in view of the limitations.

Once the film had been processed and assembled, the next step was to transcribe it in preparation for analysis. I clearly needed the assistance of a native signer for this purpose, and was fortunate to obtain the help of the senior welfare worker (a hearing native signer) who spent many hours going through the data and helping me to transcribe it. Deaf members of the club also helped in the process, particularly in transcribing the parts which they themselves had signed.

In retrospect, the main strength of my study seems to be the amount of time I was able to spend in the deaf club, and the extent to which my role there was accepted. Without the gradual build up of my competence in sign language, and their confidence in me, I would not have been able to obtain the film data. Nevertheless, the data is limited, both in quantity (30 minutes, plus data on video and in note form) and in quality (because of the continuity problem). I myself was limited in my lack of knowledge of BSL at the outset, but this limitation could have been overcome if I had had a deaf research assistant who could have helped both in teaching me sign language and in collecting and transcribing data. More sophisticated recording equipment, preferably of the kind that I could operate myself, would also have improved both the quantity and quality of the data collected. However, my lack of access to assistance and equipment resulted from financial limitations which I could not do anything about at the time, except operate within them to the best of my ability.

Having given this personal account of my experience in sign language data collection, I shall go on to a more general consideration of the problems involved, under the headings mentioned on p. 177. The first heading, *type of researcher*, refers to whether or not the researcher is a member of the deaf community, and whether or not he or she has access to financial support for the research. Clearly the ideal researcher would be someone who was both a member of the deaf community and also with access to financial support, but unfortunately these characteristics tend to be mutually exclusive. Deaf people have difficulty in achieving success in an educational system which is not geared to their needs, so that few deaf people obtain higher education, which is almost a prerequisite for access to those institutions who are likely to provide financial support. Those who have access to research grants are generally hearing people who have completed graduate work and who are employees, or potential employees, of institutions of higher education. They are rarely qualified for sign language research as native signers, unless they happen to be hearing with deaf parents, which is rarely the case. Given that hearing researchers tend to have more access to the financial support which is vital for recording equipment and research assistance, while deaf researchers have sign language skills, a good compromise in these circumstances would seem to be research teams including both deaf and hearing researchers. Such teams have already been set up in Britain, as we saw in chapter 2, p. 44. The only disadvantage in these situations would seem to be that a hearing rather than a deaf person is usually the initiator and director of research, because of that person's role in higher education, and because a project has to be planned before financial support can be obtained and a deaf researcher employed. However, as deaf people gradually gain more access to higher education, this situation may change.

The next question to be considered is the *type of* BSL *data* which is to be obtained in sign language research. The dominant trend in modern linguistics, established as a result of the work of Noam Chomsky, is to base linguistic analyses on intuitive data. These data are 'intuitive' in that they are produced by reflection about the language (rather than by using language) for the purposes of the linguistic analysis, often by the linguist himself or herself. The data commonly consist of sentences which the linguist, investigating his or her native language, considers to be possible sentences in the language. It is common for the linguist also to invent some impossible ('ungrammatical') sentences in order to work out the grammatical rules which allow the construction of certain sentence types but not of others (cf Smith and Wilson, 1979). While an apparent advantage of this approach is that an infinite quantity of data of the type required can be produced (as it does not have to have occurred in real speech situations), it does depend on the linguist either being a native speaker of the language under analysis, or having access to the 'native speaker intuitions' of another person. This has led some to criticize the approach as being 'unscientific' in that the linguist is producing theory and data at the same time, rather than building a theory of pre-existing data, and so could be open to the accusation of producing data specifically to fit the theory (cf Crystal, 1971, Labov, 1975). Linguists relying on intuitive data may defend themselves by claiming that their data would be agreed upon by anyone who is a native speaker of the language. Unfortunately, however, disagreement about intuitive data seems to be common, as shown by the frequent discussion among linguists in seminars and conferences as to whether or not a given sentence is 'grammatical': and as Labov (1972a) says, linguists often defend themselves by saying that they are only discussing their own 'dialect', which means that their data are unverifiable by anyone other than themselves. Further evidence for the high degree of disagreement about intuitive data is given by Labov (1975) who reports on studies showing the considerable extent to which linguists and non-linguists rejected sentences which certain linguists had used in publications on syntax as examples of grammatical sentences. The disagreements about intuitive data should lead us to question two assumptions on which their use is based: that people's intuitive judgments accurately reflect their actual behaviour; and that language is a homogeneous system. Trudgill (1974) shows how inaccurate people can be in reporting their own linguistic behaviour, and he and other sociolinguists (cf Labov, 1972b, Hudson, 1980, chapter 6 of this book) have also shown how far language is from being homogeneous. There is variation not only between individuals in their language behaviour, but also within the speech or signing of the same individual, according to the situation in which the language is used. The use of intuitive data forces the linguist to make categorical judgments about language when it is actually a variable phenomenon.

In sign language research, there are not yet enough native signers as linguists to make possible the exclusive use of intuitive data. In any case, anyone working on sign language cannot fail to be aware of its variable nature (and therefore the unsuitability of purely intuitive data), since the absence of a written, standard form makes it impossible to focus only on one idealized variety of the language. Native signer intuitions can nevertheless make a substantial contribution to generating hypotheses about the possible types of structures to be found in sign language, and sign language research is clearly being enriched by the participation of more native signers. However, the best approach, in my view, for research on any language, is to combine data from various sources, and to check data based on intuitions against data based on observation of language use in actual situations.

Before we discuss the collection of data by observation, and how this applies to sign language research, we should look at a type of data which is related to intuitive data, and which has been fairly widely used in ASL research: this is data based on elicitations (cf Labov, 1972a). This is related to intuitive data in that it is a type of data sometimes used when the linguist is not a native speaker of the language under investigation, but has access to native speakers of the language from whom actual linguistic data, or intuitions about data, can be elicited by direct questioning. As Labov (1972a) points out, this method became established by anthropological linguists working in the early part of this century who did not know the languages they were investigating well, but who would ask bilingual informants to translate sentences, for example from English into their own language. This is the approach taught in some courses on linguistic field methods, the implication contained in the title being that such methods are particularly appropriate for 'exotic' languages that one does not know, that one has to go to the 'field' (or the 'bush', see Labov, 1972a, p. 99) to investigate. ASL is an 'exotic' language for most

American linguists, and the method of elicitation has been used extensively with native signing informants. As I said in chapter 5, p. 120, Liddell (1978) based his data on elicitations, 'by asking native signers to translate into ASL a list of English sentences containing restrictive clauses' (Liddell, 1978, p. 67). Liddell was aware of the possibility that the informants might be influenced by the structure of English, and attempted to minimize a possible bias by giving them a few days to think about the translations. It is difficult to determine whether the time interval in fact had the effect he desired, but in any case the informants were probably influenced by the constraints of the English sentence. As several researchers have pointed out (see e.g. Thompson, 1977, Friedman, 1976a, and chapter 4, p. 83 of this book) it is not clear whether the sentence is a viable unit for analysis in ASL, and it seems likely that a larger unit, that of discourse, should be taken into account.

In addition to the problem that the linguist's native language may influence a translation elicited, elicitations share with intuitions the problematic assumptions that the data are representative of actual behaviour, and that the system is homogeneous. These assumptions seem just as questionable for elicitations as for intuitions, and particularly so when the language under investigation has low status. As Trudgill (1974) has shown, some informants are likely to report that they use more (or less) prestigious language than is actually the case, and Labov (1972a, p. 111) has suggested that elicitations from native speakers will tend toward the most prestigious variety of the language. He calls this the 'Principle of Subordinate Shift', which he states as follows, 'When speakers of a subordinate dialect are asked direct questions about their language, their answers will shift in an irregular manner toward (or away from) the superordinate dialect' (Labov, 1972a, p. 111). As we have seen in chapter 6, both BSL and ASL have varieties which are influenced by the structure of English, and these varieties have the most overt prestige in that they are used in deaf education, if signing is used at all, and on public, formal occasions. Given the extent to which English-influenced signing has particular public sanction and the generally negative attitudes to signing on the part of the hearing, it is not surprising if signers should produce their 'best' kind of signing for a hearing investigator. This problem is illustrated by a study of BSL done by Cicourel (1973), who attempted to elicit BSL translations of

English sentences such as 'The bear gives the monkey to the man'. Despite instructions to the informant to sign as she would to a friend at the deaf club, the data he obtained had an English structure, with the order of signs following English word order, and fingerspelling for English words which do not have a single sign translation, such as 'the' and 'to'. Because of the problems arising from elicitations, sign language researchers now tend to avoid using them as the only source of data, and instead to concentrate on the observation of spontaneous sign discourse.

Data collected on the basis of observation is essential in order to check data obtained in other ways, which may not be representative, and in order to give an idea of the full range of variation which, as we have seen, is inherent in any language. It is particularly important for the study of low prestige languages like sign languages, where usage may be inaccurately reported because of awareness of the low status of the language. It is also particularly important for the study of language in a medium unfamiliar to most linguists, since one cannot be sure a priori which categories of visible behaviour will be significant, and which will not. We have already seen that it is unclear whether the sentence is a viable unit of analysis in sign language, and it is only by observation that one can collect data in large chunks, without reference to English, in order to determine what the appropriate units of analysis might be.

It may seem obvious to some that *data collection* by observation of signing in natural situations should be one of the most important kinds of data to obtain, but as Labov (1972a) has pointed out, it is one of the most difficult methods. Some of the problems which it entails can be considered under three main headings: *access to the data*, *the effect on the data of the observer's presence*, and *data recording*.

Access to the data should not be difficult for a deaf signer, who is likely to be a member of the local deaf club. However, since research is not a familiar activity for many deaf people, a deaf researcher will have to explain what he or she is doing and why, in order to avoid being regarded with suspicion and possibly ostracized. A hearing researcher working with a deaf person may be able to obtain access to the data through that person, but otherwise will have to gain access directly. This is not necessarily an easy task, since it involves approaching strangers who are members of a different cultural group, having a different native language. Labov (1972a, p. 110) states that 'The strongest constraints that prevent linguists from utilizing the wealth of linguistic data with which they are surrounded are the barriers against interaction with strangers in one's own culture', so one can assume that the constraints will be correspondingly stronger when the interaction is with members of another culture. Nevertheless, barriers can be overcome with persistence, particularly if one is willing to show serious commitment, for example by attending a deaf club regularly over a certain period of time. One's chances of acceptance in the community may also be enhanced if one is able to present oneself as a 'friend of a friend' to the community (cf Milroy, 1980, for discussion of this approach). It is also useful to have a role which justifies one's presence, particularly if this role is helpful to the community, so that they are receiving something in return for providing research data. As I said earlier, in my case I acted as a volunteer driver, but other possible roles could doubtless be found, according to the needs of the community concerned. Although the deaf club may seem the most obvious place for observation to be carried out and help for the deaf community to be provided, another possibility is in deaf people's homes. Access to these may sometimes be gained through a welfare worker who knows which people would welcome visits, such as elderly or lonely people.

Once access has been obtained to the data one wishes to observe, there is an immediate problem to be resolved: *the effect of the observer's presence on the data.* The presence of someone who is not a member of the deaf community may lead those who are being observed to be particularly conscious of their signing, and possibly to modify it in what they consider to be the appropriate direction. We have already seen (chapter 6) that the type of sign language variety used may vary according to the situation, and that sign varieties approaching the structure of English are used for communication with hearing people and in formal situations. Because of the low status of sign language and negative attitudes towards it on the part of the hearing, deaf people may alter their signing not only when communicating with hearing people, but in the presence of hearing people, especially if they think that they may be being evaluated on the basis of their signing. The effect of the observer's presence on the data will depend partly on his or her obtrusiveness, which may be increased by the use of recording equipment.

The problems of observation are captured by Labov in what he calls the 'Observer's Paradox': 'To obtain the data most important for linguistic theory, we have to observe how people speak when they are not being observed' (Labov, 1972a, p. 113). In order to resolve this paradox, we have to first recognize the potential effect of the observer's presence on the data, and then find ways of minimizing this effect. A lot will depend on the personality of the observer, and the extent to which he or she is able to gain acceptance and trust by the community. However, certain practical guidelines can be followed, such as the importance of allowing as much time as possible for acceptance before introducing recording equipment, and when this is introduced, allowing people to become gradually accustomed to it. If possible, equipment should be left unused for some time, so that people get used to its presence, and it is usually a good idea not to use the first recordings for data in any case. Bright lights should be avoided if possible, as these emphasize the unnaturalness of the situation.

As we have seen, data obtained by observation presents certain problems, some of which are similar to, and some of which are different from the problems arising with intuitions and elicitations. Each method has its limitations and none is ideal alone: while data based on intuition and elicitations have the disadvantage of not being 'natural' and possibly open to influence from English, they have the advantage of being more under the control of the investigator than observational data produced spontaneously. An investigator who is interested in a particular grammatical form or function may find only a few relevant examples in a large quantity of observational data, whereas many more might be produced using another method. This is particularly likely in the investigation of the grammar rather than internal sign structure (phonology), since certain aspects of the grammar depend on what is being said. One cannot investigate negation, for example, if the signer does not wish to express negative meaning, whereas certain aspects of internal sign structure are always present, such as the parameters of place, handshape and movement. The type of data chosen will clearly depend on what is being investigated, but in order to ensure maximum naturalness as well as maximum control on the part of the investigator, a combination of the various types of data seems the most desirable. The intuitions of a deaf signer, or elicitations from a deaf informant, may be a useful way of generating hypotheses which can then be tested by comparing them with data obtained by observation. Data which is obtained from various sources but which is nevertheless similar should inspire a greater degree of confidence than data obtained from one source alone.

A practical problem facing any kind of researcher collecting any kind of data is *how to record the data*. Until the recent techno-logical innovations, researchers investigating language generally had to record their data in the form of notes. However, the invention of the tape recorder and its subsequent development in various forms, including the compact and unobtrusive cassette recorder, has made it possible to keep a more accurate record of spoken language. Visual recording equipment began with the invention of the cine camera, and recently we have seen the introduction of the video recorder, which is becoming more and more sophisticated. Recording onto video tape has several advan-tages over cine film, including the following: instant feedback, so that you can view what you are recording on a monitor while the recording takes place, and immediately afterwards (whereas a cine film has to be processed before you can know if the recording was successful); video cameras on the whole require less extra lighting than cine cameras, though the latter are being modified in this respect; video tape generally has a longer span than cine film; and once the video tape has been produced you can generally locate specific parts of it for viewing more easily than on cine film. However, disadvantages of video tape compared with cine film include the fact that its quality deteriorates more rapidly with use, and that there are often problems with playing a tape on a machine other than that on which it was recorded. As pointed out earlier in this chapter (see p. 179), video standards are not international, and even within the same country there is some incompatibility between machines of different makes, and sometimes even between machines of the same make. However, such technical problems are gradually being overcome as the technological sophi-stication of such equipment increases.

Note-taking still has a place in sign language research, in that it allows unobtrusive data recording by jotting down signs in English glosses or notation (see chapter 3, p. 59 and below), although the quantity of data that can be recorded at one time is limited by memory and one's speed of writing, and the fact that one cannot easily look and write at the same time.

Techniques of 'writing' sign language are important not only for occasional notetaking, but also for the *transcription of data* recorded on film or video-tape. For analysis, it is important to have data in a form that can be easily referred to, and where the units to be analysed are clearly marked. This is likely to be a written system, as in phonetic transcriptions of spoken language, where, according to the type of transcription chosen, information is given about the detailed characteristics of the speech sounds, or merely about those sounds which contrast with one another. Various kinds of phonetic transcriptions are used where the object of interest is the pronunciation or sound system of the language, and ordinary orthography is used, with possibly additional marking for intonation, where the grammar or discourse of the language is the focus of interest. Transcriptions of sign language will vary in a similar way according to the object of the analysis, and will involve difficult decisions about what activity is relevant to this object, e.g. manual or non-manual behaviour. In chapter 3 (p. 52) I mentioned two kinds of transcription used for individual signs: English glosses, conventionally written in capital letters (e.g. BOOK, SIGN), and a notation of individual signs which gives information about the way in which a sign is formed, in particular its place, handshape and movement. As I pointed out, there is no established notation system for the representation of non-manual activity, although it now seems that significant activity is not confined to the hands. Researchers working on different sign languages are either developing systems of notation for non-manual behaviour (e.g. Vogt-Svendsen, 1981) or using a system developed for other purposes, as in the case of American sign language researchers using the Facial Action Coding System (Ekman and Friesen, 1977, cf Stokoe, 1978, p. 72).

In most research on BSL so far, data has been transcribed using English glosses for convenience, despite their limitations (see p. 52), with the use of notation where the formation of the sign is important. Additional information about non-manual behaviour has been added where necessary. Figure 3 is a fairly typical example of transcription of data in an analysis where the possible grammatical function of non-manual behaviour is of interest:

Eyebrows	————————— raised —————————————
Eyes	widened
Manual gloss	NOW GOOD RIDER GOOD a-r REALLY THEY GOOD RIDER

Eyebrows	—— raised ——
Eyes	
Manual gloss	MARVELLOUS f-o-r-m

| Translation: | 'The present riders, are they really good riders, in marvellous form?' |

In an analysis where the phonological structure of individual signs is important, however, notation would be used, as for example in our earlier comparison of Reading and York signs in chapter 6 (p. 131).

One notation system which has not yet been mentioned seems potentially able to represent both manual and non-manual behaviour, and to be useful both for representing the internal structure of signs and for representing sign discourse. This is the 'Sign Writing' system developed by Valerie Sutton (Sutton, 1981) and has various versions, depending on what it is used for. 'Detailed Sign Writing' is used for transcription for research purposes; and then there is 'Sign Writing for Everyday Use', including 'Sign Writing Printing' and 'Sign Writing Handwriting', and finally, 'Sign Writing Shorthand' for 'sign language secretaries' (Sutton, 1981, p. 11). 'Detailed Sign Writing' appears appropriate to represent the formation of signs, since it is based on simplified drawings of head and arm position and handshapes, and of facial expression, with symbols to show types of contact and arrows to show direction of movement. 'Sign Writing for Everyday Use' is a simplified version of 'Detailed Sign Writing', and may prove appropriate for transcriptions of sign discourse where the focus is the grammar. However, although the Sutton system is being well promoted, its use in sign language research does not yet seem to be widespread.

Meanwhile, research reports make considerable use of illustrations, which, despite inadequacies such as poor representation of movement, have the advantage of being clear both to researchers who lack a standard, comprehensive system, and to the uninitiated who have no previous knowledge of either sign language or its transcription.

Summary

In this chapter I have dealt with some of the practical aspects of sign language research. I have suggested that, in the present circumstances, sign language research is ideally done by a team of deaf and hearing researchers using observations of spontaneous signing as their main source of data. I have discussed some of the problems of data collection and how they might be solved, and have given some idea of the types of transcription system available, depending on the purpose of one's research.

9
Conclusion: BSL and linguistic theory

In most of this book the emphasis has been on looking at BSL from a linguist's point of view, and using insights from linguistics to illuminate various aspects of the structure and function of BSL. In conclusion, rather than attempt a summary in the same vein, I shall review the contents of chapters 1–8 in turn, in order to determine, conversely, what insights can be derived from BSL for linguistic theory, by which I mean the theory of language as studied in the discipline of linguistics. I shall refer to BSL specifically as much as possible, but it will be understood that the contribution of research on BSL to the theory of language is partly to be seen in the context of the accumulation of findings from research on various sign languages.

The implications of research on BSL for linguistics are particularly exciting not only because of the nature of the findings themselves, but also because linguists have only recently turned their attention to sign language as a worthy object of investigation for the discipline. During the 1970s, when many publications on ASL by linguists appeared, sign language became established as an area of interest in linguistics, as is shown by the introduction of a section for sign language papers at meetings of the Linguistic Society of America. In Britain, sign language research did not become established until the late 1970s and early 1980s when a few papers on BSL were given at linguistics conferences, but the precedent of ASL meant that British linguists were generally ready to accept BSL as an object of potential interest. Nevertheless, the interest of British linguists not actually working on BSL has generally been to see how far existing concepts of linguistics can be applied to BSL, rather than to consider how the nature of BSL might lead to the re-examination of certain linguistic concepts. In the USA, however, there is some consideration of sign language in the second edition of a widely used American textbook for introductory courses on language and linguistics (Fromkin and Rodman, 1978), and an innovative textbook (Baron, 1981) looks at language from the point of view of its representation of reality, comparing speech, writing and sign. The potential interest of BSL for students of linguistics is not presented in any comparable British textbook, possibly because there have been fewer researchers working on BSL than on ASL, and the results of their work have not been widely disseminated. In what follows I shall suggest some of the implications for linguistics that may arise from this book.

Implication (1): *Language is not as arbitrary as we think.* In chapter 1, I tried to give an idea of what BSL is like by answering questions that I have often been asked about it. Linguists have asked me the same questions as anyone else, but they tend to pursue with the most enthusiasm questions (3) and (4): 'Is BSL iconic?' and 'Is BSL a language?' These two questions are related particularly clearly for linguists in that the presence of iconicity is assumed to imply absence of arbitrariness, and arbitrariness is considered in twentieth century linguistics to be one of the most important structural properties of language. So if BSL is iconic, the argument might go, it cannot be a language. However, as we saw in chapter 1, BSL has arbitrary as well as iconic aspects, and although some degree of arbitrariness may be important for the flexibility and versatility of languages, as Lyons (1981) suggests, there seems no reason to suggest that some degree of iconicity will interfere with this. In any case, as I said, some linguists have pointed out that even spoken language is not actually as arbitrary as was previously thought. Wescott (1971) has suggested that certain sounds are iconic in English in that they evoke common meanings, such as 'smallness' for high front vowels like that in 'little', and 'bigness' for low back vowels such as that in 'lot'. It is debatable to what extent one can discern 'similarity' (as required by the definition of iconicity on p. 11) between such sounds and what they represent, and Bolinger (1980) suggests that there is more iconicity in units larger than the individual sound, arguing that 'The smaller the unit, the greater the arbitrariness, as a rule' (Bolinger, 1980, p. 19). He suggests that there is iconicity above the level of the word, for example, in the placing side by side of two names referring to people who have done an action together, as in 'Jane and John came into the room', where the placing of the words 'Jane' and 'John' next to one another (separated only by 'and', which arbitrarily links them) can be related to the spatial closeness of John and Jane entering a room together.

Implication (2): *Conventionality in language may be more important than arbitrariness.* As we saw in chapter 1, not only may iconicity and arbitrariness in a language be complementary, but the two properties may co-exist with a further property, conventionality. Both arbitrary and iconic signs have the property of conventionality in that they are shared by the signing community. So one lesson we might learn for linguistics is that conventionality may be a more important criterial property of language than arbitrariness. Although Saussure (whose lectures were first published in 1915) is credited with introducing the current emphasis on the arbitrary nature of the linguistic sign (Saussure used 'sign' to refer to the relationship between form and meaning: cf chapter 1, p. 19), a close reading of his *Course in General Linguistics* shows that Saussure was well aware of the importance of conventionality in language, and he in fact stated that 'every means of expression used in society is based, in prin- ciple, on collective behavior or – what amounts to the same thing – on convention' (Saussure, 1959, p. 68). Baron (1981) argues that the issue of conventionality, or the extent to which language is shared between people, has much greater implications for the study of language than does arbitrariness. She says that 'we might decide to abandon the notion of arbitrariness altogether as a design feature of human language without changing our concep- tion of language itself or of the fundamental ways in which we analyze language' (Baron, 1981, p. 10).

Some support for this view is found in the writings of some of those working in the field of semiotics (an area concerned with meaning and communication in general, cf Crystal, 1980a, p. 317), both contemporary with Saussure and also following him. Peirce (1932), defining the sign as 'something which stands for somebody or something in some respect or capacity' (Hartshorne and Weiss, 1932, Vol. II, p. 135), divided signs into icons, indices, and symbols, and although I said on p. 13 that his category 'symbol' was equivalent to our category of arbitrary signs, his criterion for the symbol is its conventionality in the sense of it being part of shared knowledge, rather than its arbitrariness. He describes a symbol as 'a sign which is constituted a sign merely or mainly by the fact that it is used and understood as such' (Peirce, 1932, vol. II, p. 172). Peirce appears to include in his category of symbol those signs which are iconic, as long as they are conventional. Eco (1976), writing more recently, suggests that iconic signs are 'culturally coded', which we may interpret as saying that they too are based on convention. This is in line with our argument in chapter 1, p. 16.

The importance of conventionality in a language appears again in the writings of another semiotician, Charles Morris (1946), particularly in his definition of a language. Morris gives five criteria for a language, as follows: (1) it is composed of a set of signs; (2) each sign has a meaning common to a number of people; (3) these signs can be produced by the same people who understand them, with the same meaning in production as in comprehension; (4) signs have roughly the same meaning in different situations; and (5) 'the signs in a language must constitute a system of interconnected signs combinable in some ways and not in others in order to form a variety of complex sign-processes' (Morris, 1946, pp. 35–6), which can be interpreted as meaning that a language has a grammar. These criteria amount to a definition of a language as consisting of a shared vocabulary combined according to shared rules in a particular community. What is emphasized here is the shared meaning and use of language, the only reference to structural properties being that there must be a grammar.

An emphasis on conventionality in language rather than on arbitrariness is an emphasis on the social function of language rather than its structural properties. For while arbitrariness concerns the relation between signs and what they refer to, conventionality refers to relations between people in the language community. (I am grateful to Trevor Pateman for pointing this out to me.) The social function of language has been somewhat neglected in modern Chomskyan linguistics, but is difficult to neglect in the study of sign language. This may be partly because linguists' interest in sign language derives from the fact that it appears to *function* as a language, even though its *structure* appears superficially so different from spoken languages. As I suggested at the end of chapter 1, it is likely to be more fruitful to study the structure of BSL in relation to its function than in relation to the structure of spoken languages. If a functional approach cannot be ignored in the study of sign language, then we ought perhaps to pay more attention to such an approach in the study of spoken language also, as some linguists (cf Halliday, 1973, 1978, Givón, 1979a, Baron, 1981) have suggested.

Implication (3): *Linguistics can affect the status of a language.* Since chapter 2 dealt with the historical and social conditions under which BSL developed, and not with a linguistic analysis of BSL, one might not expect to find many implications for the discipline of linguistics there. However, one may draw some tentative conclusions about the way in which linguistics as a discipline can have an effect on the status of a language. I suggested on p. 30 that the difference between the British and French attitudes to sign language in the eighteenth century could be partly attributed to the stronger effect of the new intellectual climate on attitudes in France.

We then saw that, in the nineteenth century, attitudes to sign language became generally negative all over Europe, culminating in the decision at the international conference in Milan in 1880, that the oral method was to be preferred in deaf education. It is interesting to note that in linguistics in the nineteenth century, the emphasis was on the historical development of languages, particularly the Indo-European family, and on tracing this with reference to ancient languages such as Sanskrit and Greek. In the late nineteenth century the emphasis was particularly on sound change, about which the 'Neogrammarians' produced new ideas (see Robins, 1967). With this interest in the history of languages that could be traced back to ancient times, and the focus on sound change, it is not surprising if linguists paid no attention to sign language, which had little recorded history and which did not use the medium of sound. So the conference at Milan would not have had the benefit of any expert opinion from linguistic studies of sign language in taking its decisions, and its focus on speech may in fact have been further influenced by the work of Alexander Graham Bell, who was active in the mid nineteenth century in promoting his father's *Visible Speech*, a system which could be used in teaching speech to the deaf. In 1880, when he won the Volta prize for inventing the telephone, he used the prize money to set up the Volta laboratory and then the Volta Bureau, which became the headquarters of the American Association for Teaching Speech to the Deaf (Bruce, 1973). So Bell's work and the interests of linguists may well have conspired to link deafness and speech to the exclusion of sign language.

While it seems that linguistics may have had a negative effect on sign language in the nineteenth century, I argued in chapter 2 that it had had a positive effect in the late 1970s, with the common use of the term 'BSL' by deaf people following its use in linguistics. Linguistic research on BSL has not only given more confidence to the deaf community in asserting itself, as I suggested, but it has also provided information for those making policy decisions in deaf education, who previously had to rely on inaccurate stereotypes about the nature of sign language. So we can see that there are two types of practical consequences that can arise from sign language research: the possibly unplanned effect which research can have on the status of a language in general, and the planned application of the results of the research. In linguistics the second category is usually termed 'applied linguistics', which in the form of teaching English as a foreign language, speech therapy or language planning (cf Rubin and Jernudd, 1971) is often used as a practical justification for linguistics. The first category, however, the unplanned effect of research, is often not recognized by researchers themselves, who claim to be doing value-free research and not to be interested in political goals. However, it clearly is recognized by those who feel threatened by the results of such research, and explains why those working on minority languages in general are sometimes seen as political radicals. In his article on linguistic methodology, Labov (1972a, p. 105) expresses the idea of research as a value-free, neutral activity when he says 'that our descriptions should apply to the language which was spoken before we arrive and will still be spoken after we leave'. (However, see Labov, 1982, for a modification of this view.) In having an effect on the status of a language, as I suggested happened with BSL, linguistic research is likely to have an indirect effect both on the function and the structure of that language. Linguists must recognize that Labov's (1972a) goal is an impossible one, and that just as language has a social and political context, so does linguistics.

Implication (4): *Phonology is not restricted to spoken languages.* In chapter 3 we began our structural analysis of BSL, at the level of the individual sign, and saw how 'phonological' analysis could be applied to a language in a visual medium. Despite the normal association of the word 'phonology' with sound, we saw how BSL could be said to have a phonology in that one can postulate units below the level of the sign. These units can be compared to phonemes of spoken language in that they can be shown to function contrastively, distinguishing one sign from another. It is interesting from the point of view of linguistic theory that the notion of phonology, in the sense of abstract organisation below the level of the sign or word, is applicable to a language whether its concrete medium is visual or oral. However, beyond the general statement that there are sub-lexical units (units below the level of the word or sign) in both spoken and sign language, it is not clear to what extent we can expect parallelism in the details of phonological structure in languages of the two kinds, or to what extent phonological structure is constrained by the physical medium.

I suggested that the sub-lexical units of sign language, 'cheremes' in Stokoe's terminology, could be compared to the phonemes of spoken language, because of their significance in distinguishing signs from one another. However, I also noted that while we perceive phonemes as sequential, cheremes (tab, dez and sig) are simultaneous. The fact that linguists are used to the term 'phoneme' referring to sequential units may make them unwilling to accept that simultaneous 'cheremes' might be parallel to phonemes, even if they have a similar contrastive function. Some have in fact suggested that the simultaneity of cheremes makes them more similar to the phonetic features of place and manner of articulation in consonants, or to distinctive features (see chapter 3, p. 51 and chapter 5, p. 110), which may have similar labels to phonetic features. So to illustrate this argument with an example, it might be said that just as the sign, I (see p. 54), is made with an index finger touching (manner) the chest (place), so the consonant [m] is made by releasing air through the nasal cavity (manner) while a closure is made at the lips. The consonant [m] appears to have simultaneous or co-occurring features of place and manner just like the simultaneous features of place, manner and handshape in the sign I. However, the sound [m] alone does not have a similar function in the language to the sign I, which is a meaningful unit comparable to a word in spoken language.

In any case, arguing that cheremes are equivalent to phonetic or distinctive features assumes that cheremes cannot themselves be analysed as made up of distinctive features. This is not the case, since we saw in chapter 5 (p. 110) that some researchers working on ASL have proposed distinctive features for the handshape or dez in particular. This provides support for the argument that cheremes are equivalent to phonemes, the only difference being that while cheremes both combine with other cheremes simultaneously and are themselves made up of simultaneous features, phonemes combine with other phonemes sequentially, although they are themselves also made up of simultaneous features. (This is over-simplifying somewhat, given the controversial status of the phonemes and the fact that analysis in terms of distinctive features is usually seen as an alternative to analysis in terms of phonemes. However, the simplification is necessary in order to clarify the difference between the possible phonological units in sign and spoken language.)

The fact that the notion of phonology can be applied to sign language suggests that the existence of abstract organizing principles below the level of the word or sign is independent of the medium in which they are manifested. It would be easy to attribute any difference we find between the phonology of spoken and sign languages to their difference of medium, but we should also consider the possibility of using the findings from research in sign language to throw new light on spoken language, particularly its simultaneous aspects (see below).

Implication (5): *We should pay more attention to simultaneity in language.* A particularly salient aspect of sign language which we can 'explain away' by attributing it to the visual medium, but which might also be used to enrich linguistic theory, is the apparently extensive use of simultaneity. This can be useful to linguistic theory in two ways: it can encourage the investigation of parallel phenomena in spoken language, and it can lead us to be more precise about exactly what we mean by simultaneity and its converse, sequentiality. We have seen that there is simultaneity in spoken language below the level of the individual sound, if this is analysed in terms of simultaneously occurring features. In addition, as had been known for a long time before linguists became interested in sign language, prosodic aspects of spoken language such as stress and intonation, and tone in languages such as Chinese, can be said to occur simultaneously with the more sequential aspects of speech. So in spoken French for example, it is often intonation alone which distinguishes statements from questions. So the sentence 'Vouz avez du pain' will be transcribed with the same (sequential) phonetic symbols [vuz ave dy pɛ̃] regardless of its intonation, which, occurring simultaneously with the phonetic segments, will differ according to whether a statement or a question is intended. Those simultaneous or prosodic aspects of speech are sometimes not considered part of the central core of the language (see later in this chapter, p. 203) but this view might be reconsidered in the light of the finding that simultaneous aspects certainly play a central role in the phonology of sign language. (See Firth, 1957, for his conception of prosodies and Coates, 1980, for a model of phonology which is based on time-related features rather than on sequential segments.)

Another potential benefit of the salience of simultaneity in sign language is that it can lead to greater precision in establishing what simultaneity and sequentiality are. They may in fact turn out to be relative, rather than absolute characteristics in both speech and sign language. Levelt (1980), while acknowledging that 'the visual mode allows for larger degrees of simultaneity than the auditory mode' (Levelt, 1980, p. 143), mentions the finding by Grosjean, Teuber and Lane (1979) that components of signs in ASL are not actually completely simultaneous, but that they occur in the order of orientation and location first, followed by handshape, followed by movement. Levelt also points out the essentially temporal nature of movement in comparison with the other components. In speech, on the other hand, there is some acoustic evidence which blurs the notion of sequentiality: for example, plosive consonants like [p] and [t] tend to be recognized according to the acoustic characteristics of the vowels that precede or follow them (see e.g. O'Connor, 1973, p. 104, Fant, 1968).

Levelt (1980) also suggests that in a discussion of simultaneity and sequentiality (which he calls 'successivity') one must distinguish between the signal and the process, since information which is presented simultaneously might be processed sequentially, or vice versa. Levelt suggests that at the word and sign level, the sign has more information presented simultaneously than the word, but he argues that 'the recognition process for both word and sign is largely sequential in character: different components of information are successively taken into consideration' (Levelt, 1980, p. 145). This claim is supported by several psycholinguistic experiments, although evidence from only one on sign language (Grosjean, Teuber and Lane, 1979) is available. More research on the perception of sign language is clearly needed, but meanwhile Levelt's distinction between signal and process raises the question of psychological reality. Linguists disagree regarding the extent to which their analyses should mirror psychological processes, or to what extent they should be purely abstract (see Katz, 1981, for a discussion of this issue). If phonology in sign and spoken language turns out to be distinct at the level of the signal (and does this mean the physical signal, or the linguist's analysis of it?), but similar at the level of psychological processes, does this mean that phonological descriptions should have psychological reality, in order to pinpoint the similarity between speech and sign language? The decision made on this issue will probably be determined by the investigator's assumptions about the nature of language, either as an abstract object independent of the speaker/signer or as in some way part of the mind, but this example of sign and spoken language serves to remind us that different assumptions will determine different analyses, and ultimately, different explanations for the nature of language.

The salience of simultaneity in sign language (at least at the level of the signal, see above) is apparent again in chapter 4, on the level of the grammar of BSL. At the beginning of chapter 4 I suggested that if one looks at sign language through the framework of spoken language, expecting grammatical categories to be realized sequentially rather than simultaneously, we may be disappointed. The lack of sequential inflections in ASL and BSL may have led people to make statements like 'sign language has no grammar' before linguistic research on sign language started. The early linguistic researchers working on ASL seem to have accepted the idea that it had no inflections because there were no sequential ones. However, they did not think that this made sign language ungrammatical, because they knew that some languages do not make extensive use of inflections in their grammars, Chinese being one of the more obvious examples. However, since they also knew that in languages that do not have inflections, word order is often a way of indicating case relations, they were perhaps unduly concerned with the role of sign order in ASL (cf chapter 5, p. 127). The influence of what they knew about spoken language still led them to concentrate on the temporal (sequential) dimension rather than the spatial (simultaneous) dimension of sign language.

Implication (6): *Simultaneity may lead us to revise our view of morphological typology.* It was probably as a result of the work of Klima and Bellugi (1979) and their focus on the spatial dimension in ASL that the term 'inflection' began to be widely used with reference to sign language. They discovered that movement, one of the simultaneous parameters of signs, could be modified to represent a change in meaning. At first they called such modifications 'modulations', since they were not sure of their grammatical status (cf Klima and Bellugi, 1979, p. 395), but later used the terms 'inflectional' and 'morphological processes' to refer to regular modifications of movement which marked distinctions within grammatical categories such as deixis, number and aspect. As we saw in chapter 4, similar inflections have been found in BSL, again in the spatial dimension, involving movement and sometimes handshape, to indicate case, aspect, and negation in verbs, and plurality in nouns, for example.

As I said in chapter 4, Klima and Bellugi (1979, pp. 272–3) argue on the basis of their findings that ASL is somewhat akin to Latin, which is known as a language of the 'inflecting type'. The parallel with Latin is not carried further than this mere suggestion, but it is worth considering to what extent this is a reasonable parallel, since the simultaneity of inflections in sign language may have implications for the traditional classification of languages according to their morphological type. In a useful discussion of morphological typology, Comrie (1981, p. 39) says that the three 'canonical types of language' established in the nineteenth century were 'isolating', 'agglutinating' and 'fusional'. Isolating languages have no morphological variation, so there is no change of form to indicate grammatical category, and no change in verb form to indicate tense, for example. Agglutinating languages do have morphological variation, but change in form involves the addition of clearly identifiable inflections, each having a separate function. So in Turkish plural nouns, as Comrie shows, the plural inflection is placed before the case inflection, each being separately identifiable. Fusional languages also have inflections, but their functions cannot always be separately identified. In Latin, for example, the genitive plural inflection '-orum' in 'dominorum' ('dominus' means 'lord') indicates both genitive and plural, but the two are not separately marked as '-or' and '-um', for example, since they do not occur regularly in other cases as markers of genitive and plural, respectively. Latin thus belongs to the category of 'fusional' languages, which is in fact another name for what Klima and Bellugi called 'inflecting' languages. Their term is confusing, though, because as Comrie points out, both agglutinating and fusional languages have inflections; there is just a difference between the categories as to whether there is a one to one relation between an inflection and the grammatical category it marks.

So if ASL and BSL have inflections, do they belong to the category of agglutinating or fusional languages? In the discussion of inflections in BSL in chapter 4, there is certainly some evidence for a one to one relation between inflection and grammatical category: for example, repetition in nouns indicates plurality, slow repetition in verbs indicates iterative aspect, while fast repetition indicates durative aspect (for a state or process), or habitual aspect (for an event). Examples with multiple inflections are needed as conclusive evidence of this one to one relation, but must await further research in BSL. Meanwhile we may note that Klima and Bellugi (1979) have established that multiple inflections are found in ASL, and that they can be broken down into separate components analytically, even though they have a global effect on the movement perceptually, occurring simultaneously with it. Klima and Bellugi (1979, p. 300) say:

> The inflectional processes are distinguished from one another exclusively by differences in the global movement changes they impose on classes of uninflected signs. One inflectional process imposes a rapid lax single elongated movement; another inflectional process imposes a smooth circular lax continuous movement; still another imposes a tense iterated movement. Each inflectional process has its own specific properties of movement dimension by which it operates.

So are BSL and ASL therefore agglutinating rather than fusional languages? This is where the issue of simultaneity becomes significant, since although the inflectional processes can be analytically separated, they are clearly not separate in time in a way true of spoken agglutinating languages. Following Levelt (1980) we might wish to argue that processing is likely to be sequential even if there is simultaneity in the signal, but this does not answer the question as to whether the segmentability of inflections required to identify a language as agglutinating is dependent on sequentiality in time.

Allowing simultaneity as an alternative to sequentiality of inflections would be one way of accommodating sign languages within the traditional morphological typology, but this might have far-reaching implications for spoken language, since simultaneous aspects of speech would then potentially qualify as separate inflections. According to Hyman (1975, p. 214), in some languages, 'tone serves to mark different verb tenses, possession and even negation', so could such languages be considered possible candidates for the agglutinating type? The question of morphological typology is just one of the issues in linguistic theory on which simultaneity in sign language may have some bearing.

Implication (7): *The notion of the 'core' of language needs to be re-examined*. One important simultaneous aspect of sign language that we discussed in chapter 4 was the co-occurrence of non-manual behaviour with manual signing for marking processes such as negation and questions. Although little is yet known about this, I also suggested in chapter 3 (p. 75) that non-manual activity might also function at the level of the individual sign, to distinguish one sign from another. So it may be significant at several levels of the language, although research has mainly concentrated on the activity of the hands, assuming that that was the 'core' of the language with non-manual behaviour providing extra but non-essential (non-propositional) information, in a similar way to what is commonly understood as the 'non-verbal' behaviour of spoken language. (Explicit parallels have actually been drawn between the manual component of sign language and 'verbal' behaviour, and the non-manual component and 'non-verbal' behaviour.) We do not yet know enough about the function of non-manual behaviour in sign language, such as to what extent it is obligatory, providing information that no other channel provides, and to what extent it is redundant in the sense of providing extra information (although this presupposes that there is another channel providing 'central' information, and so risks begging the question). However, evidence so far suggests that at least some non-manual behaviour has a function in the language directly comparable to that of manual behaviour. This not only forces us to revise our view of manual behaviour as necessarily central, but in depriving us of a rough and ready comparison with our stereotypes of verbal and non-verbal behaviour in language in general, we may be led to review these ourselves, and to reconsider the traditional view that the 'core' of spoken language is the segmental, sequential speech signal. It may lead us to review the traditional view that intonation, for example, is outside grammar (but see Crystal, 1969, for discussion of this question), since intonation can distinguish statements from questions in some languages in a way similar to that in which eyebrow movement works in BSL. It may also lead us beyond the 'prosodic' component of language (to which intonation belongs) to what is sometimes called the 'paralinguistic' component (cf Lyons, 1972), including non-vocal movement such as gestures and facial expressions. Linguists are gradually beginning to take more of an interest in what is traditionally known as 'non-verbal communication', and to realize that linguistic functions might be fulfilled by non-vocal behaviour to some extent. An obvious example is in deixis, where 'you' (singular) can be distinguished from 'you' (plural) in a face-to-face situation by gazing or pointing in the direction of the individual concerned. I have heard it suggested (Karmiloff-Smith, personal communication) that it would be actually ungrammatical to point at the wrong object in connection with 'this' and 'that' (e.g. to say 'I want *this* book' while pointing at a pen), and it has also been observed that priority is assigned to non-verbal behaviour when it contradicts verbal behaviour. An example of this would be where a nudge or a wink indicates a lie, or where facial expression (and perhaps also intonation) indicate approval while one's words express disapproval (as in 'You're a naughty boy', accompanied by a smile in addressing a child). All this indicates that notions of what is 'central' and what is 'peripheral' in language need to be re-evaluated in the light of the functions fulfilled by each activity, regardless of the channel in which the activity occurs. We may actually want to dispense with a distinction between central and peripheral aspects of language, since such a distinction involves both acknowledging a central *function* of language, usually (erroneously in my view) the propositional or referential (cf chapter 1 p. 23), and also looking for certain aspects of structure which one assumes to be central.

Implication (8): *Sign languages may be examples of creoles.* In chapter 5 I compared the structure of BSL and ASL at two levels, those of phonology and grammar. In the first chapter of this book I claimed that sign language is not universal or 'international' and that BSL and ASL, for example, are different from one another, so the findings presented in chapter 5 provide a way of testing that claim. Some similarities and some differences were found. At the level of phonology, there were more differences in the phonological inventory (list of tabs, dezes and sigs) than in phonological constraints and processes. One might suggest as an explanation for this, that whereas the selection of elements for an inventory may be somewhat arbitrary (except that one might expect the unmarked or neutral handshapes to be present in both languages, which they are), constraints and processes might be determined by universal or 'natural' factors based on the production and perception of motor movements by the human body. At the level of grammar, the similarity was even more striking. Not only do certain ASL verbs have the properties of directionality and reversibility as found in BSL, but they apply to a very similar semantic set of verbs. Negative incorporation applies to a similar set of verbs in the two languages also, even though GOOD, HAVE, KNOW etc. are formationally different in BSL and ASL. Non-manual activity appears to fulfil some of the same functions in ASL and BSL, although there are differences of detail. Deixis of person and time are fairly similar, and aspect is a salient grammatical category in both languages, marked by modification of movement, although different distinctions seem to be marked in different ways.

How should we interpret this relative similarity of grammar in the two languages compared with relative difference of phonology and vocabulary? Four possible factors which could be taken to explain this were mentioned at the end of the chapter: the influence of English on both ASL and BSL, the constraints of the visual medium, historical relations, and language contact. To these a fifth could be added in the light of the discussion in chapter 6, that both ASL and BSL are creoles and share the grammatical structure which is typical of creoles.

I suggested in chapter 5 that the influence of English was not actually a significant factor, and the fact that the grammars of BSL and ASL appear so similar to one another, and yet so different from English, seems to bear this out. The constraints of the visual medium cannot be ruled out as a significant factor until more research has been done on other sign languages. While the visual medium certainly makes non-manual activity available as a channel in any sign language, it is not so obvious how it accounts for example, for the existence of negative incorporation in both languages, applying to almost exactly the same set of verbs. A historical relationship is generally not thought to link ASL and BSL (cf Stokoe, 1973), but there is actually very little evidence. Language contact seems more plausible as an explanation. If ASL and BSL were not directly in contact, they might have been linked indirectly through both having some contact with French Sign Language. This would at least account for the similar pattern of negative incorporation in the three languages, which we mentioned on p. 118. Studies of language contact show that it is possible for languages to influence one another in their grammatical structure while remaining distinct in their lexicon and phonology. In studies of pidgins and creoles, it is suggested that it is possible for one pidgin or creole to develop from another by adopting the other language's syntactic structure and substituting new lexical items. This is known as 'relexification'. Gumperz and Wilson (1971) have shown that contact between languages which are not normally considered pidgins or creoles can also lead to a similarity in the grammars of the languages while their vocabularies remain distinct. So following the pidgin/creole relexification approach, we could argue that ASL and BSL may have developed at least partially by relexification of the grammatical structure of French Sign Language (FSL). Alternatively, following the approach of contact between pre-existing languages as in Gumperz and Wilson (1971), we might argue that ASL and BSL have converged in their grammatical structure through contact between signers of both languages. The second suggestion seems less likely, in that there has only been contact between American and British deaf signers relatively recently, and in only small numbers.

However, the other suggestion, of contact between the two languages and FSL does seem feasible, given the geographical closeness of France and Britain (and the fact that Epée's system was finally used in Britain to some extent in the nineteenth century), and given our knowledge of the contact between French and American deaf educators (see chapter 2, p. 32).

Indirect contact between ASL and BSL might be a partial explanation for similarity in the grammars of both, but a further possible explanation, as suggested above, is that they might both be creoles, and this would account for the similarity in their grammars, whether or not they had had contact with one another. We have seen that BSL might be considered a creole both on the basis of its structure (see chapter 6) and because of the social conditions under which it is acquired and used (see chapters 7 and 6). As we saw in chapter 6 also, Fischer (1978) has suggested that ASL might be a creole too. If BSL and ASL are creoles, and creoles are similar in their grammars, we might still want to know *why* creoles should be similar in their grammars. While one explanation found in the pidgin/creole literature is 'monogenesis', or the idea that all creoles have the same historical origin, this does not seem to apply readily to sign languages. An alternative explanation would be Bickerton's (1981): he suggested that human beings are equipped with a 'bioprogram' which determines the form language can take. Creoles, he suggests, because of their relative newness, and the relative lack of exposure to external influences on their structure are likely to be closer to the form determined by the bioprogram than other languages, which have been subject to cultural and processing factors in their development. He suggests that the nature of the bioprogram accounts for the structural similarities in creoles. Bickerton's hypothesis is controversial, but its plausibility in accounting for the similarities between ASL and BSL, assuming they are creoles, is an indication of how sign language research can contribute to important debates in linguistic theory.

Bickerton's theory challenges the widely accepted dogma in linguistics that all languages are equal, and that so-called 'primitive' languages do not exist. His and other pidgin/creole studies suggest that languages can actually be at different stages of development. Givón (1979b) supports this notion in the distinction he makes between what he calls the 'pragmatic' versus 'syntactic mode' in languages. He suggests that certain languages or language varieties are characterized by the 'pragmatic' mode with a topic-comment structure (among other characteristics) while others are characterized by a 'syntactic mode' with subject-predicate structure. He argues that while pidgin, child language and informal language have the 'pragmatic mode', the 'syntactic mode' is found in creole, adult language and formal language. (He admits, however, that creole may have more topic-comment type structures than 'normal' language, so it might be more appropriate to ascribe the pragmatic mode to pidgin/creoles, and the syntactic mode to 'post-creole' or 'normal' languages.) We saw in chapter 5 that structures in both ASL and BSL appear to be easily analysed in terms of topic-comment: this would identify the 'pragmatic mode' in Givón's terms. Since Givón (1979b) also argues that languages go through historical cycles, in which topics can become subjects in a process of 'syntacticization', we might infer that the structure of BSL and ASL can be partly attributed to their early stage of development. If they are in fact creoles, as I have suggested, this would give some weight to Givón's schema.

Implication (9): *Agency may be more central to the notion of subject than topicality.* The discussion in chapter 5 of topic and subject as found in BSL and ASL can also contribute to the debate in linguistic theory as to what the criterial properties of a subject are. My proposal that topics are coded temporally, mostly in noun signs, while subjects are coded spatially in pronouns (see p. 128) can be shown to provide some support for Comrie's (1981) view of the notion of subject as the intersection of agent and topic. Comrie (1981, p. 101) suggests that 'the prototype of subject represents the intersection of agent and topic. i.e. the clearest instances of subjects, crosslinguistically, are agents which are also topics'. This implies that the subject in a language will be less easy to identify (less 'prominent' in Li and Thompson's (1976) terms) where the agent and topic do not coincide. This is clearly the situation in ASL and BSL, where agency is only marked in pronouns incorporated into verbs allowing modification of their movement, and pronouns are not generally topics. In suggesting (on p. 128) that noun signs are likely to be topics while pronouns can be subjects, I have in fact assigned the role of subject to the agent. In view of the syntactic function of the subject identified by Li and Thompson (1976) and others, while the topic is found to have more of a discourse or 'pragmatic' function, it seems correct to assign subject to the agent pronoun in ASL and BSL since this, unlike the topic, is an argument of, and governed by, the verb. This analysis of BSL and ASL might be used to support the idea that agency is more central to the notion of subject than topicality: this is certainly implied by Comrie's more detailed discussion of the correlation between subject and agent properties than of that between subject and topic.

Implication (10): *Spoken and sign languages share fundamental characteristics.* I emphasized at the end of chapter 5 that languages not only change, but also vary, and this is the theme of chapter 6. Approaches that have been used in the study of variation in spoken language were found to be useful for the study of sign language, and the fact that sign language shares the 'inherent variability' of other languages provides further support for the idea that it is similar to spoken languages in its fundamental characteristics. We saw in this chapter how BSL appeared to be creole-like in its structure, and as I suggested earlier (p. 207), the fact that a sign language shares many of the structural characteristics of spoken creoles despite the potential interference factor of the visual medium, gives some support to Bickerton's (1981) contention that the shape of language may be predicted by a human 'bioprogram'.

Some further support for Bickerton's notion of a 'bioprogram' was provided in chapter 7, where it was shown from research on sign language acquisition that children appear to be able to acquire sign language with incomplete linguistic input, or even in the total absence of input. So if language is not available, children seem to invent it, and to create a creole in the process. Sign language acquisition was shown to be unusual not only in the varying quantity and quality of linguistic input, but also in the times at which it is acquired. Only a minority of deaf children are exposed to a language from birth, but those who are appear to follow stages very similar to those in spoken language acquisition, which again suggests that sign language is structurally and functionally comparable to any other language. The main difference was that sign language acquisition began earlier than spoken language, possibly because of its mode of production. Studies of language acquisition in a visual medium can also be linked to studies of early 'non-verbal communication', which suggest that the beginnings of language are actually non-vocal, and that we should not automatically equate 'non-vocal' with 'non-linguistic'. Like the studies of the importance of non-manual activity in sign language structure mentioned earlier, sign language acquisition studies should lead us to re-examine categories such as 'verbal' and 'non-verbal'.

Implication (11): *Research on sign language acquisition may throw light on the link between brain lateralization and language acquisition.* As we saw in chapter 7, the majority of deaf children acquire sign language later than is normal for spoken language, from the point at which they enter a school for the deaf, or even later, in early adulthood. Research on BSL acquisition at various stages could throw light on the question of whether there is a critical period for language learning, and also on the controversial question of whether this is related to lateralization of the brain with respect to language functions. Lenneberg (1967) suggested that the end of the critical period would coincide with the completion of lateralization, whereby the left hemisphere would normally be established as dominant for language function. However, Krashen and Harshman (1972) provide evidence that lateralization is actually completed by the age of five, and Krashen (1973, p. 69) concludes that 'the development of lateralization may represent the acquisition of an ability rather than the loss of an ability'. In any case, as Krashen (1973) points out, the case of Genie (see Curtiss, 1977) shows that some first language acquisition is possible after the 'critical period', though in Genie's case this seemed to involve the right hemisphere rather than the left. We are not sure to what extent lateralization is different for signed and spoken languages (see Poizner and Battison, 1980, and Kimura, 1981, for discussions of cerebral asymmetry and sign language). Nevertheless, any evidence for or against a critical period in spoken and sign language acquisition could be compared with the extent to which lateralization appears to be similar in the two types of language. This should help to determine whether or not there is actually a link between language acquisition and lateralization.

Implication (12): *Children may create their own language.* As we have seen, many deaf children do not learn sign language until they go to school, which is later than the normal age for first language acquisition. Apart from this, there are two other unusual features of sign language acquisition: (a) the children learn from their peers, and (b) only about 10 per cent of their peers are likely to have learned sign language from their own parents. There is evidence in the study of spoken language acquisition that peers play a part in the process, for example brothers and sisters, who are found to modify their speech in what they consider an appropriate manner (cf Snow and Ferguson, 1977, Andersen and Johnson, 1973) and it is also known that children tend to aim to speak like their peers rather than their parents (cf Labov, n.d.). However, in these cases peer input is additional to adult linguistic input, rather than being the sole source. The only situation in spoken language learning where a child might be expected to rely almost entirely on peer input would be when learning a second language, as when their parents' language is not the language of the spoken community. Even in this case (which anyway is a second language situation) the children would have some input from adults in the community such as teachers, whereas deaf children of hearing parents very rarely come into contact with deaf adults until they leave school (since there are very few deaf teachers). So not only do many deaf children learn sign language from their peers, but as we have seen, only a few of their peers will have had contact with the adult language system. So, as in the case of the younger children in the study by Feldman et al. (1978), they probably create their own language to a great extent, perhaps producing a creole. We have almost no research evidence from sign language acquisition in schools, but the apparently normal acquisition of a language under such abnormal conditions does seem to provide some evidence for the idea that there is an innate language capacity or 'bioprogram' in human beings.

Implication (13): *Ignoring data collection problems narrows the basis of linguistic theory.* In chapter 8 we looked at the practical problems of doing sign language research, in particular, data collection and transcription. Even such practical choices have theoretical implications that are currently ignored in mainstream linguistics. Many introductory textbooks do not even mention problems of data collection, and one which does (Lyons, 1981, p. 45) expresses a somewhat ambivalent attitude to such problems:

> There are in fact quite serious methodological problems atta-
> ching to the collection of reliable data for a whole range of
> issues in theoretical linguistics. But they are no more serious
> than the methodological problems that confront those working
> in psychology, sociology or the social sciences in general. And
> in certain respects the linguist is better off than most social
> scientists, since it is fairly clear how much of what is observable
> is language-behaviour and how much is not. Furthermore, there
> are very considerable areas, in the description of any language,
> for which the reliability of the native speaker's intuitions, and
> even of the linguist's introspections, is not a serious problem.
> One must not make too much, therefore, of the methodological
> problems that arise in the course of linguistic research.

I would interpret this as meaning that we need not worry about data collection as much as our colleagues in other social sciences, since at least we are able to distinguish between data and non-data; and anyway, data collection in the normal sense can be avoided to a great extent, since we can rely on intuitions. As I hope the discussion in chapter 8 showed, I would question the assumption that linguists have the two advantages mentioned: being sure of the boundaries round their object of investigation; and being able to rely on intuitions. We saw the difficulty of using intuitions in sign language research, especially if the researcher is not a native signer; we saw also that data transcription involves difficult decisions about what activity is significant (e.g. manual versus non-manual). A non-native signer would also have problems in distinguishing between significant and non-significant activity in any one channel (could eyebrow-raising be a nervous twitch, and is the signer touching his nose to make a sign or to scratch an itch?).

These appear to be purely practical problems, but in fact they have important theoretical implications. It is because of the relatively unknown nature of sign language (compared to spoken language), that there are as yet no assumptions about what is and is not sign language, nor do we have much access to native signer intuitions. So we cannot limit our concerns to a pre-defined object of research, nor can we ignore spontaneous data, which has to be almost our only source of data. The lack of a set of assumptions and practices in sign language research makes one aware of the arbitrary nature of such assumptions and practices in spoken language research, and gives us more reason to question them. In chapter 8 we reviewed the evidence on the unreliability of intuitive data in any linguistic research, and sign language research can only make us more aware of this. It also makes us aware of the problems surrounding the identification of significant activity, and we have already suggested under implication (7) (p. 203) that this needs questioning for spoken as well as sign language.

Finally, we may note that the problems discussed in chapter 8 are not peculiar to sign language research, even if they are ignored in mainstream linguistics, but also arise in a similar way in research on non-standard and low status languages in general. This makes us aware that the traditional linguistic approach is not only based on spoken language, but in particular, the standard variety of a spoken language (such as English) as used by an educated elite who are as accustomed to writing this variety down as to speaking it. This is surely a narrow basis for general linguistic theory.

Summary

This concluding chapter has outlined some of the implications for linguistics that can be drawn from research on BSL. We have seen that they include the following: re-evaluation of the notion of arbitrariness as a criterion of language, with more emphasis on conventionality and a related functional approach; awareness of the potential effect of linguistics on a language being studied; a new application of the notion of phonology; awareness of the potential significance of simultaneity in spoken as well as sign language; re-consideration of the notion of a 'core' in language and its identification with one particular channel of behaviour; some support for the role of an innate 'bioprogram' in the structuring and acquisition of language; and finally, recognition of the narrow basis of linguistic theory when insufficient attention is paid to problems of data collection.

As we have seen, research on BSL is in its early stages, and it is to be expected that further research will not only provide more sophisticated analyses of BSL, but also contribute to a more sophisticated theory of language.

Bibliography

Ahlgren, I. (1977), 'Early linguistic cognitive development in the deaf
    and severely hard of hearing', paper presented at the National
    Symposium on Sign Language Research and Teaching, Chicago.
Ahlgren, I. (1981), 'Parental input and sign language acquisition in deaf
    children', paper presented at the Second International Symposium on
    Sign Language Research, Bristol.
Ahlgren, I. and Bergman, B. (eds) (1980), *Papers from the First
    International Symposium on Sign Language Research*, Leksand, The
    Swedish National Association of the Deaf.
Aitchison, J. (1976), *The Articulate Mammal. An Introduction to
    Psycholinguistics*, London, Hutchinson.
Allan, K. (1977), 'Classifiers', *Language*, vol. 53, pp. 285–311.
Andersen, E. S. and Johnson, C. E. (1973), 'Modifications in the speech
    of an eight-year-old to younger children', *Stanford Occasional Papers
    in Linguistics*, vol. 3, pp. 149–160.
Anderson, L. (1977), 'Towards a grammar of the American Sign
    Language on a comparative-typological basis', unpublished
    manuscript, Gallaudet College.
Ashbrook, E. (1977), 'Development of semantic relations in the
    acquisition of American Sign Language', unpublished manuscript,
    Salk Institute for Biological Studies, La Jolla, California.
Baker, C. (1980), 'On the terms "verbal" and "non-verbal"', in Ahlgren
    and Bergman (eds).
Baker, C. and Padden, C. A. (1978), 'Focusing on the nonmanual
    components of American Sign Language', in Siple (ed.).
Baron, N. S. (1981), *Speech, Writing and Sign. A Functional View of
    Linguistic Representation*, Bloomington, Indiana University Press.
Battison, R. M. (1974), 'Phonological deletion in American Sign
    Language', *Sign Language Studies*, vol. 5, pp. 1–19.
Battison, R. M. (1978), *Lexical Borrowing in American Sign Language*,
    Silver Spring, Maryland, Linstok Press.
Bellugi, U. and Klima, E. (1976), 'Two faces of sign: iconic and
    abstract', *Annals of the New York Academy of Sciences*, no. 280,
    pp. 514–538.
Bickerton, D. (1981), *Roots of Language*, Ann Arbor, Karoma
    Publishers.

Bibliography   215

Binnick, R. I. (1978), 'The Syntax of Sign', Scarborough College, University of Toronto, *Papers in Language Use and Language Function*, no. 4.

Bolinger, D. L. (1975), *Aspects of Language*, New York, Harcourt Brace Jovanovich.

Bolinger, D. L. (1980), *Language – The Loaded Weapon*, London and New York, Longman.

Bonvillian, J. (1983), 'Early sign language acquisition and its relation to cognitive and motor development', in Kyle and Woll (eds).

Bowerman, M. (1973), *Early Syntactic Development: A Cross Linguistic Study with Special Reference to Finnish*, Cambridge, Cambridge University Press.

Boyes-Braem, P. (1973), 'The acquisition of handshape in American Sign Language', unpublished manuscript, The Salk Institute for Biological Studies, La Jolla, California.

Boyes-Braem, P. (1981), *Features of the Handshape in American Sign Language*, unpublished PhD dissertation, University of California, Berkeley.

Brennan, M. (1976), 'Can deaf children acquire language?', *Supplement to the British Deaf News*.

Brennan, M. (1981), 'Grammatical processes in British Sign Language', in Woll, Kyle and Deuchar (eds).

Brennan, M. (1983), 'Marking time in British Sign Language', in Kyle and Woll (eds).

Brennan, M., Colville, M. D. and Lawson, L. (1980), *Words in Hand*, Moray House College of Education, Edinburgh, British Sign Language Research Project.

British Deaf and Dumb Association (1970), Report by a Working Party formed to study and comment on 'The Lewis Report' on the education of deaf children.

Brown, R. (1977), 'Why are signed languages easier to learn than spoken languages?', paper presented at the National Symposium on Sign Language Research and Teaching, Chicago, Illinois.

Bruce, R. V. (1973), *Bell: Alexander Graham Bell and the Conquest of Solitude*, London, Victor Gollancz.

Bruner, J. S. (1979), 'Learning how to do things with words', in Aaronson, D. and Rieber, R. W. (eds), *Psycholinguistic Research: Implications and Applications*, Hillsdale, New Jersey, Erlbaum Associates.

Bullowa, M. (1979), *Before Speech: The Beginnings of Inter-Personal Communication*, Cambridge, Cambridge University Press.

Carter, M. (1980), 'Noun phrase modification in British Sign Language (BSL)', unpublished paper, University of Bristol, School of Education.

Carter, M. (1981), 'The acquisition of British Sign Language (BSL)', unpublished paper, University of York.

Chafe, W. (1976), 'Givenness, contrastiveness, definiteness, subjects, topics and point of view', in Li (ed.).

Chomsky, C. (1969), *The Acquisition of Syntax in Children from 5 to 10*, Cambridge, Massachusetts, MIT Press.

Chomsky, N. (1957), *Syntactic Structures*, The Hague, Mouton.
Chomsky, N. (1965), *Aspects of the Theory of Syntax*, Cambridge, Massachusetts, MIT Press.
Chomsky, N. (1972), *Language and Mind*, New York, Harcourt Brace Jovanovich.
Cicourel, A. (1973), 'Cross-modal communication: the representational context of sociolinguistic information processing', in Shuy, R. W. (ed.), *Report of the Twenty-Third Annual Round Table Meeting on Linguistics and Language Studies*, Washington, D.C., Georgetown University Press.
Coates, R. (1980), 'Phonology – the state of the discipline', *Language Teaching*, vol. 15, no. 1, pp. 2–18.
Comrie, B. (1976), *Aspect*, Cambridge, Cambridge University Press.
Comrie, B. (1981), *Language Universals and Linguistic Typology*, Oxford, Basil Blackwell.
Conrad, R. (1979), *The Deaf Schoolchild. Language Development and Cognitive Function*, London, Harper and Row.
Conrad, R. (1981), 'Sign language in education: some consequent problems', in Woll, Kyle and Deuchar (eds).
Corfmat, P. T. (1970), 'The deaf idiom', paper presented at Church House, London, at Refresher Course for Chaplains to the Deaf.
Cornett, R. O. (1967), 'The method explained', *Hearing and Speech News*, vol. 35, no. 5, pp. 7–9.
Coulthard, M. (1977), *An Introduction to Discourse Analysis*, London, Longman.
Coye, T., Martin, B. and Humphries, T. (1978), 'A bilingual, bicultural approach to teaching English or how two hearies and a deafie get together to teach English', in *Proceedings of the Second National Symposium on Sign Language Research and Teaching*, October, Coronado, California.
Craig, D. (1971), 'Education and creole English', in Hymes (ed.).
Craig, E. (1973), 'The Paget Gorman Sign System: a report of the research project 1970–73', unpublished manuscript, Department of Linguistic Science, Reading.
Crystal, D. (1969), *Prosodic Systems and Intonation in English*, Cambridge, Cambridge University Press.
Crystal, D. (1971), *Linguistics*, Harmondsworth, Penguin.
Crystal, D. (1980a), *A First Dictionary of Linguistics and Phonetics*, London, André Deutsch.
Crystal, D. (1980b), 'Neglected grammatical factors in conversational English', in Greenbaum, S., Leech, G. and Svartvik, J. (eds), *Studies in English Linguistics: for Randolph Quirk*, London and New York, Longman.
Curtiss, S. (1977), *Genie. A Psycholinguistic Study of a Modern-Day 'Wild Child'*, New York, Academic Press.
Dale, P. S. (1976), *Language Development. Structure and Function*, second edition, New York, Holt, Rinehart and Winston.
DeCamp, D. (1971), 'Toward a generative analysis of a post-creole continuum', in Hymes (ed.).

Denmark, J. (1976), in Royal National Institute for the Deaf (1976a).
Denton, D. M. (1976), 'The Philosophy of Total Communication',
  Supplement to the British Deaf News.
Department of Education and Science (1968), *The Education of Deaf
  Children: The Possible Place of Finger Spelling and Signing*, London,
  HMSO.
Deuchar, M. (1978a), *Diglossia in British Sign Language*, unpublished
  PhD dissertation, Stanford University.
Deuchar, M. (1978b), 'Diglossia and British Sign Language', *Working
  Papers in Sociolinguistics*, no. 46, University of Austin, Texas.
Deuchar, M. (1978c), 'Sign language and integration in the British deaf
  community', microfiche ED 158 615, Eric Clearinghouse on Languages
  and Linguistics.
Deuchar, M. (1981), 'Variation in British Sign Language', in Woll, Kyle
  and Deuchar (eds).
Deuchar, M. (1983), 'Is British Sign Language an SVO language?', in
  Kyle and Woll (eds).
Eco, U. (1976), *A Theory of Semiotics*, Bloomington, University of
  Indiana Press.
Edge, V. and Hermann, L. (1977), 'Verbs and the determination of
  subject in ASL', in Friedman (ed.).
Ekman, P. and Friesen, W. V. (1977), *Facial Action Coding System*,
  Palo Alto, California, Consulting Psychologists Press.
El-Hassan, S. A. (1977), 'Educated spoken Arabic in Egypt and the
  Levant: a critical review of diglossia and related concepts', *Archivum
  Linguisticum*, vol. VIII, no. 2, pp. 112–32.
Ellenberger, R. and Steyaert, M. (1978), 'A child's representation of
  action in American Sign Language', in Siple (ed.).
Fant, G. (1968), 'Analysis and synthesis of speech processes', in
  Malmberg, B. (ed.), *Manual of Phonetics*, Amsterdam, North
  Holland Publishing Company.
Feldman, H., Goldin-Meadow, S. and Gleitman, L. (1978), 'Beyond
  Herodotus: the creation of language by linguistically deprived deaf
  children', in Lock (ed.).
Fenn, G. (1975), 'The development of language through signing in
  children with severe auditory impairments', final report to the Social
  Science Research Council, Grant HR 2557, 1974–5.
Fenn, G. (1976), 'Development of language in profoundly deaf children
  through the medium of manual signs', *Sign Language Studies*, vol. 11,
  pp. 109–20.
Ferguson, C. A. (1959), 'Diglossia', *Word*, vol. 15, pp. 325–340.
Ferguson, C. A. (1968), 'Myths about Arabic', in Fishman, J. (ed.),
  Readings in the Sociology of Language, The Hague, Mouton.
Firth, G. C. (1966), *The Plate Glass Prison*, London, Royal National
  Institute for the Deaf.
Firth, J. R. (1957), *Papers in Linguistics*, London, Oxford University
  Press.
Fischer, S. D. (1973a), 'Two processes of reduplication in the American
  Sign Language', *Foundations of Language*, vol. 9, pp. 469–80.

Fischer, S. D. (1973b), 'The deaf child's acquisition of verb inflection in American Sign Language', paper presented at the Annual Meeting of the Linguistic Society of America, San Diego.

Fischer, S. D. (1974), 'Sign language and linguistic universals' *Actes du Colloque Franco-Allemand de Grammaire Transformationelle*, pp. 187–204.

Fischer, S. D. (1975), 'Influences on word order change in American Sign Language', in Li, C. (ed.), *Word Order and Word Order Change*, Austin, Texas, University of Texas Press.

Fischer, S. D. (1978), 'Sign language and creoles', in Siple (ed.).

Fischer, S. D. and Gough, B. (1978), 'Verbs in American Sign Language', *Sign Language Studies*, vol. 18, pp. 17–48.

Fletcher, P. and Garman, M. (eds) (1979), *Language Acquisition*, Cambridge, Cambridge University Press.

Freeman, R. J., Carbin, C. F. and Boese, R. T. (1981), *Can't Your Child Hear?*, London, Croom Helm.

Friedman, L. A. (1975), 'Space, time and person reference in American Sign Language', *Language*, vol. 51, no. 3, pp. 940–61.

Friedman, L. A. (1976a), 'The manifestation of subject, object and topic in American Sign Language', in Li (ed.).

Friedman, L. A. (1976b), *Phonology of a Soundless Language. Phonological Structure of the American Sign Language*, unpublished PhD dissertation, University of California, Berkeley.

Friedman, L. A. (1977), 'Formational properties of American Sign Language', in Friedman (ed.).

Friedman, L. A. (ed.) (1977), *On the Other Hand. New Perspectives on American Sign Language*, New York, Academic Press.

Frishberg, N. (1975), 'Arbitrariness and iconicity in American Sign Language', *Language*, vol. 51, pp. 696–719.

Frishberg, N. (1976), *Some Aspects of Historical Change in American Sign Language*, unpublished doctoral dissertation, San Diego, University of California.

Frishberg, N. and Gough, B. (1973), 'Time on our hands', paper presented to the Third Annual California Linguistics Meeting, Stanford, California.

Fromkin, V. and Rodman, R. (1978), *An Introduction to Language*, New York, Holt, Rinehart and Winston.

Givens, D. (1978), 'Social expressivity during the first year of life', *Sign Language Studies*, vol. 20, pp. 251–74.

Givón, T. (1979a), *Understanding Grammar*, New York, Academic Press.

Givón, T. (1979b), 'From discourse to syntax: grammar as a processing strategy', in Givón (ed.).

Givón, T. (ed.) (1979), *Syntax and Semantics, Volume 12, Discourse and Syntax*, New York, Academic Press.

Goodridge, F. (1960), *The Language of the Silent World*, British Deaf and Dumb Association.

Gorman, P. P. (1960), *Certain Social and Psychological Difficulties facing the Deaf Person in the English Community*, unpublished PhD thesis, Cambridge University.

Greenberg, J. H. (1966), 'Some universals of grammar with particular reference to the order of meaningful elements', in Greenberg, J. H. (ed.), *Universals of Language*, Cambridge, Massachusetts, MIT Press.

Griffiths, P. (1980), 'Paget Gorman Sign System', *British Deaf News*, vol. 12, no. 8, pp. 258–60.

Grosjean, F., Teuber, H. and Lane, H. (1979), 'When is a sign a sign? The on-line processing of gated signs in American Sign Language', working paper, Northeastern University.

Gumperz, J. J. and Wilson, R. (1971), 'Convergence and creolization: a case from the Indo-Aryan/Dravidian border', in Hymes (ed.).

Gumperz, J. J. (1972), 'The speech community' in Giglioli, P. P. (ed.), *Language and Social Context*, Harmondsworth, Penguin.

Halliday, M. A. K. (1973), *Explorations in the Functions of Language*, London, Arnold.

Halliday, M. A. K. (1978), *Language as Social Semiotic. The Social Interpretation of Language and Meaning*, London, Arnold.

Hansen, B. (1975), 'Varieties in Danish Sign Language and grammatical features of the original sign language', *Sign Language Studies*, vol. 8, pp. 249–56.

Hartshorne, C. and Weiss, P. (eds) (1932), *Collected Papers of Charles Saunders Peirce*, Cambridge, Harvard University Press.

Haugen, E. (1977), 'Norm and deviation in bilingual communities', in Hornby, P. A. (ed.), *Bilingualism*, New York, Academic Press.

Hewes, G. W. (1973), 'Primate communication and the gestural origin of language', *Current Anthropology*, vol. 14, pp. 5–32.

Hinde, R. A. (ed.) (1972), *Non-Verbal Communication*, Cambridge, Cambridge University Press.

Hockett, C. F. (1958), *A Course in Modern Linguistics*, New York, Macmillan.

Hockett, C. F. (1960), 'The origin of speech', *Scientific American*, vol. 203, pp. 88–96.

Hodgson, K. W. (1953), *The Deaf and their Problems*, New York, Philosophical Library.

Hoemann, H. W. (1976), *The American Sign Language*, Silver Spring, Maryland, National Association of the Deaf.

Hoffmeister, R. (1978), 'Word order acquisition in ASL', paper presented to the Third Annual Boston University Conference on Language Development, Boston.

Hoffmeister, R. and Wilbur, R. (1980), 'Developmental: the acquisition of sign language', in Lane and Grosjean (eds).

Holmes, K. M. and Holmes, D. W. (1980), 'Signed and spoken language development in a hearing child of hearing parents', *Sign Language Studies*, vol. 28, pp. 239–54.

Hudson, R. A. (1980), *Sociolinguistics*, Cambridge, Cambridge University Press.

Hughes, A. and Trudgill, P. (1979), *English Accents and Dialects. An*

Introduction to Social and Regional Varieties of British English, London, Arnold.

Hyman, L. (1975), *Phonology: Theory and Analysis*, New York, Holt Rinehart and Winston.

Hymes, D. (ed.) (1971), *Pidginization and Creolization of Languages*, Cambridge, Cambridge University Press.

Ingram, R. M. (1978), 'Theme, rheme, topic, and comment in the syntax of American Sign Language', *Sign Language Studies*, vol. 20, pp. 193–218.

Jakobson, R. (1960), 'Concluding statement: linguistics and poetics', in Sebeok, T. A. (ed.), *Style in Language*, New York, Wiley.

Jones, H. (1968), *Sign Language*, London, the English University Press.

Jones, N. and Mohr, K. (1975), 'A working paper on plurals in ASL', unpublished manuscript, University of California, Berkeley.

Jordan, I. K. and Battison, R. (1976), 'A referential communication experiment with foreign sign languages', *Sign Language Studies*, vol. 10, pp. 69–80.

Kantor, R. (1980), 'The acquisition of classifiers in American Sign Language', *Sign Language Studies*, vol. 29, pp. 193–203.

Katz, J. J. (1981), *Language and Other Abstract Objects*, Totowa, New Jersey, Rowman and Littlefield.

Kaye, A. S. (1970), 'Modern standard Arabic and the colloquials', *Lingua*, vol. 24, pp. 374–91.

Kegl, J. (1976), 'Pronominalization in American Sign Language', unpublished manuscript, MIT, Cambridge, Massachusetts.

Kegl, J. (1977), 'ASL syntax: research in progress and current research', unpublished manuscript, MIT, Cambridge, Massachusetts.

Kimura, D. (1981), 'Neural mechanisms in manual signing', *Sign Language Studies*, vol. 33, pp. 291–312.

Klima, E. S. and Bellugi, U. (1972), 'The signs of language in child and chimpanzee', in Alloway, T., Krames, L. and Pliner, P. (eds), *Communication and Affect. A Comparative Approach*, New York, Academic Press.

Klima, E. S. and Bellugi, U. (1979), *The Signs of Language*, Cambridge, Massachusetts, Harvard University Press.

Krashen, S. (1973), 'Lateralization, language learning and the critical period – some new evidence', *Language Learning*, vol. 23, pp. 63–74.

Krashen, S. and Harshman, R. (1972), 'Lateralization and the critical period', *Working Papers in Phonetics*, UCLA, vol. 23, pp. 13–23.

Kuschel, R. (1973), 'The silent inventor: the creation of a sign language by the only deaf-mute on a Polynesian island', *Sign Language Studies*, vol. 3, pp. 1–27.

Kyle, J. and Woll, B. (eds) (1983), *Language in Sign: An International Perspective on Sign Language*, London, Croom Helm.

Labov, W. (1969), 'Contraction, deletion and inherent variability of the English copula', *Language*, vol. 45, pp. 715–62.

Labov, W. (1972a), 'Some principles of linguistic methodology', *Language in Society*, vol. 1, pp. 97–120.

Labov, W. (1972b), *Sociolinguistic Patterns*, Philadelphia, University of Pennsylvania Press.

Labov, W. (1975), *What is a Linguistic Fact?*, Ghent, Belgium, Peter de Ridder Press.

Labov, W. (1982), 'Objectivity and commitment in linguistic science: the case of the Black English trial in Ann Arbor', *Language in Society*, vol. 11, pp. 165–202.

Labov, W. (n.d.), 'The relative influence of family and peers in the learning of language', unpublished paper.

Ladd, P. and Edwards, V. (1982), 'British Sign Language and West Indian Creole', *Sign Language Studies*, vol. 35, pp. 101–26.

Lambert, W. E., Hodgson, R. C. and Fillenbaum, S. (1960), 'Evaluational reactions to spoken languages', *Journal of Abnormal and Social Psychology*, vol. 60, pp. 44–51.

Lane, H., Boyes-Braem, P. and Bellugi, U. (1976), 'Preliminaries to a distinctive feature analysis of handshapes in American Sign Language', *Cognitive Psychology*, vol. 8, no. 2, pp. 263–89.

Lane, H. and Grosjean, F. (eds) (1980), *Recent Perspectives on American Sign Language*, Hillsdale, New Jersey, Lawrence Erlbaum Associates.

Lawson, L. (1981), 'The role of sign in the structure of the deaf community', in Woll, Kyle and Deuchar (eds).

Lawson, L. (1983), 'Multi-channel signs' in Kyle and Woll (eds).

Lenneberg, E. H. (1967), *The Biological Foundations of Language*, New York, Wiley.

Levelt, W. J. M. (1980), 'On-line processing constraints on the properties of signed and spoken language' in Bellugi, U. and Studdert-Kennedy, M. (eds), *Signed and Spoken Language: Biological Constraints on Linguistic Form*, Dahlem Workshop, Berlin, Verlag Chemie.

Li, C. N. (ed.) (1976), *Subject and Topic*, New York, Academic Press.

Li, C. N. and Thompson, S. A. (1976), 'Subject and topic: a new typology of language', in Li (ed.).

Liddell, S. K. (1978), 'Nonmanual signals and relative clauses in American Sign Language', in Siple (ed.).

Liddell, S. K. (1980), *American Sign Language Syntax*, The Hague, Mouton.

Llewellyn-Jones, M. (1982), 'The current development of a two-year-old profoundly deaf child in relation to the use of sign language in an educational setting. The effects of the teacher's use of sign on communication and behaviour', unpublished manuscript, Plymouth.

Llewellyn-Jones, P., Kyle, J. G. and Woll, B. (1979), 'Sign language communication', unpublished paper presented at the International Conference on Social Psychology and Language, Bristol.

Lock, A. (ed.) (1978), *Action, Gesture and Symbol: The Emergence of Language*, London, Academic Press.

Lock, A. (1980), *The Guided Reinvention of Language*, London, Academic Press.

Luftig, R. L. and Lloyd, L. L. (1981), 'Manual sign translucency and referential concreteness in the learning of signs', *Sign Language Studies*, vol. 30, pp. 49–60.

Lyons, J. (1968), *Introduction to Theoretical Linguistics*, Cambridge, Cambridge University Press.

Lyons, J. (1972), 'Human language', in Hinde (ed.).

Lyons, J. (1977), *Semantics*, volumes I and II, Cambridge, Cambridge University Press.

Lyons, J. (1981), *Language and Linguistics*, Cambridge, Cambridge University Press.

Lysons, K. (1978), 'The development of local voluntary societies for adult deaf persons in England', *British Deaf News*, vol. 11, pp. 214–17.

Lysons, K. (1979), 'The development of local voluntary societies for adult deaf persons in England', *British Deaf News*, vol. 12, pp. 34–6.

McIntire, M. (1977), 'The acquisition of ASL hand configurations', *Sign Language Studies*, vol. 16, pp. 247–66.

McLoughlin, M. G. (1980), 'History of the education of the deaf', *Teacher of the Deaf*, January, pp. 18–19.

Maestas y Moores, J. (1980), 'Early linguistic environment: interactions of deaf parents with their infants', *Sign Language Studies*, vol. 26, pp. 1–13.

Mandel, M. (1977a), 'Iconic devices in American Sign Language', in Friedman (ed.).

Mandel, M. (1977b), 'Iconicity of signs and their learnability by non-signers' in *Proceedings of the First National Symposium on Sign Language Research and Teaching*, pp. 259–266.

Markowicz, H. and Woodward, J. C. (1975), 'Language and the maintenance of ethnic boundaries in the deaf community', paper presented at the Conference on Culture and Communication, Philadelphia.

Marmor, G. S. and Petitto, L. (1979), 'Simultaneous communication in the classroom: how well is English grammar being presented?' *Sign Language Studies*, vol. 23, pp. 99–136.

Matthews, P. H. (1974), *Morphology: An Introduction to the Theory of Word Structure*, Cambridge, Cambridge University Press.

Meadow, K. P. (1980), *Deafness and Child Development*, London, Edward Arnold.

Miles, D. (1979), 'Features of British Sign Language', unpublished manuscript, Newcastle Upon Tyne, Sign Linguistics Research Group.

Milroy, L. (1980), *Language and Social Networks*, Oxford, Basil Blackwell.

Mohay, H. (1982), 'A preliminary description of the communication systems evolved by two deaf children in the absence of a sign language model', *Sign Language Studies*, vol. 34, pp. 73–90.

Morris, C. W. (1946), *Signs, Language and Behaviour*, Englewood Cliffs, New Jersey, Prentice Hall.

Morris, D., Collett, P., Marsh, P. and O'Shaughnessy, M. (1979), *Gestures, their Origins and Distribution*, London, Jonathan Cape.

Mühlhäusler, P. (forthcoming), review of Bickerton, D. (1981), 'Roots of Language', *Folia Linguistica*.

Newport, E. L. (1981), 'Constraints on structure: evidence from American Sign Language and language learning', in Collins, W. A. (ed.), *Aspects of the Development of Competence. The Minnesota Symposium on Child Psychology, Volume 14*, Hillsdale, New Jersey, Lawrence Erlbaum Associates.

O'Connor, J. D. (1973), *Phonetics*, Harmondsworth, Penguin.

Ochs, E. (1979), 'Planned and unplanned discourse', in Givón (ed.).

Padden, C. (1980), 'The deaf community and the culture of deaf people', in Baker, C. and Battison, R. (eds), *Sign Language and the Deaf Community*, National Association of the Deaf.

Peirce, C. S. (1932), in Hartshorne, C. and Weiss, P. (eds), *Collected Papers of Charles Sanders Peirce*, Cambridge, Harvard University Press.

Piattelli-Palmarini, M. (ed.) (1980), *Language and Learning. The Debate between Jean Piaget and Noam Chomsky*, Cambridge, Massachusetts, Harvard University Press.

Poizner, H. and Battison, R. (1980), 'Cerebral asymmetry for sign language: clinical and experimental evidence', in Lane and Grosjean (eds).

Prinz, P. and Prinz, E. (1979), 'Simultaneous acquisition of ASL and spoken English', *Sign Language Studies*, vol. 25, pp. 283–96.

Prinz, P. and Prinz, E. (1981), 'Acquisition of ASL and spoken English by a hearing child of a deaf mother and hearing father', *Sign Language Studies*, vol. 30, pp. 78–88.

Reilly, J. and McIntire, M. (1980), 'American Sign Language and Pidgin Sign English: What's the difference?', *Sign Language Studies*, vol. 29, pp. 151–92.

Robins, R. H. (1967), *A Short History of Linguistics*, London, Longmans.

Robinson, W. P. (1972), *Language and Social Behaviour*, Harmondsworth, Penguin.

Rodda, M. (1970), *The Hearing-Impaired School Leaver*, London, University of London Press.

Romaine, S. (1982), *Socio-historical Linguistics*, Cambridge, Cambridge University Press.

Royal National Institute for the Deaf (1976a), *Methods of Communication Currently Used in the Education of Deaf Children*, London, Royal National Institute for the Deaf.

Royal National Institute for the Deaf (1976b), *Methods of Communication Currently Used in the Education of Deaf Children. The Harrogate Papers*, London, Royal National Institute for the Deaf.

Royal National Institute for the Deaf (1981), *Sign and Say*, London, Royal National Institute for the Deaf.

Rubin, J. and Jernudd, B. H. (eds) (1971), *Can Language be Planned?*, Honolulu, University Press of Hawaii.

Saussure, F. de (1959), *Course in General Linguistics*, The Philosophical Library, New York.

Schlesinger, H. and Meadow, K. (1972), *Sound and Sign: Childhood Deafness and Mental Health*, Berkeley, University of California Press.

Schlesinger, I. M. and Namir, L. (1978), *Sign Language of the Deaf: Psychological, Linguistic and Sociological Perspectives*, New York, Academic Press.

Seigel, J. (1969), 'The Enlightenment and the evolution of a language of signs in French and English', *Journal of the History of Ideas*, vol. 30, pp. 96–115.

Simpson, T. S. (1981), 'Council for the Advancement of Communication with Deaf People', *Supplement to the British Deaf News*.

Siple, P. (ed.) (1978), *Understanding Language through Sign Language Research*, New York, Academic Press.

Smith, N. V. and Wilson, D. (1979), *Modern Linguistics. The Results of Chomsky's Revolution*, Harmondsworth, Penguin.

Snow, C. and Ferguson, C. (eds) (1977), *Talking to Children. Language Input and Acquisition*, Cambridge, Cambridge University Press.

Sommerstein, A. H. (1977), *Modern Phonology*, London, Arnold.

Stokoe, W. (1960), *Sign Language Structure: An Outline of the Visual Communication System of the American Deaf*, University of Buffalo, Studies in Linguistics Occasional Paper, no. 8.

Stokoe, W. (1969), 'Sign language diglossia', *Studies in Linguistics*, vol. 20, pp. 27–41.

Stokoe, W. (1972), 'A classroom experiment in two languages', in O'Rourke, T. (ed.), *Total Communication and Psycholinguistics: The State of the Art*, Washington, D.C., American Annals of the Deaf.

Stokoe, W. (1973), 'Classification and description of sign languages', in Sebeok, T. (ed.), *Current Trends in Linguistics*, vol. 12, The Hague, Mouton.

Stokoe, W. (1978), *Sign Language Structure*, Silver Spring, Maryland, Linstok Press.

Stokoe, W. (1979), Review of Wilbur, 'American Sign Language and Sign Systems', *Sign Language Studies*, vol. 23, pp. 175–89.

Stokoe, W., Casterline, D. C. and Croneberg, C. G. (1976, originally published 1965), *A Dictionary of American Sign Language on Linguistic Principles*, Silver Spring, Maryland, Linstok Press.

Supalla, T. and Newport, E. L. (1978), 'How many seats in a chair? The derivation of nouns and verbs in American Sign Language', in Siple (ed.).

Sutton, V. (1981), *Sign Writing for Everyday Use*, Newport Beach, California, The Sutton Movement Writing Press.

Tanokami, T., Peng, F. C., Maeda, Y. and Mori, A. (1976), *On the Nature of Sign Language*, Hiroshima, Japan, Bunka Hyoron Publishing Company.

Tartter, V. and Fischer, S. (1983), 'Perceptual confusions in ASL under normal and reduced (point-light display) conditions', in Kyle and Woll (eds).

Tervoort, B. (1961), 'Esoteric symbolism in the communicative behaviour of young deaf children', *American Annals of the Deaf*, vol. 106, pp. 436–80.

Thompson, H. (1977), 'The lack of subordination in American Sign Language', in Friedman (ed.).

Trudgill, P. (1972), 'Sex, covert prestige and linguistic change in the urban British English of Norwich', *Language in Society*, vol. 1, pp. 179–95.

Trudgill, P. (1974), *Sociolinguistics*, Harmondsworth, Penguin.

Trudgill, P. (ed.) (1978), *Sociolinguistic Patterns in British English*, London, Edward Arnold.

Vernon, M. (1976), 'Communication and the education of deaf and hard of hearing children', in Royal National Institute for the Deaf, 1976a.

Vogt-Svendsen, M. (1981), 'Mouth position and mouth movement in Norwegian Sign Language', *Sign Language Studies*, vol. 33, pp. 363–76.

Volterra, V. (1981), 'Gestures, signs and words at two years: when does communication become language?', *Sign Language Studies*, vol. 33, pp. 351–62.

Wallis, J. (1670), 'Letter to Robert Boyle', *Philosophical Transactions*, no. 61, pp. 1087–97.

Washabaugh, W. (1980), 'The manu-facturing of a language', *Semiotica*, vol. 29, pp. 1–37 and *Sign Language Studies*, vol. 29, pp. 291–30.

Washabaugh, W. (1981), 'Sign language in its social context', *Annual Review of Anthropology*, vol. 10, pp. 237–52.

Watson, T. J. (1976), in Royal National Institute for the Deaf, (1976b), pp. 3–8.

Wescott, R. W. (1971), 'Linguistic iconism', *Language*, vol. 47, pp. 416–28.

Whinnom, K. (1971), 'Linguistic hybridization and the "special case" of pidgins and creoles', in Hymes (ed.).

Wilbur, R. B. (1979), *American Sign Language and Sign Systems*, Baltimore, University Park Press.

Woll, B. (1981a), 'Question structure in British Sign Language', in Woll, Kyle and Deuchar (eds).

Woll, B. (1981b), 'Borrowing and change in BSL', paper presented at the Linguistics Association of Great Britain Autumn Meeting, York.

Woll, B. (1983), 'The semantics of British Sign Language signs', in Kyle and Woll (eds).

Woll, B., Kyle, J., and Deuchar, M. (eds) (1981), *Perspectives on British Sign Language and Deafness*, London, Croom Helm.

Woll, B. and Lawson, L. (1981), 'British Sign Language', in Haugen, E., McClure, J. D. and Thompson, D. (eds), *Minority Languages Today*, Edinburgh, Edinburgh University Press.

Woodward, J. (1972), in Stokoe, W., *Semiotics and Human Sign Languages*, the Hague, Mouton.

Woodward, J. (1973a), *Implicational Lects on the Deaf Diglossic Continuum*, unpublished PhD dissertation, Georgetown University.

Woodward, J. (1973b), 'Some characteristics of Pidgin Sign English', *Sign Language Studies*, vol. 3, pp. 39–46.

Woodward, J. (1974), 'Implicational variation in American Sign Language: negative incorporation', *Sign Language Studies*, vol. 5, pp. 29–30.

Woodward, J. (1975), 'Variation in American Sign Language Syntax', in Fasold, R. W. and Shuy, R. W., *Analyzing Variation in Language*, Washington, Georgetown University Press.

Woodward, J. (1976), 'Black southern signing', *Language in Society*, vol. 5, pp. 211–18.

Woodward, J. (1978), 'Historical bases of American Sign Language', in Siple (ed.).

Woodward, J. and DeSantis, S. (1977), 'Negative incorporation in French and American Sign Languages', *Language in Society*, vol. 6, pp. 379–88.

Woodward, J. and Markowicz, H. (1975), 'Some handy new ideas on pidgins and creoles: pidgin sign languages', paper presented at the International Conference on Pidgin and Creole Languages, Honolulu.

World Federation of the Deaf (1975), *Gestuno. International Sign Language of the Deaf*, Carlisle, British Deaf Association.

Worswick, C. (1982), 'Interrogatives in British Sign Language', unpublished manuscript, Department of Language, University of York, (BSL Research Project, Edinburgh).

Wright, D. (1969), *Deafness, A Personal Account*, New York, Stein and Day.

Index

acquisition of sign language,
   17–18, 151–76, 209
adjectives, 83, 103
adverbials, 102; of time, 97, 122
agent, 86, 208
Ahlgren, I., 161, 172
American Sign Language, *see*
   ASL
anaphora, 97
Anderson, L., 126
arbitrariness, 11, 13, 16–20, 26,
   192–4, 213
Ashbrook, E., 167
ASL, 3, 6, 7, 8, 23, 25, 27, 49,
   74, 106–29, 132, 133, 191,
   204–8; acquisition of, 159–61; as
   a creole, 145–6, 205–8;
   grammar of, 81, 90, 201; history
   of, 3, 32, *see also* as a creole;
   notation of, 52, 53, 64, 107–12;
   phonology of, 60, 69, 70, 73,
   78, *see also* notation of
aspect, 82, 87, 94, 99–103, 122,
   201, 205; continuative, 116,
   117; durative, 102; habitual,
   102, 103; interative, 102, 117,
   124
assimilation, 79, 113, 118;
   progressive, regressive, 113
attitudes to sign language, 35, 37,
   38, 134, 139–40, 195

Baker, Henry, 30
Baker, C. and Padden, C. A.,
   120, 121

BATOD, *see* British Association
   of Teachers of the Deaf
Battison, R. M., 4, 49, 78, 79,
   110, 112–13, 114–15
Bell, Alexander Graham, 195
Bickerton, D., 146–7, 153–4, 207,
   209
bilingualism, 32, 39, 139, 158,
   161, 175, 176
Binnick, R. I., 126
bioprogram, 155, 207, 209, 211,
   213
Bolinger, D. L., 19, 192
Bonvillian, J., 18, 162–3
Boyes-Braem, P., 110, 111, 163,
   166
Braidwood family, 31–2
brain lateralization, 209–10
Brennan, M., 99, 102
Brennan, M. *et al.*, 53, 59, 60,
   64–5, 69, 71–2, 74–6, 112
Bristol Sign Language Group, 44,
   72
British Association of Teachers of
   the Deaf (BATOD), 36, 39
British Deaf Association (BDA),
   41–3
British Deaf News, 42
British Sign Language, *see* BSL
Brown, R., 161–2
BSL, as a creole, 28, 144, 150,
   157, 204–9; definition of, 1;
   grammar of, 22, 81–105; history
   of, 27–46, 79, 129, 205; and
   linguistic theory, 191–213;
   phonology of, 47–80, 131; status